20 years of
PSYCHOANALYSIS

20 years of PSYCHOANALYSIS

A Symposium IN CELEBRATION OF
THE TWENTIETH ANNIVERSARY OF THE
CHICAGO INSTITUTE FOR PSYCHOANALYSIS

Edited by

FRANZ ALEXANDER, M.D., *and* HELEN ROSS

W · W · NORTON *&* COMPANY · INC · *New York*

FIRST EDITION

PRINTED IN THE UNITED STATES OF AMERICA
FOR THE PUBLISHERS BY THE VAIL-BALLOU PRESS

Contents

PART TWO. Training and Research
at the Chicago Institute for Psychoanalysis

Foreword

THE FIRST part of this volume presents the Proceedings of the Scientific Meetings held in Chicago on October 11, 1952, in celebration of the twentieth anniversary of the founding of the Chicago Institute for Psychoanalysis. These papers deal with the influence of the basic concepts of psychoanalysis on medicine and medical teaching in general, on psychiatry in particular, and on the social sciences. Formal discussions follow the papers.

The second part presents in four papers an account of the specific training and research activities of the Chicago Institute for Psychoanalysis during the two decades of its existence. Added to these is a list of the publications, 1932–1952, by members of the staff of the Institute during the period of their association with it, thus rounding out the history of the twenty years.

Contributors

FRANZ ALEXANDER, M.D.
Director, Chicago Institute for Psychoanalysis; Clinical Professor of Psychiatry, College of Medicine, University of Illinois

JOHN D. BENJAMIN, M.D.
Child Research Council, Denver

HENRY W. BROSIN, M.D.
Director, Western Psychiatric Institute and Clinic and Professor and Chairman, Department of Psychiatry, School of Medicine, University of Pittsburgh

THOMAS M. FRENCH, M.D.
Associate Director, Chicago Institute for Psychoanalysis

ALAN GREGG, M.D.
Vice-President, The Rockefeller Foundation

ROY R. GRINKER, M.D.
Director, Institute for Psychosomatic and Psychiatric Research and Training, Michael Reese Hospital; Clinical Professor of Psychiatry, College of Medicine, University of Illinois

MARTIN GROTJAHN, M.D.
Chairman, Educational Committee and Director, Training School, Institute for Psychoanalytic Medicine of Southern California, Beverly Hills

GEORGE C. HAM, M.D.
Professor and Chairman, Department of Psychiatry, University of North Carolina Medical School

9

ADELAIDE M. JOHNSON, PH.D., M.D.
Associate Professor of Psychiatry, University of Minnesota;
Consultant in Psychiatry, the Mayo Clinic; Faculty Member,
Chicago Institute for Psychoanalysis

LAWRENCE S. KUBIE, M.D.
Clinical Professor of Psychiatry, School of Medicine, Yale
University; Faculty, New York Psychoanalytic Institute

MAURICE LEVINE, M.D.
Professor of Psychiatry and Director of the Department, Col-
lege of Medicine, University of Cincinnati

I. ARTHUR MIRSKY, M.D.
Professor and Chairman, Department of Clinical Science,
Professor of Research Psychiatry, Department of Psychiatry,
School of Medicine, University of Pittsburgh

GEORGE J. MOHR, M.D.
Dean of Students, Chicago Institute for Psychoanalysis; As-
sociate Clinical Professor of Psychiatry, College of Medicine,
University of Illinois

TALCOTT PARSONS, PH.D.
Professor of Sociology, Harvard University

GERHART PIERS, M.D.
Staff Member, Chicago Institute for Psychoanalysis

JOHN ROMANO, M.D.
Professor of Psychiatry, University of Rochester School of
Medicine and Dentistry; Psychiatrist-in-Chief, Strong Memo-
rial and Rochester Municipal Hospitals

MILTON ROSENBAUM, M.D.
Professor of Psychiatry, College of Medicine, University of
Cincinnati

DAVID SHAKOW, PH.D.
Professor of Psychology, College of Medicine, University of
Illinois

JOHN P. SPIEGEL, M.D.
Associate Director, Institute for Psychosomatic and Psychi-
atric Research and Training, Michael Reese Hospital

THOMAS S. SZASZ, M.D.
Staff Member, Chicago Institute for Psychoanalysis

PART ONE

Twenty Years of Psychoanalysis

A Review of Two Decades

FRANZ ALEXANDER, M.D.

TWENTY YEARS is not a long period in the lifetime of an academic institution. Time, however, particularly in the era of Einsteinian physics, is a relative concept. In the field of our young discipline in which organized teaching can look back only thirty years, two decades represent a considerable portion. And teaching is only one aspect of academic institutions. Organized, collective research carried out by a staff of co-workers has an even shorter history in psychoanalysis. Prior to the founding of the Chicago Institute for Psychoanalysis, this type of research existed neither in Europe nor in this country. The twentieth anniversary of organized teaching and research in a psychoanalytic institute may be considered a noteworthy date.

Thirty years ago when I decided to leave the well-established areas of the medical sciences to devote myself to the study of psychoanalysis, quite a few of my medical and nonmedical friends expressed their skepticism, nay, consternation, about this decision. Even those who recognized the historical significance of Freud's discoveries in the evolution of human knowledge doubted that psychoanalysis as a method of treatment was here to stay and that a psychoanalyst would ever become a recognized specialist in the field of medical therapy.

Thirty years ago, for a physician to decide to become a psychoanalyst was, no doubt, a grave matter. That the new knowledge of the unconscious mind would become the foundation of a new profession was still to be determined. There was only a handful of psychoanalysts, practicing in different countries but united in the International Psychoanalytic Association. They were trained by themselves or by each other and they were recognized by no other existing authority in the field of medicine. To make the decision to become a psychoanalyst meant to embark upon a highly insecure career; no psychoanalyst at that time could foresee his future status as a member of a larger group of professionals. He could have been certain of one thing, however: namely, that by becoming a psychoanalyst he placed himself outside the fraternity of medical colleagues and he abandoned all that aura of prestige which surrounded the modern descendants of "medicine men," the graduates of the standard medical schools.

It is true that the national psychoanalytic societies, unified under the aegis of the International Psychoanalytic Association with the leadership of Sigmund Freud, gave the new adept a spiritual haven, a kind of citizenship in a small but devoted group. In the early twenties there was scarcely a cultural center in Europe where the young psychoanalyst, once recognized by his local society, would not have found friendly acceptance by the local psychoanalysts. Among them he felt at home at once, with the sensation that he belonged to the chosen few who were enlightened by Freud's teachings about the nature of man and society. An important part of his outlook was that he and the other analysts were surrounded by a hostile world, by people who, because of their emotional resistances and ignorances, continued to live in their traditional hypercritical self-deception. Whether he was visiting his confreres in Vienna, Zurich, Berlin, Munich, Budapest, Rome, Amsterdam, Paris, or London, the conversation soon turned to the hostility and prejudice which the local analysts met on the part of the medical societies and the universities. Soon a well-told anecdote about a slip of the tongue or an observation about the Oedipal behavior of a little son or daughter, an account of an interesting dream fragment, created the feeling of complete solidarity, the feeling that we all shared the same new knowledge for which the rest of the world rejected us. Such is the psychodynamic soil in which all new spiritual movements thrive. In our minds we had no doubt that psychoanalysis was here to stay, and that it would gradually change the outlook of contemporary men and reform the sciences, including medical therapy, the principal object of which is man.

I cannot forego this opportunity to confess that it is a great privilege to have had the fortune to spend the early part of one's life as a member of such a courageous pioneering group which was destined to have a deep reforming influence upon our western civilization. One felt that whatever one's contributions were, one lived for a worthy cause and that the results of one's efforts would continue to live. This feeling is the strongest defense against the fear of personal death and explains why those who are devoted to a cause they believe in show more courage and less concern about their personal fate. They extend the boundaries of their ego by identifying themselves with something outside of themselves.

The great inner gratification derived from being a militant member of a new spiritual movement, be it in religion, art, science, or social reform, explains also the difficulties of reorienting oneself after the cause for which one fought has become accepted and respected. Every leader of an opposition, when elected to govern, faces the same difficulty. The transition from the heroic phase of a movement into its consolidation represents a particularly difficult emotional situation for the devotee. The whole personality was geared to pursue the truth in spite of a hostile world. Now the world turns to you not to fight, but to ask you to teach and to lead. The gratification of martyrdom is over. Your responsibilities increase tremendously at once and you must seek satisfaction from teaching those who want to learn and from fulfilling the promises which you implicitly made while you were fighting your opponents. This is a critical period of re-evaluation of the new truth which you have professed to own. This is the day of accounting. As long as all that you stated was contradicted, and contradicted mainly because of emotional prejudice and not because of reason, your moral position was comparatively easy. In the fervor of the battle, it was no time to look for precision and validation. In the main, *you* were right and the *world* was wrong. Even at the first rough approach to your subject, there was sufficient evidence for your teachings. You knew positively that not all human motives are conscious, that neurotic symptoms and dreams express something meaningful, that repressed sexual impulses were the main source of neurosis of the Victorian and post-Victorian Westerner, and, above all, that sexuality was there from the beginning of life and its objects in the infant were incestuous. As long as all these facts were denied, your position was easy: you were fighting for the truth. The whole dynamics of the interpersonal field change, however, as soon as all that you have professed is accepted and the world is asking you sincerely and avidly to explain the new truth. They turn to you now: "Please tell us all about it. How does this new knowledge help us, how can we use it constructively to cure a neurotic or psychotic patient, to improve child rearing, to alleviate social prejudice and international tension, and to prevent war?"

And you are bombarded with more and more embarrassing questions. "Many of my friends were analyzed for years without any results. How can the majority of people afford such long treatment? Why does training in psychoanalysis last so much longer than in any other specialty? Why is it so expensive?" The most pertinent and penetrating questions, however, are asked by our scientific confreres in other fields of knowledge, concerning the precision and validity of our formulations and the nature of our evidence. The time is past when you could retort with the once-valid formula: "You are asking all these questions because of your emotional resistances." Today we must answer these sincere and pertinent questions in good faith, and in order to do so we must search our own souls and evaluate what we know and what we do not know. This is the moment when our field, which was a combination of a nucleus of a new science with a new creed, begins to change into a rigorous science which has to accept universal standards of validation in research and to adopt academic standards of teaching established by tradition in all other fields of knowledge. Since psychoanalysis is not only a body of theoretical knowledge but also a medical specialty, this is the time when it must accept the established principles of medical practice.

Whenever such a transition from leading an opposition to participating in government, from heroic fight to responsible teaching and practice, takes place within a short period of time, there is danger that the pioneers will not be flexible enough for the required emotional reorientation; that they may remain— as we psychoanalysts say—fixated to an attitude which has become outmoded. The result is the tendency to misinterpret the attitude of others, a Don Quixote fight against windmills. Every question is misunderstood as a sign of hostility based on resistance. Valid criticism provokes, instead of reconsideration and re-examination, violent counterattacks. Smug complacency can only partly cover up the inner insecurity which accompanies the new position of responsibility. Instead of progressive improvement of knowledge and practice, the tendency to rest on the laurels of the past appears in the form of dogmatism. Repetition of the common historical pattern of a once progres-

sive movement changing into stagnant doctrinairism is immi-
nent.

The questions pertaining to psychoanalysis as a theory and
practice must be met. They can be satisfactorily answered only
by a self-critical re-evaluation of all that we can offer; else
we must evade the answers by ignoring the questions. This re-
evaluation necessarily leads to changes and requires improve-
ments in theory and practice. The complacent reiteration of
earlier achievements and the routine continuation of former
practices result in sterility.

In this country, with the general acceptance of the fundamental discoveries of psychoanalysis and of psychoanalytic treatment based on these discoveries, we have left behind the heroic
era of psychoanalysis and have entered a new phase of responsibility. And here is where the story of the Chicago Institute for
Psychoanalysis begins.

At the International Congress of Psychiatry in Paris in 1950
one of the keynotes of the meeting was the recognition of the
fact that in the United States of America, not in Europe, psychiatry has assimilated Freud's principles and has become what
one may call a psychoanalytically oriented psychiatry. I am
happy to say that our great master was wrong in his pessimistic
prediction in this one regard. He did not consider America
a fertile soil for his teachings. He spoke of the danger that here
his teachings could be accepted only in a diluted fashion. His
genius, however, foresaw even in this erroneous prediction an
element of truth. The question before us is: What is dilution?
Is what is happening today a change in meaning or is it a penetration of our knowledge into neighboring fields during which
process our previous discoveries and formulations appear in a
new perspective? The fact that today in this country the majority
of psychiatric residents consider their training in psychoanalysis
an indispensable part of their preparation, that many depart-

ments of psychiatry encourage their residents to undergo training in analytic institutes, that some medical schools undertake full training in psychoanalysis, that the U.S. Public Health Service grants fellowships for training in psychoanalysis and supports teaching and research in psychoanalytic institutes without any strings attached—all this cannot be regarded as "dilution" of psychoanalysis, but as "penetration" into medicine. This means genuine "acceptance."

You may expect that at the celebration of the twentieth anniversary of this Institute, our accomplishments should be reviewed. I feel, however, that it is not my job or that of my collaborators to evaluate our work. That we shall leave to the members of the American Psychoanalytic Association and the representatives of the neighboring fields of education, biology, and the social sciences who have joined us on this occasion. Instead of reporting our work, let me make a few remarks, not about our accomplishments, but regarding our intentions. To estimate what we have achieved is up to others, but as to what we intended to do, we are the best judges. Let me say a few words about the ideals which have animated our work.

The word "ideal" comes from the Greek and its meaning came to its clearest expression in Plato's philosophy. All later so-called idealistic philosophies are reformulations of Plato's conceptions. To Plato, the idea was the essence of all things, a directive principle, never achieved in reality, only approached. The essence of all existence is the realization of the idea. Plato's conception is particularly applicable to human phenomena such as personal destiny and history. It would be difficult for modern biology to explain the evolution of organisms as an approach toward the fulfillment of an idea, although if we omit the teleological implications, progressive adaptation might be described in somewhat similar terms. On the other hand, even such material things as a man-made machine can be described as an attempt to realize an ideal design. Fichte interpreted history as the gradual realization of an abstract idea. For him the supreme idea was the state. For Hegel, history was a continuous pendular movement between ideas, the thesis, the antithesis, which finally coalesced in a synthesis. American historians like to describe the epic of America as the realization of the American dream, a free country for all men.

This reference to dreams is appropriate. The dynamics of dreaming offers possibly the best opportunity to demonstrate the Platonic thesis. The dreamer tries to overcome in his dream all the external and internal obstacles preventing him from the fulfillment of his needs and desires. That it is difficult to reconcile our desires with all of the external interferences, as well as with the obstacles set by our own standards, is best shown by the complexity of our dreams. Why could we not otherwise simply dream of complete fulfillment of all that we want and strive for?

What was the dream of the Chicago Institute? Only the recognition of the underlying ideas which we have tried to realize can explain our history and predict our future. The central idea, around which all the other objectives can be understood as subsidiary parts of something which French calls a goal structure, was conceived twenty years ago when the Institute was founded. It was based on the conviction that psychoanalysis in this country was about to enter a new phase of its development; that it was emerging from a heroic into a responsible period. This new era required first of all a change in our attitude toward the nonpsychoanalytic world, particularly the field of medicine in general and psychiatry in particular. At the same time, it required a change in attitude toward our own knowledge, our methods of teaching and treatment. The attitude toward ourselves is easier to describe. First of all, it was an emphasis on systematic collective research based on recorded clinical material, on the comparative study by different workers of cases belonging to the same category, on the re-evaluation of what we consider as evidence, on the development of methods to check the validity of interpretation, and on the testing of our formulations by the technique of prediction. One example of systematic comparative clinical studies is our work on the psychological factors in gastrointestinal disturbances and other organic conditions. Benedek's correlational studies of the ovarian cycle are an example of testing psychological formulations by physiological methods. French in his studies of dream sequences uses an elaborate technique for checking the validity of interpretations. Study of borderline fields in other sciences has proved particularly suitable for improving methods of validation. In such studies the same phenomenon is approached by two independent techniques and by conceptual tools belonging to different disciplines. This offers opportunity to check the validity of each approach against the other. Our studies of the specific emotional factors active in organic conditions show the use of borderline concepts. For example, a certain psychodynamic configuration is noted consistently in all patients suffering from peptic ulcer. The validity of such a psychological finding can be tested by making a diagnosis on the basis of the psychological findings alone, a diagnosis which can be verified by the methods of roentgenology.

Our emphasis on research as the primary objective of our Institute in itself was a sign of a reorientation. It expressed our deep conviction that psychoanalysis is not a static body of knowledge inherited from Freud, but a developing discipline. This emphasis upon research also expresses our conviction that in our young field new knowledge is paramount and even more important than teaching the little which we know about the human mind.

However, research without teaching is as incomplete as teaching without research. First of all, we need new workers to explore and develop our discipline. And there is also the great practical need for treatment and our responsibility to utilize all that we know at present for relieving human suffering, no matter how incomplete this knowledge may be. Our dream was to build a really advanced school of learning, patterned after the university, with salaried teachers who could devote the major part of their time to teaching. We could approach this ideal only to a limited degree.

A further ideal in teaching was to emphasize from the beginning that instruction should be based on the students' own observations. We thus reversed the traditional sequence of analytic training in which early theoretical indoctrination was followed by the application of theory to the patient. Thus we tried to avoid the danger of producing students who find in their patients only what they are prepared to find as a result of instruction in theory. This is the only sound way to promote the development of a field rather than merely to consolidate it. In such an early stage as that of psychoanalysis at present, rigid indoctrination is equivalent to paralysis.

Our goals in regard to therapy are of too wide scope to be discussed in any detail. We hold to the principle that our method of treatment is far from being advanced enough for consolidation. The greatest contribution of Freud was to develop a method of studying human behavior, thus acquiring a knowledge which gradually can be converted into effective and economic treatment. This requires constant revision of techniques of treatment and steady experimentation. About seven years of our brief existence has been spent primarily on such experimentation in therapy and on a critical evaluation of the therapeutic factors in psychoanalysis.

Underlying all these strivings is the conviction that in the present era of acceptance of psychoanalysis our principal responsibility is to evaluate what we know and what we can offer in good conscience to advance both our theoretical and practical knowledge, to avoid dogmatic consolidation by emphasizing that psychoanalysis is a developing discipline and not a finished product.

Our attitude toward others—the medical community and the neighboring fields—follows logically our attitude toward our own field. In this era in which the medical profession, particularly psychiatrists, want to learn all they can about psychoanalysis, our responsibility is to open up our gates and to give all we can. Instead of working in splendid isolation, we must find ways and means to reunite with the medical community which Freud had to leave for compelling historical reasons. His conceptions and findings were too novel and revolutionary to be accepted by contemporary medicine and he was forced to take the course he chose: to build an organization of his own with his own societies, journals, teaching institutions, and press.

Twenty years ago the founders of this Institute came to the conviction that in this country the time was ripe to begin the liquidation of the academic isolation of psychoanalysis and enter upon a new era of unification with the other sciences of man. The Chicago Institute was founded to create a model which might show the way for the future incorporation of analysis into the traditional places of teaching and lecturing, the universities. The Associated Psychiatric Faculties of Chicago,* of which our Institute is a vital component, is the nearest we have come thus far toward the realization of this goal: the co-ordination of residency training in psychiatry with the psychoanalytic curriculum.

Twenty years' work in this Institute represents the major portion of my professional life. This may explain my need to add on this occasion a few autobiographical remarks. By tem-

* "Psychoanalytic Training," George J. Mohr, p. 235 of this volume.

perament and predilection I am not a revolutionary. I believe in evolution and synthesis. I know well enough, however, the function of revolution in biology and social development as well as in physical nature. It was not long ago that Schroedinger called attention to the fact that the physical principle of quantum mechanics prevails also in biology, in the phenomenon of mutation. Events in nature—physical or biological—do not always take place in continua but sometimes in distinct jumps. Schroedinger showed why it would be disadvantageous in biology if mutations occurred too frequently. I should like to extend his generalization by calling attention to the fact that in history, too, gradual change by evolution and sudden changes by revolution can be observed side by side. The Platonic approach toward the realization of ideas follows both principles, evolution and revolution.

About thirty years ago when I joined the psychoanalytic fraternity, it was not because its revolutionary nature attracted me. It is true that I partook thoroughly in the gratifications derived from belonging to a group of militant innovators. I enjoyed this role not because of fighting a skeptical world but because it appealed to the most consistent tradition in my personality. I grew up in an academic environment at a time in Europe when the heritage of the nineteenth century's cultural ideology was still powerful; indeed, it was at its peak. I mean the religious adoration of the arts, literature, and the basic sciences. When I read Freud's analysis of religion in his *Future of an Illusion,* it struck me forcefully that in dethroning the formal religions, without noticing it he injected his own nineteenth-century religion of science, which was first formulated by the French encyclopedists of the eighteenth century. My earliest memory is of when I was five years old, playing in my father's library. From the top of the high bookcases the busts of Aristotle, Plato, Spinoza, Kant, Voltaire, and Diderot were looking down on me. Sitting on the floor, I tried to decipher the golden letters on a heavy volume at the bottom of a bookcase. Finally I succeeded and triumphantly exclaimed the word, "Diderot." My father was sitting at his desk engaged in writing a book on Diderot, the greatest rationalist, the most erudite exponent of the religion of reason and science. Psychoanalysis, when I turned to it, did not represent a revolution at all, but the purest tradition, that of rationalism, the unerring pursuit of knowledge, an attempt to understand the irrational components of human behavior on a rational basis. Its revolutionary history—only incidental—is due to the inertia of the human mind which cannot at once assimilate a novel combination of ideas. My loyalty to Freud in his feud with the universities and medical societies did not in the least interfere with my admiration for the temple of science, the university, where my father had taught for fifty years. If I may try to reconstruct the Platonic ideal or, in our analytic language, the psychodynamic formula, which determined my own fate, it consists in relentless striving to reconcile these two loyalties, the one to the truth represented by psychoanalysis and the other to the traditional places of learning. This is the emotional source of a continued effort to lead psychoanalysis back to its original and legitimate place: to the university. I can only thank fate, which brought me to this country which believes in change and development and where the feud between Freud and official science was not so deeply rooted, where the repatriation of psychoanalysis was a realistic possibility.

It is difficult to foresee the course which the development of psychoanalysis will take in the future. There are those who would like the *status quo* to be preserved, psychoanalysis remaining an autonomous independent field apart from the other sciences of men, with its own teaching organizations and accreditation procedures. Others, like those in the Chicago Institute for Psychoanalysis, consider the isolated development of psychoanalysis a historical incident, the sources of which lie in Europe. We feel that as a method of treatment, psychoanalysis belongs to psychiatry, from which it sprang and with which it should be reunited. We feel that this is basically the only logical trend, that it cannot be checked, although it can be retarded by administrative measures which are dictated by the old fears and mistrusts. Those who want to see psychoanalysis become an integral part of psychiatry differ among themselves only as to the optimal speed with which this unification should take place. We believe that if not *de jure,* then *de facto,* psychoanalysis in the United States, where the majority of psychiatric residents consider training in psychoanalysis as the most important part of their curriculum, has already become an integral part of psychiatry. This course of events is not different from all social processes: legislation lags behind actual social change; legislation actually ratifies, sometimes quite belatedly, a state of affairs which has arisen according to the immanent logic of historical evolution.

We believe that the historical function of our Institute was and still is to liquidate the last remnants of mistrust and tension which in the past separated psychoanalysis from the rest of medicine, from psychiatry, and from the other social sciences. This requires more than effective teaching and demonstration of our methods, conceptual tools, and results. It requires that we abandon those defensive attitudes which developed at a time when psychoanalysis was emotionally rejected both by the public and by the academic world. I daresay that these defensive attitudes today are a greater obstacle than the emotional resistance of nonpsychoanalysts.

One of the most undesirable forms of defense is intolerance of criticism from others and insistence upon uniformity, both in theory and practice. The Institute in true academic tradition will continue to invite criticism from others and encourage differences of opinion among ourselves. Above all, we shall continue in our teaching to make students constantly aware of the preliminary nature of knowledge in our youthful field. In other words, we shall continue to have a greater reverence for what is still unknown in the complex field of human nature, than to be proud of the little we now know.

The Place of Psychoanalysis in Medicine

ALAN GREGG, M.D.

THE CHICAGO Institute for Psychoanalysis is twenty years old. At about this age institutions as well as individuals deserve congratulations. These they usually get, though commonly such greetings contain an undertone of warning and advice that might offend were it not for the cheerful insouciance of youth.

In seeking for some general principle that may inform an address that I had sooner made one of unadulterated congratulatory delight, I remembered a warning I heard in college, also in my twentieth year. I venture to offer it for your reflection, for I think it as applicable to psychoanalysis as to many another activity of our lives together in these times.

It was a comment made by Professor Thomas Nixon Carver, in a course in sociology, in the year 1910. He said that the history of the human race could, of course, be written from many points of view. It could, for example, be written in terms of the struggle to survive adversity. He considered the three main types of adversity to be disease (especially epidemic infections), starvation (or varying degrees of malnutrition), and war. He said that he was prepared to admit that the human race might in the future experience more wars, but in point of the other two great classes of adversity—epidemics and famine—a fundamental change was in progress. Medical science had mastered disease to a degree never knowingly attained before by the human race. And such machines as the telegraph, the steamship, the railroad, and agricultural machinery had already converted the danger of famine into a minor risk for large parts of the human race. Two major forms of adversity were then virtually controllable, if not all but controlled. Taking off his glasses for a moment, he looked out over the class and added this prescient observation: "I suspect that some of you young gentlemen may witness the beginnings of a new kind of struggle for survival. The question for you may be not 'Who will survive adversity?' but 'Who will survive prosperity?' And, gentlemen, to guide it in the struggle to survive prosperity, the human race has as yet but little of experience, knowledge, or tradition."

I cannot help thinking that those who are making the history of psychoanalysis could sensibly reflect upon the problems of surviving prosperity. It is all but needless to say that I do not have in mind the charges or the income of psychoanalysts when I speak of prosperity. The issue transcends that petty consideration. A greater task confronts you. Psychoanalysis has survived the adversities of opposition, obloquy, disdain, disgust, hatred, and fear. It has been evaded by academic psychiatrists, condemned by universities, condemned by churches, ignored by hospitals. Ridicule, persecution, and ostracism (if such winnowing may appear to deserve the name of adversity), psychoanalysis has survived. But now it faces the task of surviving prosperity—prosperity in the form of admission to academic status, of being tolerated, of being accepted, of having attention and deference, and, most important of all, of being in demand. If surviving prosperity be a relatively new task, you have had but little experience, tradition, or knowledge to steer by.

If only because of the oncoming obligations imposed by prosperity, this celebration of your twentieth anniversary deserves attentive reflection. For, as it seems to me, mere congratulations upon survival, though they come ever so eagerly and spontaneously, come soon to be as a tale that is told, in a banquet hall without windows, a murmuring reverie with eyes closed.

At this point let me introduce a word to cover my certain incompetence to do full justice to the title of this talk, "The Place of Psychoanalysis in Medicine." The word is *stochastic,* and it is defined as "apt to discover truth by conjecture." For if I can contribute to your brooding upon psychoanalysis, I can do so at best only stochastically—only by conjecture, not from experience or erudition or by argument or proof. The stochastic brilliance of Freud has led and perhaps at times misled his followers. He was apt to discover truth by conjecture, but in addition an epic courage enhanced his stochastic power. Now, merely to witness courage is to be encouraged. Such encouragement is a great temptation to me, for my subject so far transcends my abilities.

In considering the place of psychoanalysis in medicine, let us begin on a big canvas and with an analogy. Imagine an athlete running a hundred-yard dash on some cinder track near the equator. If he is running due west at the rate of 100 yards in 10 seconds, his speed is easy to describe in terms of the track. But his speed, reckoned on other and broader criteria, requires some further reflection. The track, the judges, and the onlookers are all moving eastward with the rotation of the earth at the rate of 5,087 yards in 10 seconds. So, excellent as his pace may be, our champion is actually moving backward at the rate of 4,987 yards in 10 seconds. But if the race be held around noontime on January 1, the earth's motion westward in its orbit around the sun aids our runner to the extent that he is actually moving westward 326,457 yards in 10 seconds. This is with respect to the sun, which, unfortunately for our champion, is moving eastward—at this time of year—at such a clip that he is moving backward 2,313,543 yards in 10 seconds flat. Even without benefit of correction from astronomers (which I have had), the point of making such calculations is clear. For the point is that medicine itself is moving, in a big way, and therefore to describe the place of psychoanalysis in medicine we must give more than a hurried glance at psychoanalysis in relation to medicine. We cannot rest on the assumption that our frame of reference, medicine, is static.

Medicine itself is moving, and if we are to try to comment on the place of psychoanalysis in medicine, we can sensibly begin by noting the character and direction of changes in the medicine that is our frame of reference. Indeed, the task of discussing the place of psychoanalysis in medicine calls for more than purely spatial metaphors and similes. One thinks of parallelograms of forces, of magnetic attractions acting across existing gaps, of pressures and suctions, of actions, reactions, and interactions, of influences almost as subtle as interpersonal relations, of multiple variables, and of sequences in time, as well as of location in space.

For the purposes of exposition only, let us divide, perhaps a little arbitrarily, the changes now occurring in medicine. First, let us consider those that concern its theory or fundamental concepts; and second, the changes that concern the practice of medicine—the practical application of theoretical concepts.

Now, the general concepts in medicine that seem to me important in this mid-century decade are: (1) an increasing interest in the natural history of disease, which includes, of course, the potentialities of prevention and the maintenance of health; (2) the attempt to express the phenomena of living tissues, both healthy and diseased, in terms of chemistry and physics; (3)

the holistic and ecological approaches to the understanding of the total organism; (4) an awakening desire to put the benefits of medicine within the reach of everybody.

The astonishing successes in the control of infectious agents, both bacterial and virological, have placed doctors in a Dionysian position. They can not only protect from disease but, through surer knowledge of etiology of disease and the laws of nutrition and growth, can also almost create health. Remember that in the Oath of Hippocrates there is no reference to the duty of the doctor to prevent disease. This is vivid evidence of the novelty of the current concept of prevention in changing the whole horizon of medicine. By its very successes the idea of prevention has confirmed the view that many diseases have each their specific cause, a characteristic course they run in time, and a clearly definable nosological identity. Following refinements of observation, the concept of convergent predisposing causes has supplemented the oversimple notion that a single precipitating agent is a sufficient cause. Largely because our observations on disease have been made mostly in the so-called acute hospitals, greater interest and attention have been given to diagnosis than to the natural history of disease. The triumphs of diagnosis, prevention, and prompt treatment leave us now looking at what is left—the chronic and degenerative diseases whose natural history awaits a less brisk but more comprehensive study. Medicine as a whole bestirs itself to study the natural history of diseases—a movement not entirely new but rather freshly awakened to its own importance and its inherent promise. In this, medicine is greatly aided by increased attention to another development.

This is the attempt to analyze and formulate in the terms of physics and chemistry what have been called vital processes. This trend continues its steady and triumphant way unabated. Chemotherapy, radiation effects, ACTH, and the antibiotics all seek their final formulations in chemical and physical terms. The study of enzymes now extends even into the field of heredity and genetics. Indeed, as biochemistry and biophysics forge forward, some physiologists at times experience emotions that remind one of involutional melancholia or at least the rigors of the climacteric. Such physiologists are wondering what will be left for physiology to do. I would not despair, since this very differentiation of analytical approach to the chemical properties of tissues calls for a proportionate increase of emphasis upon integration of all the variant aspects of living tissues, organs, and organisms. Synthesis appears as a raft to save us from drowning in an ocean of knowledge.

Thus it comes about that there begins currently a sort of corrective emphasis on the holistic view of human life and its processes and on the value of an ecological approach. The dictum that the whole is more than the mere sum of all its parts begins to reassert itself and recalls the Old Testament warning, "With all thy knowledge, get understanding." Of course, the holistic concept is not synonymous with ecology. But both share a refreshing inclusiveness of view. They both allow for more variables in their equations and cover a wider range of disparate and hitherto neglected factors than can be contained in a test tube or a psychological law. The social circumstances of a patient are coming to demand a synthesis of attention beyond the vocabulary of the chemist. Very naturally, and for reasons more cogent than mere expediency, medical psychology and psychiatry are beginning to bear not merely upon the treatment of disease but upon the very concept of what some kinds of disease are, and what a healthy organism is. Treatments that before seemed treatments of disease are beginning to be doubted—to be suspected as no more than masking or mitigating the symptoms of an underlying or submerged disease process.

Lastly, another factor seems to me to be entering the lists of the dominating forces that are now changing medicine. By so much as knowledge increases, we face the inescapable sequence that leads from curiosity to research, from research to knowledge, from knowledge to power, and from power to responsibility. Reflect upon this sequence in the field of atomic energy, if you ever took casually this unavoidable cataract of consequences. By so much as there was ever an ethical obligation on a physician to apply a tourniquet to a man bleeding to death, there is now a similar obligation upon the doctor to take the major responsibility in providing plasma, in the light of our new knowledge of the value of plasma or its fractions. Indeed, the control that medicine now has over the maintenance as well as the recovery of health might be claimed as a substantive contribution to human thought. It has all but removed the fatalistic view of health and disease. It has challenged the age-old assumption that good health is a matter of good luck. The inscrutable ways of Providence are coming in for positive scrutiny. Mere man must assume the moral responsibility that used to be shouldered onto Destiny. And what were considered to be acts of God are obviously due to man's failure to act. This entrains an enormous increase in the ethical responsibility of the physician.

So much for this brief review of the changing concepts of medicine. Let us turn to the changes in the practice of medicine before we attempt to place psychoanalysis somewhere in both of these changing frames of reference.

First among the changes through which medicine is passing is the lengthening of the required period of preparation. Medical education is no longer the four-year period we have all talked about. Even the armed forces want the experience of an internship as a minimum preparation for military medical recruits. Ten thousand internships now bid for a scant seven thousand graduates. Advanced courses compete with the blandishments of an opportunity to earn a more immediate living in practice. With or without explicit or organizational acknowledgment of the fact that it is happening, the direction and control of the last three years of a good medical education are in the hands of practitioners, not teachers. The schools of public health are almost the only university institutions explicitly in the graduate field: other forms of graduate training, especially in clinical subjects, are given in hospitals. Specialization increases, but on terms formulated by the specialist boards. The control of the later years of medical education is almost as much in the hands of practitioners as were the four-year schools of medicine when Abraham Flexner in 1910 called attention to the fact that medical education deserved to be regarded as a form of university education.

The view of medicine as a whole that society is coming to hold is shifting from regarding the task as that of meeting the *demand* for medical care to that of trying to meet the much larger *need* for it. This is of tremendous significance. When four million young people have been given—I repeat, given —free medical care in World War I, and fourteen million the same in World War II, and medical care, also paid for by taxation, is furnished in veterans' hospitals, including care for non-service-connected disabilities, a good many citizens have had a demonstration of the value of medical care even if it be tax supported. Add to that lesson the spreading utilization of the insurance principle in the form of Blue Cross and Blue Shield, and you have a changed context for the practice of medicine— a changed economic, social, and political context. Medical care begins to shift from being considered a boon to the poor or a privilege of the rich to being thought of as something worth having and to be paid for—somehow—by everybody.

Further, a change is coming in the character of disease as doctors encounter it. In 1900, one-quarter of the deaths were

reported as due to chronic disease. In 1950, over two-thirds of
the deaths were due to chronic illness. Certain diseases like
mastoiditis and lobar pneumonia have become far rarer or far
less dangerous. In 1900, 17 per cent of the population were over
forty-five years of age; in 1980, we may expect that 40 per cent
—not 17 per cent, but 40 per cent—will be over forty-five. Medicine faces increases in chronic and degenerative disease. More
emphasis is due and overdue on rehabilitation, as well as on
the care of old people. And one further change: in certain countries, streets where infants' funerals used to pass in the shadow
of the church can now all too readily fill with bread riots in the
shadow of the town hall. Thus we become aware of "population problems."

Lastly, we may consider the present emphasis upon research
not so much in itself a single change in the teaching of medicine
but as the source producing innumerable changes, far-reaching
and profound, both in concepts and in practice. The discovery
of the method of research was really the discovery of discovery
and the first outbreak of countless revolutions of the mind.
Research has become the chief origin of change. In increasing
measure, such stability as wont and usage and tradition supply
to society becomes now precarious and labile. We are, as Elton
Mayo believed, no longer in a traditional society but in an
adaptive society.

Before we turn to the place of psychoanalysis in medicine,
let me recapitulate the changes in the theory and the practice
of medicine. In point of the fundamental concepts of medicine,
first, we are in a period of increasing emphasis upon the natural history of disease. Advances in our knowledge of etiology
reinforce our interest in the time factor of disease, and in predisposing and perpetuating causes as well as the specific precipitating cause. Secondly, immense progress continues in the description and comprehension of the properties of living tissues

in the exact denotative terms of physics and chemistry. This knowledge is as fecund as it is firm and exact. Moreover, it is in a language widely understood and understandable. Then, as though to counteract the almost infinite partitive and scattered predicates of chemistry and physics, we are witnessing the growth of the holistic and the ecological view of organisms and their capacities. More and more we are coming to realize that the organism has the intrinsic ability to *become* as well as to *be,* and to experience as well as to exist, and to take part in its environment as well as to react to it. And lastly, among the changing concepts of medicine I think I see evidence that its ethical sensibilities are awakening to the inescapable responsibility that follows the new power of new knowledge.

In the field of practice, the following changes in medicine may be discerned: a lengthened and specialized preparation; an increased attention to the need for medical care, a pressure for medical care, a pressure so great that it places the provision of medical care in the realm of political issues unless care can be provided by voluntary insurance; an increasing proportion of elderly people in the population; and the further virtual certainty that knowledge will be advanced by research and that new potentialities will be added to the physician's sphere of desirable services. What, then, is the place of psychoanalysis among all these forces that are changing medicine?

Psychoanalytic theory seems to me to have developed with admirable care and remarkable success the narrative aspect of disease, the significance of sequences, and the importance of early, indeed, infantile, experiences. Perhaps the phrase "the narrative aspect of disease" fails in some measure to do justice to the deeper significance of the narrative nature of psychoanalytic theory. Perhaps calling it "the principle of continuity" would be a better way of saying it. For I take it that underneath the assumption of the subconscious there is the assertion of continuity, or, in negative terms, the denial of discontinuity of process. Like a western river, it doesn't stop—it just goes on out of sight, with its continuity intact. If infantile impressions or desires were completely ephemeral and absolutely discontinuous, if each day of our lives began as a *tabula rasa* and not a palimpsest, what use would we have for the narrative as a form enabling us to understand human behavior? The physical or psychological examination, the laboratory tests, the sudden single sampling, well observed, recorded, and interpreted —this would be all. As a matter of fact, the incapacity to take a good history is a common fault of American doctors. I cannot imagine an internist who, on obtaining a fair familiarity with psychoanalytic theory, has not gained thereby a finer sense of narrative and a deeper insight into the importance of the natural history of disease. In this sense, at least, it seems to me that psychoanalysis has contributed and can further contribute to the growing sense of the decisive role of time sequences and continuity in growth and development as well as in disease processes, of becoming rather than being.

Two factors in medical education have inclined us away from the narrative or historical approach. In the first year and a half the student devotes himself almost exclusively to the description of the timeless uniformities of tissue structure and behavior. It is only later that he finds that sequences or patterns of sequences reveal important truths. And then another type of experience dulls the student's attention to the narrative method. The usual teaching hospital is a place for acute disease or for only a short sojourn for diagnosis, operation, or the early stages of treatment, and then—good-by! "Discharged relieved." Sometimes I used to wonder if hustling the patients out didn't have the suspicious advantage that the question of cure never had time to come up. So flagrant and extreme was the pressure to get what was called "fresh teaching material" that the natural history of any disease could not be shown to the student. Indeed, the surgeons in about 1912 discovered something so new that they had to find a name for it—"the follow-up method." In such a climate of frantic disregard of the natural history of disease, psychoanalysis insisted upon the overwhelming importance of the narrative aspect of disease and focused attention upon the sequence of forgotten as well as remembered events. Far deeper than that, psychoanalysis postulated a primary significance for the concept that the organism carried its past experiences as long as life endured. Incidentally, it is just for this reason that I have felt so eagerly the supplementary character of Pavlov's concept of the conditioned reflex. Conditioning enables a new meaning to be attached to a familiar stimulus—which to me is of cardinal importance in the understanding of the narrative of the organism.

I do not believe that psychoanalysis furnished the only or the first pressures in favor of the historical study of disease. But I do believe that psychoanalysis reaffirmed and effectively reiterated the essentially historical character of the organism and did so at a time when medicine needed just this insistent affirmation.

In proportion to its admirable contribution to the role of narrative and in comparison also to the rest of medicine, psychoanalysis seems to me, nonetheless, to have somewhat neglected one of the potentialities of its mastery of the narrative understanding of disease. I have never heard much mention of prevention as a salient feature of psychoanalysis. Is it foolish to wonder whether a new form of psychoanalytic interview could be devised whose purpose would be entirely preventive? The analysts' attitude seems but rarely Dionysian—in orchestral control of the factors they have defined. Like the pathologists of 1890 or 1900, their attention seems fixed on traumata and lesions already acquired. I have been puzzled at the rarity of books or articles that might indicate where and when and how forces of the psyche could be engaged or employed to prevent developments that by common consent are agreed to be harmful. Is this because each individual's experiences are so peculiarly *sui generis* that no general counsel can be formulated? It would seem to me that the great advantage I have enjoyed from learning a little about psychodynamics came quite simply from generalized statements on psychodynamics that could serve an excellent preventive purpose, were they pushed a little harder by psychoanalysts.

To subtract from the sum of human knowledge again, I would venture the opinion that psychoanalysis, as compared with other fields in medicine, lays less stress on the predisposing and the perpetuating causes of illness than upon the precipitating causes —and this to its disadvantage. Surely, in the natural history of any condition, attention could well be given, and given generously, to the predisposing and the perpetuating factors—and to the *sequelae,* too. Maybe these aspects of psychoanalytic study await development in the future.

In any event, the emphasis that psychoanalysis has placed on narrative is more than an accent on method. It seems to me to have risked everything on assuming the essentially historical character of the organism—that the individual carries his past experiences with him as long as life endures. Certainly medicine as a whole needs, and has to some degree, at least, been influenced by, this part of psychoanalytic theory.

In a sort of resonance with the present physical and chemical interpretations of cell growth and function characterizing present-day physiology and medicine, some psychoanalysts, especially in this Institute, have contributed to broadly significant studies in psychosomatic medicine. Such efforts may seem to some psychoanalysts a dereliction or even a sort of treason—

likely to compromise the integrity of their field and certain to add nothing of substance. With this attitude few physiologists, psychologists, or internists would agree. Indeed, the active pursuit of psychosomatic studies has done more to bridge the ravine between internal medicine and psychoanalysis than any other activity. And it would seem to me to be a signal step forward for both biochemists and psychoanalysts to find that the subjects they study present certain phenomena that lend themselves simultaneously to comparable expression in two different terminologies, like a man whose portrait in oils, or even in words, shows a usable similarity to a photograph taken on acetate film impregnated with silver bromide.

During the past three decades, while physiologists and clinicians found increasing satisfaction in learning to think with biochemical concepts and in biochemical terms, the psychoanalysts developed a different dialect and, indeed, a different dialectic. Of the two methods of validating a hypothesis, the physiologists prefer experiment; the psychoanalysts are usually limited to the criterion of the accuracy of their predictions. Competently used, either way of validation is good. So, for the tensions and intolerance that attend the remarkable divergence between the concepts and terminology of chemists and those of psychoanalysts, I can only revert to a motto I saw in the office of the secretary of a Viennese professor—*"Nicht ärgern: nur wundern."* For, to record a song both musical notation and written words are necessary: I cannot believe that the task of understanding a human being requires or can be satisfied by but one system of notation. Like the Scottish trial law which allows one of three verdicts—guilty, not guilty, and not proven —I decline the logic that forces acceptance of one or another of the two alternatives.

It is to the credit of psychoanalysts that they have more often attempted to correlate their observations with those of the chemists and physicists than has been the case the other way around. I do not know that I am speaking for the rest of medicine in my appreciation of the intellectual restlessness of psychoanalysts. At times I despair of mutual recognition by observers placed on opposite sides of that blinding beacon, Truth. They seem unable to see beyond the great light into the faces of other observers who see the light, too. How generous is the Moon to show us in her penumbra her thanks for the illumination we on Earth have passed on to her, having received it originally from the great source of enlightenment, the Sun. Must each graceless discipline in the study of man refuse to show a penumbra to another? Is each too insecure to give—even to give thanks?

In comparison with the rest of medicine, psychoanalysis shows a creditable openness of mind toward the holistic and the ecological. But I am not devoid of suggestions for a further advance in comprehension. It has long seemed to me that psychoanalysts would have much to gain in their equations if they showed more familiarity with heredity, conditioned reflexes, learning theory, and the work of Ames and his colleagues on the nature of experience. The besetting failure of the scientist is to assume that his equation contains all the pertinent variables. To mix metaphors, his blind spot proves to be an Achilles' heel. I haven't the time to press the arguments for thinking that heredity, conditioned-reflex theory, learning theory, and the demonstrations of Ames could all enrich psychoanalytic theory—I can only hope that there is some stochastic merit in such suggestions. Meanwhile, as I think, psychoanalytic concepts would seem to have greatly enriched the holistic approach in the study of man.

The ethical aspects of the use of the power that comes from new knowledge will always deserve sober attention. The power that comes from psychoanalysis is no exception. But it should be noted that the troubled history of the psychoanalytic movement could be adduced in defense of the charge that psychoanalysts abuse their power. It is not from groups that have known ostracism, ridicule, and hostility that one can immediately expect equanimity, tolerance, and a naturally ingenuous forgiveness. Nor does the intensely personal and individual character of analytic therapy direct your attention inevitably to your responsibilities toward large numbers of persons, as, for example, is the case with the epidemiologist or school physician. But the phenomena of transference and countertransference bear clearly, directly, and heavily upon the ethical responsibilities of the psychoanalyst. I simply do not know whether in psychoanalysis there is clear evidence of a current increase in the acceptance of responsibility. Since in ethical matters the tempo of rewards and punishments lags notoriously, but at long last proves to have unimagined strength and intensity, I would expect to find that the moral responsibilities of the psychoanalyst resemble a game where huge stakes are slowly won— slowly lost. The attempts at short therapy have much of the best kind of ethical concern for the patient's welfare. On this point, too, the motives of this Institute deserve admiring acknowledgment. But by a process of inclusion, psychoanalysis must be prepared to stand with the other branches of medicine before ethical judgments that could very naturally be as stern and searching as the power of doctors and psychoanalysts over human life and conduct is already great.

Following the order already set forth in our discussion of changes taking place in medicine, we leave the changes in the theories and come to the changes in the practice.

The teaching of psychoanalysis has been, for obvious reasons, outside the walls of most medical schools. Though this independence has provided a sort of protection whose advantages for a decade or two outweighed its disadvantages, the present demand from students for training in psychoanalysis threatens to engulf the scholarly study and singular freedom provided by isolation.

The avid interest of the oncoming generation in training analysis reflects, I think, not merely curiosity but an intense appreciation of a form of teaching that is deliberately and delicately individualized. Our medical educators could wisely brood upon the eagerness of students for intimacy in the relationship of teacher to student. The teaching of psychoanalysis provides, I think, a rare and valuable exception to the general run of impersonal exposures from which the medical student is expected to extract an education. It seems probable to me that all teachers in medicine could usefully regard the truly educative experience of a student not as a steady continuum but as a discontinuous set of moments of acute receptivity, yearning, sometimes unconscious yearning, for satisfaction. Such receptivity is the priceless product of bewilderment, but all too few of our students realize that bewilderment is the beginning of knowledge and not the first step into failure. Here again, psychoanalysis sets an example by seeking salvation through the very elaboration or working out of distress and confusion.

You have some very serious problems to solve. How can you teach so many applicants? More important still, how can you keep them under competent direction long enough to train thoroughly reliable practitioners plus an elite of investigators? At what stage of a young man's studies and personal maturity does the training analysis come best? How best to present psychoanalysis to other students than those intending to enter the field as specialists? None of these questions is trivial. How to present psychoanalysis to all medical students in general may decide the measure of understanding and acceptance that psychoanalysis will have in 1975 or the years following. How can the financial cost of training any appropriate number of applicants be carried without institutional support? Variant as the preliminary opinions would be, I should think that, since to foresee is to govern, the psychoanalysts might be wise to exchange views as to the solutions of these pressing questions, since in point of educational organization their future seems very likely to depart from their past.

Psychoanalysis suffers at present from its popularity with laymen. Here again, we have the task of surviving prosperity, perhaps confused a bit by the fact that a considerable proportion of your patients present in their personal difficulties a similar failure to survive prosperity. The solution offered by the high cost of psychoanalysis can hardly be called a permanent solution. As in medicine, persons needing psychoanalytic care greatly outnumber those who can afford to pay the analysts' charges. Being without large charity hospitals effectively devoted to the psychoanalytic study and care of indigents, you are, if anything, behind the stage of medicine a hundred years ago in the task of meeting the need for your services. A profession trained and structured to meet explicit individual requests for care is being forced to heed a general pressure to meet the far larger task—the needs of all who could be helped by medical care. Can psychoanalysis afford to neglect or ignore this change affecting the rest of medicine? Where are you headed? For a cyclone cellar built of explanations? Is a partial relief from the pressure of numbers to be expected from the economy of using better criteria for the selection of the cases psychoanalysis is uniquely fitted for? Have psychoanalysts begun to wonder whether their charges could be adjusted to the coverage of Blue Shield or any other application of the insurance principle for meeting the cost of care? In other branches of medicine many aspects of the care of patients can be delegated—to assistants, nurses, and technicians. In sharpest contrast, psychoanalytic care can be delegated almost not at all. The cost of psychoanalytic care becomes invidiously conspicuous and the danger of commercialism correspondingly difficult to avoid. It is not what the rich have to pay that worries me: it is what you will lose.

Is psychoanalysis likely to feel and react to the increasing proportion of persons over forty-five, or to the increasing proportion of chronic and degenerative disease, or to the most interesting psychological accompaniments of rehabilitation therapy?

Almost certainly you will have a contribution to make to the reproductive as well as to the sociological aspects of the population problem. Unless you do, other branches of medicine will think you are lagging at the very points where you would be expected to give some measure of help.

And now to take up the last category we considered as a part of the structure of modern medicine, namely, research. Perhaps you will think me obdurate if I say that in psychoanalytic research the findings are more intimately affected by the researcher than is the case in any other medical field. That does not *ipso facto* make the findings less reliable, but it makes them less easily verifiable and perhaps more open to qualification or rejection. Oscar Wilde's remark that all criticism is a form of autobiography comes to mind when I try to reconcile two different interpretations of but one history of a patient. So, almost unique among medical specialties, psychoanalytic research, as well as psychoanalytic teaching and patient care, requires long hours exclusively from highly trained personnel. I would hope that you will find a way to preserve the devotion to scholarly research that is the undoubted heritage you have received from days when psychoanalytic research was pursued in isolation— sometimes enforced, sometimes deliberate. No administrative regulations can secure or preserve the wonderful freedom of the outcast or the hermit. Such liberty cannot be given: it can only be taken. I venture to incite you thus only because if you expand or intensify your contacts with the rest of medicine, you will be under a powerful pressure to collaborate at the expense of the very identity and tradition that Freud developed so wonderfully in isolation from the university. Virtue of that sort is deliberately lonely business, as is walking any tightrope, with falls possible on either side.

With such reservations, it is nonetheless consistent to help to bridge the gap—at times the canyon—between psychoanalysis and the rest of medicine. Part of this chasm is due to differences of dialect and dialectic, of terminology and semantics. The guerdon will belong to those who can speak both languages.

Now, doubly dangerous as is the lot of the go-between and the self-appointed interpreter of one side to the other, my assignment this morning implies something of that perilous obligation.

To begin with, medical men have for years regarded psychiatry as an island lying off the coast of the mainland of medicine, doubtless connected geologically with the mainland but not very accessible to less than adventurous spirits. For the past ten years psychiatry has been a sort of St. Michel, an island only when the tides of feeling are at the flood. You need no reminder of the somewhat similar status accorded by psychiatrists to psychoanalysts. The history of psychoanalysis has involved all the tensions and complexities that may be expected when an eclectic minority forms within an already half-ostracized and supersensitive clan. The status of psychiatry in medicine is precarious enough: to discuss the place of psychoanalysis in medicine suggests an imaginary epic of how Cinderella's unacknowledged child got into the Social Register. Your history reminds one of William the Conqueror, for it takes strong wings to fly in the face of the correctitudes and right into the eye of the wind of doctrine. You must be strong to have done that, and you must be strong if you are to continue doing that.

But you have scarcely reached as yet such a degree of acceptance by medicine as a whole as to make it quite safe to ignore your critics. Doubtless you could secure the services of the Gallup poll to find the place of psychoanalysis in medicine. I don't know what the figures would have been if that method had been applied in each decade beginning in 1910, but I am sure that the proportion of those completely ignorant of, as well as those completely hostile to, psychoanalysis has steadily diminished.

If I were to try to express the more superficial aspects of the attitude of American doctors to psychoanalysis, it would run something as follows: they admit psychoanalytic theory in much the same way that they admit the existence and the occasional usefulness of a foreign language they can't read or speak—useful to those who like to travel, doubtless an accomplishment, but somewhat suspect and unreliable, and hardly essential. While admitting psychoanalytic theory and borrowing convenient fragments as they borrow occasional French words like "brazeer" and "liaisong," they watch your practice with uninformed skepticism as to your successes and jealous suspicion of your charges per hour. When you take on cases carelessly, they snort with a disdain that finds righteous solace only when they hear that you are quarreling among yourselves. They resent your neglect of experimental corroboration and the dogmatic nature of your assertions and formulations. Your efforts in the fields of correlation or connection with the accepted forms of clinical study occasion among American doctors almost exactly the same range of responses they show when a foreigner tries to speak English —no resentment, occasional sympathy, a sort of provincial and pleased respect, and a tolerant but not very imaginative approval.

You will perhaps think this comment flippant. But I beg you to realize the capital importance of the problem of the Tower of Babel. Much of the effectiveness of living in modern society depends on our ability to get ourselves understood: it even requires effort! The alternative is infinite confusion.

Let me conclude this talk by reverting again to a larger canvas and a more extensive horizon. I pose this question: Is medicine influencing human thought as deeply as it might? How, for example, do physicians compare today with physicists in contributing to the world's store of ideas? Copernicus, a physician, revolutionized our ideas of the universe, but certainly not from his medical knowledge nor in the mood of confining his mind to his occupational problems. But have physicians as human beings contributed greatly of late to human thought? There are areas such as the population problem where the general advances of medicine have posed problems related to the survival of prosperity. But where have physicians contributed in a substantive way to extending the horizons of the mind in any way comparable to the contributions of Sigmund Freud? And if you were to answer, in happy acquiescence, "Nowhere!", I would pose again the question, "Is medicine influencing human thought as deeply as it might?"

The Impact of Psychoanalysis
on Training in Psychiatry

MAURICE LEVINE, M.D.

THIS MEETING has meaning and purpose in various ways. We are here to do honor to the Institute and to the faculty which has guided its growth with such warmth and tenacity and energy and productiveness, and which has contributed so much to the development of the practice of medicine and the science of man. We are here, especially the alumni among us, to acknowledge our debt of gratitude to an institution which has meant so much to us personally. And we are here to speak, not only of this Institute and its achievements, but also of some of the general problems of psychoanalysis, of psychiatry, of medicine, and of the other fields of human activity in which the Institute has been concerned.

But, first of all, we must speak of the Institute and its achievements. Perhaps I can do this best by saying that when one thinks of the psychoanalytic institute in which one has had one's training, one's thoughts go back automatically to the material of one's own analysis and to one's childhood. And so I think of an experience of my childhood which has pertinence, shall we say, to the achievements of the Institute. It is the religious celebration of the Seder, the Passover dinner which expresses thanksgiving for the deliverance of the Jews from Egypt. One Hebrew word in that service is memorable—the word *Dayenu,* which means "It would have been enough." During the ritual, the father of the family recites the fact that God separated the Red Sea, and everyone at the dinner table responds with the emphatic word *"Dayenu."* Then the reader mentions the manna from Heaven and everyone chimes in with an emphatic *"Dayenu."* This continues pleasurably for a long list of miracles and grateful *"Dayenus."*

And certainly this childhood memory fits our celebration of the miracles of the Institute and the deliverance of the alumni from the Egypt of descriptive psychiatry. When we mention the fact that Alexander and the others of the Institute played a central role in bringing psychoanalysis into close contact with the general field of psychiatry, we can all say, *"Dayenu,*—it would have been enough." Then today's ritual must mention the fact that the Institute played a vital role in bringing psychoanalysis back to the major stream of medical theory and practice and research, with the enormously significant psychosomatic studies, and again an emphatic *Dayenu* is in order. And certainly the fact that throughout these twenty years the Institute has served as a center of training for many psychoanalysts and others and as an active center of treatment deserves the response of, "This also would have been enough." And then we must list the research on therapy and the attempt to delineate the essential factors in therapeutic technique and procedure. This, too, deserves the accolade of *Dayenu,* although were I enough of a linguistic scholar, I could add a word that would mean "Hold on now, this might be too much."

Surely the pleasurable memory, with its theme song of *Dayenu,* represents our feeling toward the Institute. Today's celebration, like the other, is one of respect and warmth and devotion, and bespeaks our pride in the history of the Institute.

But now we must turn from the past to the present, and from paeans of praise of the Institute to the more general problems

of psychoanalysis and psychiatry in which the Institute is playing a major role. I shall focus on the impact of psychoanalysis
on the training of psychiatrists. Perhaps I can point up my comments historically by making a brief contrast between the status
of psychoanalysis and of psychiatry twenty-five years ago and
the status today. Then the two were relatively independent and
represented fairly disparate streams of activity, of theory, of
practice, and of research. Only a very small number of psychiatrists were interested in psychoanalysis or included analytic
training in the preparation for their careers. In some specific
and circumscribed aspects, psychoanalytic understanding had
influenced psychiatric work and teaching, but the main stream
of psychiatric thought was relatively untouched. Psychiatric
teaching was essentially nonanalytic, and academic promotion
in the field of psychiatry was seriously jeopardized if the psychiatrist was outspoken in his psychoanalytic orientation.

Today the pendulum has swung far in the opposite direction. Psychiatry is in many ways deeply and basically psychoanalytic in approach; psychiatric residents in large numbers
recognize the urgent necessity, either of specific analytic training, or of a meaningful psychodynamic basis for their psychiatric work; and most of the new professors of psychiatry are
analysts or are understanding of psychoanalytic material.

In short, the historic situation is that we have witnessed an
amazing vitalization of the field of psychiatry. An essentially
static and descriptive discipline has become dynamic and vital
and energetic. Psychoanalysis has played an outstanding part
in the transformation, but it has not been the sole agent of the
change. The development of the shock therapies and other
somatic methods, despite the absence of an acceptable theory
of their action, and in spite of their not infrequent misuse, has
energized the hospital care of psychiatric patients and given
its practitioners a sense of being active therapeutic participants

rather than passive observers. And from another angle the field of psychiatry has been vitalized. The growth of community clinics, with their emphasis on family dynamics and the meaningful impact of interpersonal relations and environmental stress, has stimulated the field of psychiatry to a much more dynamic approach. And here the role of child psychiatry is of high consequence. Further, in our reference to the factors that have transformed and vitalized psychiatry, we cannot forget the influence of psychiatric military experience, nor the historic role of Adolf Meyer in preparing American psychiatry for its fusion with psychoanalysis.

Although shock therapy, child psychiatry, and other developments have played their part in the vitalization of psychiatry, the influence of psychoanalysis in the past twenty-five years is predominant. In everyday psychiatric work, the impact of psychoanalytic understanding is outstanding. The emphasis on a nosology of clear-cut and rigid descriptive entities has given way to a subordination of clinical diagnosis to dynamic and genetic formulations. Fact-finding question-and-answer examinations have been subordinated to interviewing which is much more spontaneous and free-flowing and permits the appearance of significant emotional sequences and dynamic trends, and which fosters the sensitive development of good physician-patient relations and communication. The emphasis on heredity and constitution has been subordinated to an understanding of anxiety and defenses, of drives and patterns of adaptation. The emphasis on intellectual understanding is joined by understanding based on empathy. In the training of the psychiatrist, the psychoanalytic influence is obvious in the growth of the system of individual supervision and case seminars. The therapy of the psychiatrist, now largely a psychotherapy, is based more and more on serious consideration of the patient's conscious and unconscious conflicts and dynamics, and his distortions in the therapeutic situation. Even the psychiatrist's prescriptions to an occupational therapist, to include one specific sample of the psychiatrist's job, are based on dynamic understanding—for example, the ways in which occupational therapy may be planned to fit into a patient's guilt or with his destructive drives. A long list could be given of the specific ways in which general psychiatry today shows the extensive impact of psychoanalytic understanding, but, for this group, such a list would be merely a statement of the obvious. Perhaps some excerpts from experience with actual patients will be more relevant than descriptive statements, even though for many of the audience today such case material is taken for granted.

A young man of nineteen who had poliomyelitis, with paralysis of all four extremities and the diaphragm, was unable to come out of the respirator for more than seven minutes at a time, even though his somatic status would have permitted independent breathing for many hours. The forcing insistence, by the hospital personnel, that he stay out of the respirator, eventually expressed in a rejecting critical attitude, led only to anxiety attacks and panic when he tried. Psychiatric study rather quickly revealed the following facts: His dominant emotions were those of extreme anger and expectation of disaster and death. He had been struggling to suppress his resentment at those who, throughout his illness, had been admiring the fact that he had taken its onslaught with such stoicism, and who had urged him to be a good sport whenever he began, in the slightest, to complain. Actually he had a violent resentment at being sick and paralyzed, and toward those who were unaffected and could walk and be independent. And with this surging resentment, he was, in reality, completely dependent on those toward whom his resentment was directed. He was afraid that any show of hostility to the nurses might lead them to neglect him and so endanger his very existence. And in this setting of complete dependence on others and on mechanical apparatus, he had regressed to the level of symbiotic dependence on others and on the respirator, and then developed the deep anger which often goes with such dependence. He was like a child, who, feeling hateful toward its parents, is unsure of their protection and expects punishment and disaster. He had pervasive doubts that the nurses would place him in the respirator in time, and had intense fears of disaster and crisis. Therapeutic dealing with the dependency-hatred problem, in relation to current figures and to the therapist, led to a marked increase in his ability to stay out of the respirator. Further, it was clear that in his regression, the iron lung became not merely a loved protective mother-figure who gave life and strength, but also the hated mother-figure, who might die and leave him to die unprotected. His enormous fear that the respirator might stop, particularly when he was not in physical contact with it, led to memories of his fears in childhood that when he was angry at his mother, his mother might stop breathing, and he himself would die. A clarification of this neurotic symbiosis with the hated and loved respirator led to further clinical improvement.

A second patient, a man of thirty, had been on the surgical service for two years, following the first stage of a two-stage chest operation. The first-stage operation had been surgically successful, but it was followed by a downhill course with serious loss of weight, persistent draining infection unchecked by antibiotics, and a general state of debility which made the surgeons refuse to take the risk of the second-stage operation. Finally he was transferred to the psychosomatic ward. For the first time he was given an opportunity to talk and to develop a productive relationship with a physician. Many dynamic factors became apparent quickly and easily, the most pertinent revealed by the fact that he had married a dominating woman of whom he was afraid; that he had had recurrent dreams, long before his chest disorder, of being hurt and damaged by women with knives; and that, in reality, and this was crucial, the second stage of the chest operation was to be done by an aggressive surgical resident who was a woman. Obviously, in part at least, his downhill course was based on his fear of being in a helpless anesthetized state while a woman wielded a surgical knife on his chest. This story, I can add, had a happy ending.

The third case, to indicate the present vitalized and dynamic state of psychiatry, was a forty-five-year-old man, admitted to the medical service with a severe cardiac decompensation. He was gravely, critically ill. He was given the usual heroic medical treatment, which, however, was interrupted every hour or two by the patient's insistence on getting out of bed, throwing wide the near-by window, and doing deep knee-bends and gymnastics. Psychiatric consultation revealed that his primary orientation had to do with pseudomasculine strength; that his cardiac decompensation had directly followed a fight in which he had been knocked down for the first time in his life; that he then had raced up four flights of stairs to show that he still was a man; and that when the decompensation began, he developed enormous fears of weakness. His deep knee-bends were his method of proving to himself that his cardiac disorder would not leave him weak and helpless. The medical residents thought that it might be necessary to force him to stay in bed, since there was serious danger that his gymnastics might lead to sudden death. The psychiatric consultant advised taking the calculated risk, and the patient continued his combined myocardial and athletic regime, gradually improved, and was discharged from the hospital. He failed to return for outpatient care, and several weeks later he was again admitted to the hospital in cardiac decompensation, of approximately the same degree of severity. In the meantime the medical residents had rotated to another hospital service and a new medical resident was in charge. When the patient began hopping out of bed to do his knee-bends at the window, he was tied to his bed, struggled vehemently for a short period, then lay completely quiet and inert, and in two hours, was dead.

Now problems such as these three are characteristic of a large portion of the current work of the psychiatrist and exemplify the fact that psychiatric work, in the hospital and in office practice, must rely in many ways on the insights and methods which are basically psychoanalytic. And one must add that at present only a tiny fraction of the patients who could respond will receive this kind of therapy.

Certainly, one can say that tremendous progress has been made in the integration into the general field of psychiatry of the pertinent contributions of psychoanalysis. But this highly desirable development leads to many problems which are far from solution. And today I want to concentrate on the problems that we face, rather than to amplify further the details of the ways in which psychoanalysis already has influenced the general field of psychiatry—details which most of you know. Essentially, the question can be phrased this way: How are we to make an integration and application of psychoanalysis to general psychiatry that will be effective and sound and safe? How can we preserve the values of such a development and avoid the dangers of flabby psychiatry and of wild analysis? Twenty-five years ago, psychiatrists and psychoanalysts were not confronted with such problems. Psychiatrists could do their limited job, protected from the complexities of dynamic thinking by a variety of defensive strictures against analysis, and analysts could do their limited job with the point of view that only those who were fully trained should work with analytic or dynamic concepts.

The simple solution now recommended by some psychoanalysts, a solution simple in concept but not in execution, is that any psychiatrist who wants to do more than a minimum of psychotherapy should have full psychoanalytic training. Such a solution is ideal, and I would recommend it heartily, whenever it is practicable, for those residents who are suitable as candidates and want to have such thorough training. But I feel convinced that such a solution is not the only good plan, that in part it represents an unnecessary expenditure of time and energy and money, and that at times it may represent a diversion of some of the basic goals of an analytic institute. In fact, there are many objections to such a plan as the predominant goal in our thinking. One obvious objection is that it is impractical, on a large scale, to meet community needs. The effort must be made to have several times as many residents in psychiatric training as we have now, and any large increase in the enrollment of institutes, or the setting up of many new institutes, provides serious risks for the institutes and for analytic training. But of even greater importance, there now is a growing body of evidence that something less than full analytic training is adequate to produce a group of psychiatrists whose dynamic training prepares them to do a first-rate job.

To rephrase the problem, I might say that I quoted three typical cases not only to characterize the historic situation of the development of a dynamic psychiatry, but also to pose the central problem of those of us who function as medical educators in the current scene. The problem can be stated in this way: How can we reconcile the enormous social and community need for good psychiatric care and facilities with the fact that the training of the psychoanalyst is a protracted and arduous process and limited to a relatively small number? Can such patients be handled only by those who are psychoanalysts, or is it possible to give enough training in psychoanalytic understanding and method to a very much larger group of psychiatrists, so that they will be able to do a worth-while job with such patients? To me, the answer is clear. On the basis of experience, we now can say with assurance that many such patients can be handled effectively by psychiatrists who do not have full analytic training. We are not yet ready to present careful studies of such a dynamic psychiatric approach to patients, but we can say that in seminar after seminar we have presented to us good studies of such patients, with dynamic understanding of a respectable sort, and often with a predictable therapeutic response.

At this point, I think it imperative to attack directly one of the unfortunate by-products of the emphasis on full analytic training in the education of the psychiatrist. One current distortion is that a psychiatrist, no matter how good, is a second-class citizen if he does not have full psychoanalytic training. In reality, a well-trained psychiatrist, whose training has included the vitally pertinent aspects of psychoanalytic understanding and technique, is a first-class citizen of the medical community. He has certain limitations in that his training does not qualify him for some aspects of protracted reconstructive therapy and for an understanding of some patterns of genetic and dynamic sequence. But he has enough understanding to permit him to work effectively at his chosen level; he has the advantage of touching therapeutically on a larger number and variety of troubled human beings; and in his training and subsequent growth and development, he can use the time that psychoanalysts use otherwise for his own accumulation of a mass of experience that makes him qualified to deal effectively with many problems in which the psychoanalyst has not had time or opportunity to develop competence. In short, when one contrasts a physician who had good dynamic psychiatric training and then psychoanalytic training and then concentrated on psychoanalytic work for five years, with a physician who had good dynamic psychiatric training and then concentrated on psychiatric work (in good part psychodynamic and psychotherapeutic) for five years, one would conclude that each was doing a good job in a somewhat different fashion, that each had assets that the other did not have, and that the label of second-class citizen had nothing to do with reality.

If, so far, my approach is acceptable, many inferences and problems follow. One inference is that a man may choose to be a psychiatrist (psychoanalytically oriented, of course) rather than a psychoanalyst, and may make his choice on a rational basis, not on the current situation of a shortage of training analysts. And it is my conviction that many residents should make such a decision. They can have an effective, productive, self-respecting career. And a psychoanalytic institute may feel freer in recommending that a man not have full analytic training without feeling that it is excluding him from the ranks of the saved and the best. Actually the institute is recommending a valuable alternative career.

Now let us concentrate further on this man who will choose to be a general psychiatrist rather than a psychoanalyst. He may decide to have full psychoanalytic training, wanting to be able to do analysis part time in his later practice, or because he wants to have the thoroughgoing understanding of psychodynamics and psychotherapy in his psychiatric work which only full analytic training can give him. (And I should hope that many would so decide.) He may, however, decide that deeply penetrating or thoroughgoing understanding is not necessary, that a good understanding is enough. In such a circumstance, it is his job and that of his training center to see to it that in his psychiatric training he does develop an understanding of dynamics and therapy that in reality deserves the label of good although not thoroughgoing. And I am sure that all of you will agree that this is not an easy job, and that we are not at the moment certain of the content or the methods to be used in such training.

At this point, we must face a serious objection to my point of view. Some analysts are of the opinion that a practicing psychotherapist must have thoroughgoing training to be able to handle any type of development during the course of therapy. The argument would be that in the course of any psychotherapy, dynamic problems may arise which may call for a more thorough understanding and more radical therapy than one not fully trained might handle, and that he must be prepared for any eventuality. To this, I would say that it is a counsel of perfection and an approach in which one asset dictates a total situation. And the answer to such an objection seems to me fairly obvious, when one considers other medical areas and specialties. It certainly is true that the usual general surgeon does not have a thoroughgoing training in orthopedics, but he still can include the handling of many dislocations and fractures, many patients with low back pain, in his practical work. And certainly in the handling of such patients, eventualities may arise in which he would be more effective if he had had thoroughgoing training in the principles and practice of orthopedics. But he knows a good amount and in most circumstances it is enough, and if he is a person of integrity, he recognizes his limitation and works collaboratively with the orthopedist. And all of us have known some excellent pediatricians and general practitioners who knew enough of dermatology, or cardiology, and so on, without being thoroughgoing, and who had built up a working concept of the levels of their own understanding and competence and skill in many areas. By sacrificing thoroughness and depth they preserve their capacity for breadth and widespread usefulness, and call on others to add depth when necessary.

This, then, leads to the most difficult question: What constitutes good but not thoroughgoing understanding of psychoanalytic dynamics and methods? Can there be some answer to this problem in terms of levels of practical working understanding and competence?

Perhaps I can clarify my comments on this problem by saying that medical education in general is confronted with the question of how to plan teaching which is to be good but not thoroughgoing. Many of you recall the weeks and months of learning the data of human anatomy. The essential concept in your medical school days was that all physicians should have a complete and thorough understanding of anatomy, in great detail and at all levels of complexity and organization. It was obvious to most of you that this was a tremendous waste of time and energy and had value for most students only if it led to some emphasis on ideals of careful work and tenacity if such ego patterns were inadequate. It was apparent to you that apart from its disciplinary effects, such studies in anatomy were pertinent only for those who planned major surgery as a career, and that it should be possible to teach anatomy more effectively to most medical students by limiting the teaching to the inculcation of a point of view, of a limited number of basic facts and principles, of good but incomplete levels of understanding, of clear demonstration of patterns.

And essentially such a change has taken place. Recently I have been on the curriculum committee of a medical school. My conception of the teaching of the first two years, especially of the anatomy course, was based on my memories of my own medical school days. To my surprise, I found that the course had changed radically, that a large part of the old course in anatomy was condensed, and was amplified only in the later elective course in surgical anatomy and in the graduate teaching of the clinical subjects themselves, for example, orthopedics. Exactly the development which I am recommending as one alternative in the field of psychiatry was taking place in the field of anatomy, namely, the course for all students was limited in scope and stressed good but not thoroughgoing understanding.

And in other fields, the same problem exists—mathematics is one of the basic sciences in the education of the atomic physicist, the research chemist, the engineer, the business executive, and the public accountant. Yet, the teaching of mathematics to the executive and the accountant can be different from the mathematics taught to the physicist.

And so this is our problem: if, as now seems clear, psychoanalysis provides our closest approximation to a satisfactory body of knowledge about the anatomy and physiology of the personality, how can we teach its substance, not only in detail and depth to those who are to be psychoanalysts, but in usable form to those who are to be psychiatrists, and in still less extensive form to internists and others?

Now let me try to phrase very briefly some of my ideas about what of psychoanalysis is to be taught to the resident in psychiatry. If he simultaneously is in psychiatric residency training and in psychoanalytic training, the two of course should be interrelated, but can be thought of essentially as the integration of modern psychiatric residency work with the modern curriculum of a psychoanalytic institute. Problems arise, but they are largely problems of organization and institutions, the matter of timing and sequences, the selection of candidates, and so on. But when the psychiatric training is not associated with concurrent full analytic training, we are confronted with a different set of problems, in an area largely uncharted and unexplored. Let me summarize my experience in this way: The resident should be given great breadth of experience with a wide variety of types of cases, but with time enough to work in concentrated fashion with a limited case load. He should have full and well-supervised experience with both inpatients and outpatients, with greater emphasis on experience with patients than on theory. He should have adequate training in neurologic and other medical disciplines pertinent to his work. He should be trained in hospital management; he should deal with psychotic as well as neurotic patients, have experience with children as well as adults, be at ease with shock therapy as well as other somatic methods of treatment; he should be able to work with psychologists, social workers, and various agencies; he should develop a research attitude, and perhaps research interests, and be competent in clinical diagnostic work. In addition, then, in a psychoanalytically oriented center, he should learn an adequate psychodynamics and psychotherapy. I attempted to indicate my conception of the workable level of such understanding in my chapter on treatment in the recent book, edited by Alexander and Ross, *Dynamic Psychiatry*. To amplify a bit: In the area of psychodynamics, as I see it, the resident should try first to achieve a fairly full understanding of environmental stresses and strains and of conscious problems and conflicts. This, then, should lead to a limited understanding of unconscious patterns. Essentially, in this area, his understanding would be of current dynamic problems rather than of infantile neurosis, although he certainly can include some understanding of the effects of gross childhood influences in the production of later dynamic problems. He need learn little of the subtleties of overdetermined sequences, of thorough interpretation of dreams, of symbol interpretation, of the dream screen, and the like. But he would learn a great deal about the indications of anxiety and its typical defenses, of patterns of conflict at various stages of development, of current repressed hostility, of guilt and its consequence, of unrecognized envy, of the wish to be protected and fed, of the problems of love and human relations. He would learn a fair amount about ego strength and weakness. And he would learn something of the difference between fixation and regression.

In the field of psychotherapy, he would learn largely the ways of applying his limited dynamic understanding to the choice of, and the carrying through of, appropriate techniques. By and large, he would use procedures which fall under the category of supportive and relationship therapies and would do a restricted uncovering psychotherapy. The relative infrequency of his appointments with patients and his face-to-face interviews would largely prevent the development of a reactivated infantile neurosis, the elucidation and solution of which are regarded by many analysts as the crux of analytic therapy. Incidentally, the recommendations with regard to therapy by the Chicago Institute, even though they are the focus of disagreement in psychoanalytic circles, are of the highest significance as they are applied to psychotherapy suitable for the dynamically oriented psychiatrist.

Perhaps I can express my conception of the level of the resident's understanding and therapy by a series of comparative phrases: He would deal more with conscious and preconscious problems than with unconscious; he would deal more with current dynamics than with genetics; he would use relationship therapy more than an uncovering therapy; he would use the technique of clarification much more than the technique of interpretation; his goal would be more of symptomatic relief and improvement in current relations than of character reconstruction; he would deal more with reality problems than with basic fantasies.

And I express my conviction that the development of wild analysis can be averted by a constant emphasis in supervision on countertransference attitudes, by a persistent teaching of the avoidance of direct interpretation of symbols and the unconscious, by an emphasis on limited therapeutic goals, and by a constant emphasis on the value of clinical diagnosis, as a way of prevention of inept therapy with fragile and explosive patients.

Now, if such an analytically oriented program for the training of psychiatrists proves workable and effective, a number of desirable ends will be reached. The psychoanalytic institutes will be freed of the unbearable pressure of training all psychiatrists. A much larger group of adequate psychiatrists can be trained to meet community needs. Psychiatrists will not regard themselves as second-rate citizens or develop unfortunate defenses against such feelings. And an incidental by-product will be that many residents who plan to have full analytic training can postpone that portion of their program. In their psychiatric residency, they can develop not only the usual skills of the psychiatrist, but also the capacity to do a self-respecting psychotherapy. With this in prospect, the rush to have analytic training concurrent with psychiatric training can be avoided; and the resident then can finish his psychiatric training, take a post as psychiatrist or go into practice, and have his analytic training at a time when it will not jeopardize his financial status and his ability to support his family, will not put his personal life under undue strain, and will not lead to an overemphasis on financial stability and income. Further, his decision to have analytic training will be made at a point when his experience will have clarified for him the question of whether he actually wishes to function as a psychoanalyst.

In summary, I have attempted to show the impact of psychoanalysis on psychiatry, not only by indicating the ways in which such an influence now is obvious, but also by pointing up the problems which have arisen from this impact, particularly in the field of the training of the psychiatrist. And in all of this impact, of course, one predominant force has been the Institute we honor today.

Discussion

HENRY W. BROSIN, M.D.

IT IS NOT easy to express deep gratitude publicly without approaching the unseemly. Yet many of us share the feelings that this faculty, largely self-sustaining, has adhered consistently and with high fidelity for twenty years to the highest ideals of the experimental method. This courage and steadfastness has made its members powerful and significant figures in the lives of many of us and those with whom we are associated. We can only hope that this faculty will be permitted to continue to exercise its many functions for many more years to improve the quality of psychoanalysis and psychiatry.

There is little need for me to add to Doctor Levine's splendid exposition of the different levels and goals of training in psychiatry. He has shown us the problems in the integration of psychoanalysis and psychiatry, and the dangers inherent in flabby psychiatry and wild analysis. He faces the problem of enormous community needs realistically, for he does not want to dilute the training of psychoanalysts nor does he believe that everyone who wants this training can utilize it to the full.

There are excellent teachers who will question his support of the concept of limited training. Perhaps this concept applies more to the acquisition of skills through supervision than to the acquisition of knowledge or even understanding of the patient's behavior. There are so many variables operating in this situation that only prolonged discussions will permit even a good description of the more basic issues, because some real issues are hidden by verbal obscurity.

Perhaps I would better point out several other familiar areas in which psychoanalysis has an impact on psychiatric training. In a chapter in the Alexander and Ross text, *Dynamic Psychiatry* (1),* these and other related topics are mentioned, but a few merit reconsideration.

In less competitive days, before 1930, most psychiatrists learned their skills by the apprenticeship system at a state hospital without the benefit of highly formalized curricula. A few university or community hospitals were gradually built up after 1900, but they had no specific psychological methods to develop their therapeutics or research, and anyone who persisted could enter the field. With the influx of psychoanalysis we are now challenged more pointedly by the questions: Who is best fitted to become a good psychiatrist? What are the qualities of a good psychiatrist? What are the various functions performed by psychiatrists in their highly varied settings and how shall we train them for their manifold duties? Is it theoretically feasible to train men of widely varying abilities and experiences in a single pattern within a core curriculum? What worth-while qualities are sacrificed in demanding high compliance during a long period of a student's most imaginative years?

Testing methods of the quantitative types susceptible to treatment by factor analysis and projective techniques give us interesting but not conclusive criteria. Psychoanalysis encourages us to go on along this difficult road because we can see much more clearly now than ever before why some men function well in chosen areas and not in others, and we can perceive the nature of the difficulties which prevent some men from even a modest development of their abilities. Freud's suggestion that a trial analysis was the best method of estimating a candidate's capacities for growth as a therapist may still be the best screening

---

* Numbers in parentheses refer to references at end of paper.

device we have, but the combined skills of many training analysts will eventually give us much more sound and publicly verifiable data as to who may become a proficient therapist (2). As we find better means to describe the therapeutic process in its many ramifications, we shall be able to sharpen our ability to differentiate men according to their growth potential, their intuitiveness, their integrity, their resistance. A much deeper understanding of the nature of individual differences and methods for detecting them in small samples is now becoming possible. The psychiatric scene is also changing because we can give much more depth to the concepts of motivation which are essential to an understanding of personality. For example, why does one man pursue at wearisome length purely verbal methods of dealing with human problems while another indefatigably insists on a physical metier whether it be gas, heat, electricity, or water? It seems as if analysis may help provide methods for detecting such career patterns before the eighteenth year as well as help us understand those unusual workers known as "dedicated" men (5). Much time is devoted to emphasis on this selection of residents as an important phase of psychoanalytic learning because it may be one of the most important things we do. If we could encourage the most gifted men to work in the field, we should not need to worry about the continuity of original contributions and a high level of practice. Without them we face a growing sterility, so dourly suggested by Sachs (8).

Levine has pointed out that if we train more residents in psychoanalytic psychiatry we shall have a much larger pool from which to choose those men who are genuinely devoted to psychoanalysis and able to practice it at the best levels.

It is obvious that progress in this field will make enormous differences in the amount of pertinent information we shall have about the choice of occupation in many other areas, and thus will add considerably to the probability of a man's finding himself in a proper sphere of activity in a rapidly increasing complex world.

Although patient-doctor relations are usually a function of the cultural level of the community where they occur, it seems to me that psychoanalytic methods have done much to improve the level of doctor-patient relations in our time. The best standards of therapeutic relations as outlined by Hippocrates, Osler, and Peabody and practiced by thousands of cultivated men did not always permeate to all practitioners. Most of us have seen sheer power operate in doctors for quite ignoble motives, to the disadvantage of the patient. The methods of psychoanalysis, properly applied, make such attitudes improbable because the therapist must study himself and the patient with real respect and with a minimum of self-deception. While human frailty will always result in some failures in execution of the ideal deportment, it seems apparent that psychoanalysis through its influence upon psychiatry, psychology, pediatrics, education, the social sciences, and literature has been one of the most powerful humanizing forces of the twentieth century. It has compelled a more sensitive handling of the individual and has consequently forced a more respectful attitude toward the dignity of the individual man. This is in the best tradition of eighteenth-century enlightenment, both European and American, but is strongly needed to withstand the authoritarian attitudes so prevalent since the two wars. Most psychiatrists now understand much more thoroughly the need to treat patients in a decorous manner in order to treat them at all. Even proponents of mechanical or physical therapies are aware that with some psychological preparation and aftercare their patients will do much better. With the growth of group practice, insurance and industrial panels, and huge government agencies, the much-lauded private doctor-patient relationship is under severe stress, but psychiatrists are helping all doctors understand why this contract is a particularly delicate one, which should not be altered carelessly. It is notable that psychoanalysis, which is hated and feared in so many quarters as degrading to the highest human values, including those of art, ethics, and creativity, should be so potent a method to improve human conduct for scientific reasons.

Psychoanalysis has had an important share in altering the types of investigation used by psychiatrists. While anatomic and neurophysiologic research methods are absolutely essential to a better comprehension of central nervous system activity, they do not answer the need for concepts and working methods of psychological problems at their own distinctive level of organization. Psychoanalysis provided both concepts and methods for doing so and has enabled us to break away from the rigid statistical designs of Karl Pearson and the earlier workers in comparative psychology into more flexible techniques. This reflects itself in training, but much more energy should be spent in helping psychiatric residents understand the postulates and the methods of psychoanalytic processes. Every psychiatrist as well as every good doctor should be a trained observer and interpreter so that he may be a true scientist in a clinical setting. The discoveries of Planck and Einstein have shown us how quite improbable solutions to vexing old dilemmas have been found, and we can hope for similar enlightenment if a sufficient number of gifted men apply themselves freely to the problems in our field.

It is quite probable that even without psychoanalysis, the training programs for residents in psychiatry would have become more formalized, with many fixed didactic courses in the basic physical and social sciences as well as in medical and psychological management of patients. It is also fair to say that the teachings of Freud as they have come to centers of residency training—whether federal, state, city, university, private clinics, or hospitals—have awakened large therapeutic ambitions in many young men. They definitely favor those clinics where there is psychoanalytic supervision of their early treatment cases; in fact, the more the better. This pressure from students has been another force for the growth of psychoanalytic ideas in the medical world. Students and residents have accelerated the spread of Freudian concepts and practices to such an extent that the approved training centers are embarrassed by their responsibilities. Levine has described this burden and presented some solutions in the direction of limited training in psychoanalytic psychiatry. I should like to stress one aspect of continued training for gifted men in psychoanalytic psychiatry which will probably emerge as an increasingly important problem in the future. If we improve our selection methods, and then are able to give the best training to those who are most likely to profit by it and make good use of it, we shall have the problem of improving the emotional and intellectual climate in which all of us work, so that an individual's productivity will be encouraged rather than discouraged by the heavy apparatus of training and scholarship. Most of us are aware that sometimes subsidies and supports by departments and foundations are not unmixed blessings because these grants and their attendant loyalties impose more or less subtle limitations upon the freedom of the individual. The spiritual price paid for the support given may be too high in many instances, as when it permits only mediocre recapitulation or feeble preoccupation with trivia.

Reik in his book *Listening with the Third Ear* (7) understood that scientific training alone will not make anybody a good analyst. This is probably true for psychiatrists, also. Grotjahn in his review of this book stresses the following quotation from Reik as the best summary:

"If I were asked what quality I regard as most important for an analyst, I should reply: *moral courage*. It would be absurd to assert that an analyst must be superior to his patients in brains or knowledge or acumen. But in this matter, in moral courage, or, as we might call it, in inner truthfulness, he must be superior. The training of analysts should be directed less toward the acquisition of practical and theoretical knowledge than the extension of intellectual independence. It is not so much a question of acquiring technical ability as inner truthfulness." Later follows the optimistic note: "Inner truthfulness is infectious like lying." (6, p. 64)

Freud in the second chapter of *The Interpretation of Dreams* quotes a letter of Schiller's to Körner which is appropriate not only to this theme of dealing with patients, but also to the vital question of how to improve the quality of our work.

"The reason for your complaint lies, it seems to me, in the constraint which your intellect imposes upon your imagination. Here I will make an observation, and illustrate it by an allegory. Apparently it is not good—and indeed it hinders the creative work of the mind—if the intellect examines too closely the ideas already pouring in, as it were, at the gates. Regarded in isolation, an idea may be quite insignificant, and venturesome in the extreme, but it may acquire importance from an idea which follows it; perhaps in a certain collocation with other ideas, which may seem equally absurd, it may be capable of furnishing a very serviceable link. The intellect cannot judge all these ideas unless it can retain them until it has considered them in connection with these other ideas. In the case of a creative mind, it seems to me, the intellect has withdrawn its watchers from the gates, and the ideas rush in pell-mell, and only then does it review and inspect the multitude. You worthy critics, or whatever you may call yourselves, are ashamed or afraid of the momentary and passing madness which is found in all real creators, the longer or shorter duration of which distinguished the thinking artist from the dreamer. Hence your complaints of unfruitfulness, for you reject too soon and discriminate too severely." (Letter of December 1, 1788.) (3, pp. 111–112)

My favorite passage dealing with this problem of how to encourage productivity is also from Freud, "A Note on the Prehistory of the Technique of Analysis," 1920. Freud tells of his early reading of Börne's essay "The Art of Becoming an Original Writer in Three Days" as a boy, and his recollections of it much later. Freud particularly cherished the following paragraph and quotes it:

"A disgraceful cowardliness in regard to thinking holds us all back. The censorship of governments is less oppressive than the censorship exercised by public opinion over our intellectual productions. (Moreover there is a reference here to a 'censorship,' which reappears in psychoanalysis as the dream-censorship.) It is not lack of intellect but lack of character that prevents most writers from being better than they are. . . . Sincerity is the source of all genius, and men would be cleverer if they were more moral. . . ." (4, p. 104)

It has been a privilege for me to have been associated with this Institute for fifteen years, not only for personal ties but also because of the idealism and courageous enterprise which have been actively present. The members of this faculty have done much in discovering new ways for the liberation of man's repressed abilities and for the improvement of human relationships.

REFERENCES

1. Alexander, Franz, and Ross, Helen, editors. *Dynamic Psychiatry*. Chicago, University of Chicago Press, 1952.

2. Ekstein, Rudolf. Trial Analysis in the Therapeutic Process. *Psychoanalyt. Quart.*, 19: 52–63, 1950.

3. Freud, Sigmund. *The Interpretation of Dreams*. New York, Macmillan Co., 1933.

4. Freud, Sigmund. A Note on the Prehistory of the Technique of Analysis. (In his *Collected Papers*, Vol. V. London, Hogarth Press, 1950. pp. 101–104).

5. Ginzberg, Eli; Ginsburg, Sol W.; Axelrad, Sidney; and Herma, John L.

The Problem of Occupational Choice. *Am. J. Orthopsychiat.*, 20: 166–201, 1950.

6. Grotjahn, Martin. About the "Third Ear" in Psychoanalysis; a review and critical evaluation of Theodor Reik's *Listening with the Third Ear; the inner experience of a psychoanalyst. Psychoanalyt. Rev.*, 37: 56–65, 1950.

7. Reik, Theodor. *Listening with the Third Ear; the inner experience of a psychoanalyst.* New York, Farrar, Straus & Co., 1948.

8. Sachs, Hanns. Observations of a Training Analyst. *Psychoanalyt. Quart.*, 16: 157–168, 1947.

Discussion

ROY R. GRINKER, M.D.

THIS IS a day for congratulations to the faculty of the Chicago Institute for Psychoanalysis, its director, and the students who have obtained the benefits of a liberal, scholarly education at this Institute. All of them should have great satisfaction and pride in what has been accomplished in the past. They may likewise be permitted a legitimate hope that future achievements of this Institute in research and training will be even greater.

It is very difficult at this point in time to determine what qualities, what skills, and what knowledge will be essential to fit a man for adequate functioning in a rapidly changing field ten or even five years in the future. Persons in our specialty should know better than any others the restrictions and constrictions that are imposed upon a developing mind by a formalized education that sets rigid patterns of standards, ideals, and values. Even more is this true in the behavioral sciences, the present nature of which is controversial and poorly defined. No one can imagine what new and startling developments will take place in this field in the near future.

We cannot define or delimit our field of today and, therefore, can hope less to do it for the future. Since we cannot reach an agreement in regard to the functions and aptitudes of psychiatrists or psychoanalysts, how can we agree as to content of a training program? One of the most outstanding achievements of the Chicago Institute's staff has been its unwillingness to formalize or rigidify a training program. I think we should hold fast to the concept that it takes many sorts of people to make the psychiatric-psychoanalytic or medical world and that the more diverse are the personalities—with different internal psychodynamics, with varying knowledge and experience—the more chance is there for the development of new therapies and original investigations.

As a participant in this symposium I feel called upon to make some statements based on trials and errors in setting up training programs, even if these are generalizations incapable of detailed specification. In the first place, speakers on this program representing medicine, psychiatry, and psychoanalysis seem to form a trichotomy which in my opinion does not exist. What makes a man good for one is the same for all. Especially do I want to emphasize that a good psychiatrist, yes even a good psychoanalyst, should be a good doctor. We tend to forget that we are specialists in medicine, which means that we hold the patient's welfare to be primary and vow to do him no harm. For this function a man needs a modicum of intelligence and an interest in accomplishing beneficial results for others. He should have a sound medical education, for which today we can rely on all the American medical schools and on the general hospitals to which the interns match themselves. But without the acquisition of a broad educational background no special skills will make a man a truly good doctor. He needs to know much about life and living that is not obtainable in a specialized curriculum.

It has been said repeatedly that in addition to his medical education the potential psychiatrist or psychoanalyst should be a warm, sensitive person with intuitive grasp of hidden feelings and a sincere liking for people. In fact, candidates who strive to be selected for training all tell us that they have these characteristics in correct proportions. Our acceptance of such characteristics as criteria would be just as bad as the rejection of candidates on the basis of some nosological diagnostic classification of their particular neuroses. What living being isn't to some degree and at some times warm, sensitive, intuitive to other humans? Contrariwise, what living person is not to some degree paranoid, phobic, compulsive, homosexual, depressed, or what not? A psychiatrist cannot be defined by his temperature, rate of oxygenation, sensory thresholds, nor by his neurosis.

The problem really concerns information and the processes of its communication. At what times or situations and in what degrees are special forms of communication utilizable to a person in his attempt to assist another? The selection of potential psychiatrists depends primarily on the recognition of potential or developed processes necessary for functions in relation to another person, and these are all dependent on various forms of communication. The patient communicates to the psychiatrist, the psychiatrist undergoes a process of internal communication or association and communicates through a feed-back mechanism to the patient. Patient and doctor exist in a two-way, circular, transactional process within a special environment, each assuming a role pertinent and specific to his position in this process. The result is that the stronger personality who assumes the role of the physician or the psychiatrist communicates an effect on the sicker personality who has been assigned by fortuitous circumstances the role of the weak, dependent, and helpless patient.

To perform the functions assumed in the role of psychiatrist a person should *first* have the capacity to communicate with others. He must know the implicit and explicit social roles which his patient enacts and those that are expected of him in transaction with his patient. Therefore, he must be able to understand and accept the cues of others and be able to express himself to, and be understood by, the other human being with whom he is in transaction. Such a process of rapidly shifting social roles which are cued by the patient's needs is most significant for the psychiatrist's skill. Equally significant within the scope of the psychoanalyst's job is the capacity to prevent himself from passively following the cues and commands of the patient, at the same time thoroughly understanding them and their internal motivations. It is only by remaining away from these tempting relationships that the psychoanalyst can press for the patient's understanding of what he is asking for by turning his attention inward.

The *second* necessary function which the potential psychiatrist should possess with endurance is the process of communication with himself. If he has an open system which permits transactions among the various foci within his own personality, he may draw from the codification of his previous experience and feed-back to the patient the benefits of a knowledgeable communication which is more than a simple response to a stimulus. This kind of open system or communication with self is often extremely painful. The analyst or psychiatrist should be able to recognize many of his own emotions and have the capacity to endure the suffering of feelings such as anxiety, guilt, or depression which are evoked within him. This characteristic causes much divergence of opinion among the selectors of potential candidates. Health or illness is the end result of a variety of transacting factors, from constitutional structuralization to genetic and current life-situations. These reach a more or less stabilized state of ease (comfort), or disease (suffering). If ease, health, and comfort are attained at the cost of rigidity or intellectual repression, the flexibility of the psychiatrist is decreased. If disease or suffering becomes too great, then there is an attendant over- or under-evaluation of one's own problems and, therefore, of the patient's suffering.

The *third* process which seems to be important for the functioning of a psychiatrist is his integrative capacity. This concerns the ability of the intrapsychic transactional systems to maintain themselves as an organization without disintegration under conditions of stress severe enough to strain the dynamic equilibrium. What external events disturb him, how much does he become disturbed, to what degree or type of equilibrium does he return, and how fast does this occur are parameters of his integrative capacity. These need to be measured in terms not only of the stress which the psychiatrist must endure in his own life-situations, but also of those stresses which patients constantly impose on him. Over and above this is the fact that the life of a psychiatrist or a psychoanalyst is especially hard. He has to live in a particular environment, he is constantly bombarded with all sorts of disturbing emotions, and at the same time he is called on to maintain a stability and equilibrium not expected of any other person.

Finally, the psychiatrist or psychoanalyst should have personal value systems derived from the ethnic and cultural influences of his early human environment which are sound and healthy in comparison with the contemporary culture in which he exists. These values are expressed in terms of integrity and incorruptibility of his superego and by sincere and constant operations which lead toward the realization of his ego ideals. All these indicate adequate but not fixed systems of primary values and social roles which correspond to the changing need and demands of his environment.

There is another aspect to the problem of selection for training of the doctor-psychiatrist and psychoanalyst that I should like to make clear through an analogy. During World War I the Air Force pilots were chosen through no special selection methods. They had no knowledge of scientific aeronautics, but flew by the "seat of their pants." They used their semicircular canals for learning their position in space, their vibratory sense and hearing for knowledge of their machines. Each man developed his own methods and tricks of flying through his own research. The early psychoanalysts also worked by the seat of their pants. They called it intuition, empathy, third ear, and so on. Each did his own research and published papers concerned with his own tricks and knowledge of certain kinds of dreams and his personally developed techniques.

But the first pilots were not as hot as they thought. In fogs they often flew upside down without knowing it and crashed when visual contact with the land was absent. Analysts too were in the fog of the deep unconscious, for they were involved within a single system which constituted an internal function with nothing to "take a fix on." In spite of the resistance of the first pilots, the job of flying eventually was analyzed and pilots with the necessary special aptitudes were subsequently selected. Machines were improved to indicate position in time and space and gauges registered the functioning of the important engines which maintained the ship aloft. Sadly to say, many analysts, like the old pilots, refused to analyze their jobs, recognize their participant functions and countertransferences, or utilize landmarks for time and space. Today we do not have an adequate definition of the field of psychoanalysis nor any valid concept of what constitutes a good analyst. We have no criteria, therefore, because of the absence of a job analysis to determine what kind of people make the best kind of analysts.

We must now come back to the problem of communication which is the essence of psychiatry and psychoanalysis. This cannot be self-corrective and thus constitute a true transactional communication as long as one system is utilized. For adequate development of a circular, self-corrective system the psychiatrist needs to know more than just the psychic system and the psychoanalyst more than the unconscious. Both need to know what forces transact with the personality from the environment on the one hand and the body on the other, both of which constitute in varying directions and at various times the input-output system of the mental apparatus.

I should like to use another term for the psychiatrist or psychoanalyst, differentiating these only in accordance with their special techniques. I should say that they are practitioners in a field of behavior in which they try to understand the psycho-somatic-environmental systems as processes in transaction, within a particular universe or field. The psychiatrist or analyst is usually interested most intensely in varying levels of the psychic system. The physiologist or physician penetrates into the depths of activities of the somatic system. The sociologist is more concerned with the interaction of individuals as total persons within various social or environmental settings. However, it is not possible for any person to understand fully a system from a structural analysis of it attained by working inside that system alone. One can learn more about interrelations between somatic and psychic or between psychic and social systems by making observations at the boundaries of their interactions. However, in order to understand more adequately the processes at work in the total psychosomatic-social field one must understand the processes that go on in transaction among at least three systems by assuming a more distant position outside the system but within the field.

Putting it in other ways, the psychiatrist or psychoanalyst must know the signs of somatic and the symbols of environmental processes affected by the ego as it assumes varying social roles in the transactions which involve himself and his patient. By doing so he will not accentuate one aspect of these transactions nor will he overlook others. He will not be accused of diving deeply into the lower levels of the unconscious mental processes nor will he be accused of completely ignoring the effects of reality on the personality nor the influences of physical dysfunctions on behavior. For these functions he need not have a highly specialized knowledge of more than one discipline. He needs to know, however, the extent of his own field, its boundaries beyond which he cannot skillfully reach where he requires other professional help in multidisciplinary operations.

These transactional principles can be taught only in rudimentary form. The student must learn most of them through his own participation and through his own researches. What we can do, however, is to select those who have the potentialities for developing and recognizing transactional communication and early weed out those who cannot. Those who succeed in developing or perfecting their fluidity in these processes with the factual instruction given in any accredited psychiatric training center will find that the little that is known about psychiatry or the behavioral sciences will fall into logical and usable operational facets. More than knowledge, they will acquire skills which will make them investigators of process and developers of a technique of a psychiatry that is a science.

Along with the advances of psychiatry and psychoanalysis in their penetration into the field of biological, medical, and social sciences there is today a growing resistance to these changes. On the one hand there is an extreme attempt to hold back any involvement of psychiatry and psychoanalysis in the study and utilization of somatic processes developed in the modern biological sciences. On the other hand, warning may be given of the temptation to reread the findings of psychoanalysis in terms of sociology, and warning that unceasing vigilance will be needed to avoid such temptations and that it is the duty of psychoanalysts to observe, to study, and to try to understand only the inner meaning of the extraordinary events around us. The intensification of both these counterreactions as resistances toward progress of psychiatry and psychoanalysis in transactional processes with somatic events on the one hand and social phenomena on the other is a gauge of the degree to which progress is threatened. Curiously enough, Dr. Levine's expression, by means of a series of comparative phrases, of his concept of the level of the resident's understanding and therapy points out not so much what the nonpsychoanalytically trained resident should know more about, but what the psychoanalyst who is doing psychiatry should know in addition to his highly specialized knowledge of unconscious processes.

I think that the point of view which I have stressed may be brought out more clearly by a formal definition of the psychological system with which psychiatrists and psychoanalysts work in varying depths. The psychological system functions in transaction between the soma which communicates by means of electrical and chemical signs and the social and cultural environment which uses symbolic processes of communication. Through such a process of transaction the psychological system differentiates, grows, and maintains its functions. Within it develop varying degrees of awareness or consciousness of the space-time continuum of the individual and his species. It expands in function as a confluence of the projection of all inner and outer surfaces of the organism and its environment.

Subscribing to this definition makes the psychiatrist or psychoanalyst a disciple of a science of behavior possessing a variety of tools suitable for special points of observation of special foci. Training according to this as a principle prepares a student to become a sound therapist or a capable investigator, whichever way his interest turns.

Present Trends in Psychoanalytic Training

WHEN psychoanalytic training was taken over by Institutes, it became customary to organize training in three major phases: (1) the personal analysis ("preparatory" or "training" analysis); (2) theoretical instruction in the form of lectures and seminars; and (3) practical clinical training in the form of supervised analytic work and case discussions.

The function of the personal analysis is to prepare the student psychologically for his training, to overcome those psychological impediments, blind spots, emotional resistances, which would interfere with the understanding and adequate handling of his patients.

The traditional concept of training was to have the student pass through the phases in this chronological order: personal analysis followed by instruction in theory, and then actual clinical work. In the following presentation, I retain this sequence but will show a present trend to synchronize the second and third phases. This follows a universal trend in modern medical education: to teach theory on the basis of the student's firsthand clinical observations.

The Training ("Preparatory") Analysis

The emphasis of my presentation lies upon the postulate that a training analysis under present conditions is different—

84

but should not be different from a therapeutic analysis. The existing difference between therapeutic analysis and training analysis is comparable to the difference between a patient and a sick physician. When a physician gets sick, one of his first announcements when consulting a colleague will be that he wants to behave and wants to be treated "just like any other patient." It is evident that this is not easily done and the difficulty lies both in the sick physician and the treating physician.

First of all, the goal of the training analysis is not *primarily* therapeutic. Its purpose is learning. Even the knowledge that the doctor may need analysis for therapeutic reasons does not change the fact that he is being analyzed not only to be freed from his neurotic patterns but primarily to be prepared for training.

Accordingly, the atmosphere of the training analysis is different from a merely therapeutic situation. We employ rules and regulations dictated by academic considerations which are not necessarily indicated by therapeutic considerations. For example, the length or the approximate length, and the timing of the interviews, are determined by training standards and not necessarily by therapeutic exigencies. In my opinion, any rules inhibiting flexibility and enforcing regularity in analytic training are dangerous and perhaps disastrous. Only with constant change of technique, including changes in frequency of interviews, interruptions in the therapy, and many other variables, can we bring the doctor-student into the situation where he will accept himself as "just another patient in analysis." Only then will the old maxim that there is no difference between training analysis and therapeutic analysis be approximately realized. Probably this postulate can never completely be realized in actual practice.

This, however, is a difficulty which can be met by such flexible training standards, which the American Psychoanalytic Association is in process of adopting at the present time. By flexibility is meant the ability of the analyst "to be consistently inconsistent," to change the therapeutic environment as required in order to activate those trends in the patient which may lead to the necessary therapeutic experience. Flexibility is a special aspect of the analyst's skill in dealing with the student's resistance to therapy before he gives verbal interpretations. It belongs to that nonverbal communication between analyst and patient which is inherent and essential to analysis. It is of special importance in the didactic analysis because of the close relationship between verbalization and intellectualization.

Flexibility in training is an essential demand of analytic technique (36). It is one way of counteracting the always-present intellectual defenses of the student. It includes shifts in the time axis around which psychoanalytic training revolves: in the frequency of weekly hours, in the interruption of all treatment for months at a time, in the resumption of analytic interviews even after years of not having seen the analyst.* A flexible approach is needed in order to prepare the transition from

* Recently and after the completion of this paper, Kurt Eissler has made suggestions which could show the way from "wild discussion of psychoanalytic technique" corresponding to wild psychoanalysis to a more rational discussion of controversies of psychoanalytic technique and training. Eissler defines in this paper the concept of a "parameter" as a variation both quantitatively and qualitatively from basic modern psychoanalytic technique, which requires interpretation as the exclusive tool. Applying Eissler's concepts to the ideas expressed about psychoanalytic training here, it is clear that the "parameter" of flexibility and similar analytic techniques here discussed are introduced into didactic analysis only when the basic model technique does not suffice; furthermore, the recommended technique leads up to its final self-elimination. At all times all suggestions of changes in the technique of psychoanalytic training can be understood in terms of the effect of the parameter on transference relations with the aim to keep or to lead the transference neurosis of the analyst in training as closely as possible to the transference neurosis as it exists in the original therapeutic relationship of psychoanalytic therapy. Interpretation becomes again the basic tool as in the model technique, and ego integration remains the final aim. (14)

analysis to self-analysis; it guides the future analyst to use analysis for himself as efficiently as for his patients.

A basic complication of the training analysis lies in the fact that the transference neurosis is of a more complex nature than in a regular therapeutic analysis. The incognito of the training analyst does not exist; the patient is not an individual out of anonymity but lives in an environment and in a reality which is partly the environment and the reality of the training analyst. The doctor-patient, therefore, is invited to form a transference neurosis on a screen which is not smooth but distorted by reality. In this connection the impact of modern institute training on the relation between candidate and his training analyst must be considered. Originally training was almost exclusively an affair between the analytic teacher and his individual student. Today, candidate and analyst are members of an analytic group and institute; the former apprentice-type of training has been replaced by a new type in which a large faculty participates with different roles and with different degrees of responsibility. This is a decisive change: group responsibility has replaced the individual responsibility of our teachers. It reduces the intensity of the emotional involvement both in transference and in countertransference. It frees the training analyst from certain restrictions and realistic implications which increased the differences between therapeutic and training analysis in the past.

These differences are most marked in the beginning of the analysis but they persist throughout the training. For instance, at the end of the training analysis, the doctor-patient does not melt into anonymity as does the average patient. He remains within sight of the analyst and within sight of the analyst's colleagues. He will become a monument of work done or undone. This will reflect upon transference and countertransference. In the hope of remaining a pupil of the training analyst or of his substitute in the form of the psychoanalytic institute or society, a part of the transference neurosis will spill over and will, if not properly recognized and handled, lead to "acting out." Much of the necessary frustration provoked by the termination of an analysis is reduced because of the student's hope of continued contact with the analyst. This makes it more difficult to work through this crucial terminal phase of the analysis. The full emotional impact of the analytic experience, as Adelaide Johnson (26) describes it in recent publications, cannot be expected from a candidate who may hide his last-ditch resistance against separation from his analyst behind the quite realistic hope and expectation that he and his analyst will remain at least colleagues, members of the same analytic group, and perhaps friends. The analytic working-through of the separation anxiety is of fundamental importance and usually does not come to the fore in training analysis, since there is no real separation from the analyst who will remain an important figure in the analysand's life after the termination of the treatment.

Not all of the difficulties which typify analytic training can be eliminated. Therefore, the training analysis is essentially an "interminable analysis" which has to blend gradually with something which can best be called "self-analysis."

Another danger comes from the same situation. Freud once said, as Alexander (2, 3) has reminded us, that after awhile, patients no longer come in order to be cured but to be treated. Similarly in the training situation, the student does not come in order to undergo the analytic experience but to be analytically trained. Since this does not work, it requires constant alertness from the analyst to make his training candidate feel like a patient.

During the course of years I have referred many neurotic physicians to analysts. Originally I thought that such work with colleagues would serve as a kind of "training for becoming a training analyst." Clinical experience showed that the analysis of these physicians outside the institute atmosphere seemed to be healthier and sometimes more effective because of the more favorable transference neurosis. In several cases, it was possible later to accept some of these doctors for analytic training. This experience may serve as a lead that a preparatory analysis could be conducted more favorably outside the half-public scene of the institute environment. Such analysis would then be a preparatory requirement preceding the candidate's matriculation in an institute.

This raises a question as to future policies. Candidates for psychoanalytic training may not then be selected by the members of the Educational Committee before they start their preparatory analysis. The selection may be made after the preparatory analysis instead of before. Then we would no longer face the seemingly impossible task of determining in advance the suitability of an applicant to become an analyst. The outcome of the training analysis could serve as a real evidence of suitability.

In mentioning such a change in training policies, I do not overlook other practical difficulties which would arise under this system; for example, the possible waste resulting from unsuccessful preparatory analyses undertaken without sufficient screening. A method of double screening, before and after the preparatory analysis, may be the answer.

Before concluding my remarks about didactic analysis, I wish to mention the important role of countertransference. Possibly countertransference reactions have changed generally during the last twenty years of institutionalized training. The fact that we can now discuss it with greater ease may be indicative of this change. It would seem that an increasing group responsibility for training has brought this about.

The best summary of the problems of countertransference was given by Therese Benedek (5) in her unpublished remarks in a panel discussion of the American Psychoanalytic Association. In these remarks she said: "The most significant manifestation of the counter-transference is the training analyst's unconscious or conscious tendency to foster the candidate's identification with him, his dependence on him. For training analysts tend to project themselves unduly in the candidate; they tend to identify themselves—as parents do with their children—with the candidate. One of the most conspicuous manifestations of this identification is the training analyst's overprotective, unobjective attitude toward his training patient. He, the analyst, often takes it as a personal insult if someone is critical of the student. The training analysts often behave as overprotective parents do." (See also 6 and 37.)

We may expect that the growing integration of training in psychoanalytic institutes, in addition to the increasing number of training analysts and students, will further reduce the intensity of countertransference reactions in the preparatory analysis.

The more we recognize the complexity of training, the more we are inclined to distribute the responsibility for training. As a result the training analyst will become less anxious, less overprotective, guilty, or competitive toward his training analysand. This will improve our chances in bringing about meaningful changes in the personality of our candidates and eventually result in a more harmonious spirit within our psychoanalytic fraternity.

In the Conference of the American Psychoanalytic Association on "Problems of Training," 1952, in Atlantic City, some of the ideas here represented were formulated. Sandor Rado said, and I quote here from Kardiner's and L. Stone's summary of the conference: "One of the aims of analytic training is to free the student's mind of the prejudices contracted by exposure to medical disciplines." (28, 31)

Carl Binger (8) expressed himself a little differently in his book *The Doctor's Job*. He interprets the difficulty for the physician in relating himself to his patients as a result of the fact that his first "patient" was a cadaver.

Sigmund Freud encountered many of the difficulties of the medical man in relation to psychology. His changing attitude is revealed in his autobiography (20) and particularly in the recently published correspondence with his friend and "analyst by correspondence," Wilhelm Fliess (19, 23). These documents show Freud's original ambivalence and resistance toward the psychology of the unconscious. His way of overcoming these difficulties by self-analysis is not open to the average psychoanalyst, yet his experiences give us clues to effective training (21). Many of our present difficulties with the analytic training of physicians can be met today by a training analysis which is conducted not with uniform rigidity but with flexibility, never losing the principal aim to afford the student a genuine "analytic experience." As Freud (18) in another place later suggested, such an experience terminates the first phase of analytic training and introduces the interminable process of self-analysis to which the training analysis was an introduction and preparation.

Freud's letters to his friend Wilhelm Fliess show that all the great discoveries of psychoanalysis were made in connection with Freud's self-analysis. This is especially obvious in letters (Nos. 67, 68, and 71) written in August 1897, when Freud discovered the Oedipus complex first in himself. In these letters Freud reveals and describes the limitations of self-analysis (19).

Forty years later Freud discusses the same problem of self-analysis in a modified form in his paper "Analysis Terminable and Interminable": "We hope and believe that the stimuli received in the learner's own analysis will not cease to act upon him when that analysis ends, that the processes of ego transformation will go on of their own accord and that he will bring his new insight to bear upon all his subsequent experience."

In the same paper Freud makes that frequently quoted statement: "Every analyst ought periodically himself to enter analysis once more, at intervals of say five years, and without any feeling of shame in so doing. So not only the patient's analysis but that of the analyst himself has ceased to be a terminable and becomes an interminable task."

Perhaps it is possible to review what I consider the essence of Freud's thought as expressed in his letters and his paper "Analysis Terminable and Interminable" with remarks of Alexander in Atlantic City during the meeting on training in 1952, and ideas stated by Erik Erikson (17) in his book *Childhood and Society*. I would reformulate the aims of analytic training in the following way:

The training analysis aims at an inner experience of "ego-identity." This experience takes place in the transference neurosis with the help of analytic interpretation and insight into the psychodynamics of such ego-identity. The analysis should free the individual's potentialities for further development. The term "ego-identity" embraces not only the emotional experiences of one's self but also includes his relationship to the environment.

The experience of ego-identity is not solely a conscious process. It must include the knowledge, the understanding, the insight, and the final integration of the unconscious or parts of it. It is the aim of training and therapy to establish an anxiety-free communication between the conscious part of the ego, the preconscious, and the unconscious.

Ego-identity is defined by Erik Erikson as an inner institution derived from the experience of increasing social health after each of the major childhood crises. It should correct the emotional impact of major childhood crises and should teach lessons which were missed on previous occasions. The ego-identity can be studied in three ways: (1) introspectively, as a quality of experience expressing a sense of sameness and continuity in the individual's conception of what he is and of what others perceive him to be; (2) in the individual's life history, as the objective evidence of an energy-releasing synthesis of the ego in the past life-situation; (3) projectively, in the individual's imagery, as it relates to ideal prototypes which can be realized, and undesirable ones which can be avoided.

According to Erikson, patients in the early phases of psychoanalysis suffer most from inhibitions which prevent them from being what they are and think they are. This is only partly true for our psychoanalytic students today. They suffer most from the uncertainties of their professional life and beliefs; they do not know whom they should follow. The answer lies not in identification with the training analyst. The training analysis should not be a refuge from uncertainties and scientific doubts.

The solution is a new ego-identity, which is new insofar as it includes the entire person and not just his consciousness. It may be claimed that this is the goal of all education; it certainly agrees with the ideal of humanistic philosophy. It is a combination of a psychoanalysis and education which we would expect from training.

If this is so, we may find an answer to the question of ending the training analysis. There is no end to training. There should be only a transition from the terminable analysis with the training analyst to an interminable continuation of the analysis in the form of self-analysis.

Self-analysis does not take place solely within the candidate. It may take place between him and his patients. It may take place in other interpersonal relationships as, for instance, in his marriage. Even the former training analyst may again find a place in this lifelong process of working through; occasionally, the former candidate, by now a member of the analytic society or institute, may return to his former training analyst for something I call, for want of a better term, supervision of his self-analysis.

Lectures, Theoretical Seminars, Clinical Demonstrations, and Case Discussions

Formal lecture courses and theoretical seminars have always been considered of secondary importance in psychoanalytic training as compared with the preparatory psychoanalysis and supervised analytic work. Their significance today is further reduced because many students go through a considerable amount of psychoanalytic indoctrination prior to their acceptance by an analytic institute.

As a child's education should begin at least one hundred years before birth, as Oliver Wendell Holmes once remarked, so the training of an analyst should and actually does begin before his acceptance as a candidate of an institute. The student of today has lost his psychoanalytic virginity—or naïveté in Schiller's sense—almost before he starts medical school. I suggest, therefore, that Harvey Cushing's ideas concerning medical education should be applied to analytic training. In his address "Experimentum Periculosum: Judicium Difficile," he contrasts the usual and time-honored way of teaching the medical student about *diabetes mellitus* with the way he would like to teach it:

Even when the relation (of preclinical subjects to ultimate goal) is obvious, it would seem to be a needlessly long and uninteresting process. The anatomist describes the form and situation of the pancreas; the embryologist shows how it buds off from the gut; the histologist in turn points out the acini and the islets; the physiologist presents the accepted theories of the manifold functions of the normal organ; the biochemist discloses the complicated ways of detecting and of quantitating the various sugars; the pharmacologist perhaps demonstrates the action of the newly discovered insulin and explains how it is prepared; the pathologist, getting down to more solid ground, shows in turn the diseased organ; and finally, after two years of this, the student first sees a patient with symptomatic evidence of pancreatic disease, possibly brought to light by a carbuncle or a gangrenous toe.

How much simpler to have shown the patient first, to have briefly explained how diabetes came to be recognized and what its complication may be, how step by step the mysteries of carbohydrate metabolism have partly been unraveled and the principles of our present-day treatment established—in short, the solid facts of the matter in the order in which they were discovered. Is this not the logical method of presenting our increasingly complex subject? . . . Could science be prevailed upon to concede to the clinic from the beginning of the course a single hour a day if necessary from eight to nine in the morning . . . the average run of students would certainly face their subsequent laboratory hours not only with greater interest but with a clearer appreciation of why it is necessary to get the best possible scientific grounding for their future career. (12)

One good way to prepare or actually to start analytic training has been found in clinical case seminars. I avoid theoretical discussions and center the seminar around presentation and discussion of cases and case material. I do not try to teach how to analyze patients in this preliminary seminar, which is designed for students waiting or just beginning their psychoanalytic training. I try to demonstrate with my example the human therapeutic relationship between the seminar leader as the central figure and the presenting doctor, the group, and finally the patient under discussion, whether he is present or not. I try to show through my behavior how to develop and to sustain that kind of human relationship which I consider the fundamental of psychiatry and the basis of psychoanalysis. The psychiatrist or psychoanalyst is in a more difficult position to demonstrate his skill in public than the surgeon. Therefore, we must try to demonstrate the psychotherapeutic attitude not only in actual case presentation but also in the consistency of our behavior as a teacher before the group of students.

As a rule the seminar is divided into two parts. In the first twenty minutes or half an hour I report about a personal experience, or some thoughts, observations, or reading matter which I have done since the last meeting. The rest of the time is taken up by a case demonstration, occasionally with the patient present.

I try to teach more than a therapeutic attitude in my seminars. I try to teach and to demonstrate to the students the understanding of the primary process and the language of symbolism. From the beginning I make it clear that this is not "symbol analysis" (35). The symptoms from which the physician diagnoses measles are not symbols which must be explained to the sick child or his mother. The understanding of these diagnostic signs, however, is of great importance for the physician. In a similar manner, the understanding of symbols and of subliminal cues helps the therapist to understand the patient regardless of eventual interpretation. It is better that this understanding of symbols again becomes preconscious. Only then can it be used with ease and spontaneity as an instrument of empathy, so closely related to intuition (22, 24, 25, 32). If it has been made conscious once, it can easily be activated again and perceived with that kind of surprise which is so important in psychotherapeutic work. Such a seminar becomes an analytic exercise in the anxiety-free communication with one's own preconscious (34).

Teaching the analytic understanding of the living primary process is not done by words alone. Pictures, for example, may be used. I have found that advertisements in our magazines with their obvious symbolism and often crude, primitive, regressive appeal are highly suitable for demonstration. I may use an advertisement from a fashion magazine to talk about the psychology of woman. The same point may be repeated at another occasion with a picture of Toulouse-Lautrec standing in front of the Venus in the Louvre of Paris or of an actress "washing that guy out of her hair," or an aerial photograph showing the African desert. I may show the startling reaction of people to the gaping mouth of a hippopotamus as pictured in another magazine. I may discuss why people get startled; what a startle-reaction is in psychodynamic terms, and continue to discuss shock, trauma, anxiety, and fear. At another time, I may show the pictures of Salvador Dali or the even more impressive pictures of Hieronymus Bosch. I mention movies frequently because they are like a dream which we all can see together on the screen, associate to it, and possibly gain some analytic insight into an experience which was common or at least visible to all of us simultaneously (33).

Case discussions in which a number of students discuss cases are perhaps the least complicated phase of the training. Their aim is similar to that of supervision. They give greater opportunity to evaluate the discussed case *in toto,* however, and give the leader of the seminar an occasion to estimate the candidate's capacity to understand not only the details of a treatment, but its whole course and effectiveness and to understand the principal factors of therapeutic successes and failures. In many institutes participation in case seminars is requested of students during practically the whole duration of training. The beginners are admitted to more elementary discussions chiefly as listeners, in order to be exposed to as much firsthand clinical observation as possible. They begin to participate actively in the more elementary case seminars, gradually progressing to the more advanced.

Supervision of Psychoanalytic Treatment

The technique and dynamics of psychoanalytic supervision have rarely been described in analytic literature. Thoughtful and carefully worked out papers have been read, but never published. At the Innsbruck Congress, 1927, of the International Psychoanalytic Association, Helene Deutsch (13) read a paper about control analysis which cannot be found in the publications of that or later years. Other papers concerning supervision were read in 1935 in the Congress in Vienna, and in 1937 in the Congress of Budapest (15, 16).

Edward Bibring starts his paper on methods and technique of control analysis with a description of the psychological situation (7). A special form of free reporting is described which is designed to give simultaneous insight into the patient and into the psychoanalytic situation between patient and reporting doctor. The training analyst has more practical psychoanalytic experience, and supervision aims at the avoidance of the beginner's mistakes. Bibring mentioned that supervision should not be used to analyze the candidate. Whatever the training analyst has to say should be given in the form of advice, not as personal interpretation and not as an order.

In the same year, 1937, and at the same Congress, Karl Landauer (29) reported his experiences. He found that candidates may react to the permission to start analytic work with a state of anxiety, depressive discouragement, or hypomanic elation. Of special interest is Landauer's statement about the transference situation in supervised work. According to him, a positive transference should be regarded as transference and a negative one as reality. The candidate's hostility toward the supervisor should be answered by self-sacrifice on the part of the control analyst. The greatest possible consideration should be shown in the matter of fees; there should be no time limit on the need for supervision, and the atmosphere should be friendly. The supervisor should function as an older brother and colleague, and he should allow the younger colleague to participate in his own more experienced technique. The candidate should be guided into research and he should learn to recognize his own unconscious fixation in his work. One most important function of supervision is the guidance of the younger doctor in the direction of continued self-analysis.

A thoughtful and penetrating contribution to the science of psychoanalytic training was written by Michael Balint (4). It is directed—and this may be significant—not only to training analysts, but to all analysts, including those in training. (See also 27.)

Balint quotes the regulations of the London Standing Rules Committee, 1947: " 'The analyst undertaking the student's personal analysis does not undertake the supervision of his cases.' So far as we know, this statement is not the result of carefully planned and controlled observation: it sounds to me like yet another dogmatic compulsory ruling." Indeed, many rules and regulations in analytic history were made under the pressure of time and then have been taken over without proper scientific doubt; they have not been tested and retested.

It is of historical interest that neither Freud nor Ferenczi, Abraham nor Jones, liked to conduct supervised work. They took a prominent part in psychoanalytic training, but supervised work was not an equally important part of their activities. "Somehow," states Balint, they "seemed to be satisfied with analysis only." These men were not interested in indoctrination and not interested in developing disciples. They were more interested in developing independent workers in the field of psychoanalysis.

Supervision, according to Balint, can be used for the purpose of indoctrination. The candidate's best defenses are his free associations while on the couch. They do not help him when he faces a determined "supervisor," who represents his views and convictions with an unchecked authority if he chooses to do so.

Recent developments and experimentations in psychoanalytic supervision have not yet been fully reported. Henry W. Brosin (10) attempted to use supervision for a research project of analyzing the essentials of psychotherapy. Experiments in group supervision have been made in other places. In Philadelphia, an interesting variation of an old method has been introduced under the name of "preceptor system." Some other variations, especially in regard to the timing of the start of supervised work, have been reported in a short communication by Edith Weigert and Robert Morse in their work at the Washington Institute (30).

In an unpublished paper, Lionel Blitzsten and Joan Fleming (9) have discussed the problem of analytic supervision. The authors advocate close co-operation between supervisor and training analyst. The supervisor is supposed to give his analytic interpretation of the student's blind spots and difficulties as they become visible in his analytic work and supervision. The supervisory analyst then gives his observation and interpretation to the training analyst who, in turn, is supposed to try to analyze them in the student as he continues his didactic analysis. The supervisor supervises, so to speak, not only the candidate but also his training analyst. Blitzsten and Fleming do not discuss the possibility of the student's witnessing this communication between the two analysts, which I consider a necessary safeguard against the complex transference-countertransference situation in analytic training. We must also consider the reaction of the training analyst to supervision, whether direct or indirect.

Alexander (1) describes the technique of collective supervision and evaluation of the candidate's progress as it is handled in the Chicago Institute. His main point is the emphasis on the collective responsibility of the Institute as it has developed in the last twenty years. The student's blind spots, his various difficulties and their eventual analytic interpretation, are discussed at the faculty meeting in the presence of the training analyst. Alexander states: "Training in institutes is a coordinated collective enterprise and not a loosely juxtaposed series of procedures as it was in the old, pre-Institute days." In Alexander's opinion, development of the Institute goes "from the fully unorganized apprentice system to loosely organized Institute training to a well-planned, coordinated Institute training in which the whole faculty works as a unit."

The first problem of psychoanalytic supervision is to decide when the student should start supervised work.* Theoretically this question is easily answered. The candidate is ready to start supervised work when he has learned how to activate the unconscious of his patients with due understanding of transference and resistance and without reacting himself with undue anxiety or unrecognized feelings of countertransference; and when he has learned how to use interpretation as the essential tool of psychoanalytic technique.

The timing of supervision offers practical difficulties. It is my experience that the "dangers" of an early start of supervised work are overestimated and not founded on clinical observation. Too many rules and regulations are contradictory to a free development of analytic training. Today most students as residents of psychiatric departments treat psychiatric patients

---

* The term "patient" is used for the patient in analysis; "doctor," "student," "candidate," or "analyst in training" for a physician undergoing his training analysis and having started supervised work. The "training analyst" is the analyst who conducts the didactic analysis of the doctor-candidate. The term "supervisor" or "controlling analyst" is used to differentiate this function from the psychoanalysis of candidates.

with psychotherapy before they begin the supervision of analytic work. The transition from this psychotherapeutic work
to psychoanalytic treatment is gradual. The student gradually
recognizes when his patients or some of his patients are "in
analysis" and no pledge can or should prohibit this development. The doctor's medical conscience will slowly guide him
into analytic work if he feels free and treats his patients according to the best of his knowledge. It is the serious-minded and
sincere candidate who feels a strong obligation to use what he
has learned from his own analysis in the treatment of his patients. Not all therapeutic activities of the candidate necessarily
constitute an "acting out," since his residency training requires
him to treat patients to the best of his ability.

The training analyst feels that he owes it to his medical conscience to safeguard the patient in treatment with his candidate
against misuses and avoidable mistakes of analytic technique.
If the candidate begins to make mistakes with his patients, his
training analyst will be tempted to step out of his analytic role
and interfere with his patient's outside activities. Occasionally
I have recommended that the candidate begin his supervised
work in order to delegate this policing function to a colleague.
If this is the case, then the beginning of supervised analytic
work looks—for a while—more like a supervision of psychotherapeutic activity than of psychoanalysis. This may be a favorable start. The main point here is that the student and supervising analyst should know what they are doing. The transition
from psychotherapy to systematic analytic work may help the
supervising analyst to judge the psychological acumen and pre-
paredness of the candidate.

The training analyst needs the cooperation of the educational
committee and of the faculty of the institute to evaluate the
candidate's progress. This collective responsibility is the most
important trend in current psychoanalytic training. The evalua-

tion of a student is no longer a private affair between analyst and candidate as in the days of apprenticeship.

There is no doubt in my mind that a collective evaluation of the candidate's supervised work, as well as of his contributions in case seminars, is the best possible method of judging the results of the training analysis. The faculty thus can learn what has been accomplished and what remains to be done. In such evaluation meetings, the training analyst should participate primarily as a listener because his countertransference may influence his judgment.

In supervision, I do not encourage the candidates to wait until they find a "suitable" case for analytic work. I assume that they want to start with a discussion of their entire work, not of one case. I assume that they want to show their analytic attitude and not necessarily their analytic knowledge. I prefer to discuss many of their cases before we settle down for the supervised analytic work of one case. During this process, many things can be learned about the qualities and limitations of the candidate.

The search for a "patient fit for analytic therapy" is frequently a sign of resistance to beginning supervised work. To be resistant is not the exclusive privilege of the candidate. Under the disguise of not having found the proper patient, the supervisor may rationalize his resistance against spending an additional hour with the tedious work of supervising. The assumption that there are patients especially easy and well-fitted for supervised work nourishes a tendency in the therapist to suit the patient to therapy, and not to suit the therapy to the patient.

An investigation conducted by Heinz Hartmann showed that the patients chosen for analysis by the candidates themselves and taken from their own practice have a better prognosis and are most frequently carried through to completion than the assigned cases. This gives a hint that the candidate may be the best judge in the selection of his cases for supervision.

Supervision may be divided into three parts which frequently overlap:

First, the period of preparation. This is the time in which the doctor and supervisor get acquainted with each other, and in which the supervisor gets an impression of the entire patient-load of the beginning analyst. The main aim is to avoid the typical mistakes of the beginner.

Second, the period of deepening insight into the dynamics of psychoanalytic treatment. Mistakes are analyzed, blind spots are investigated, and technical rules of interpretations and concepts of transference and resistance are explained in the actual setting of the treatment.

Third, the period of working through with the patient. The psychodynamics of the patient's personality, and the technical and emotional aspects of the therapeutic experience are discussed and worked out comprehensively.

I frequently use one hour during the first weeks of supervision in order to visit the colleague in his office. His report to me makes more sense when I can visualize his "field of operation." It is important for me to see the arrangements of the waiting room and the secretary's and doctor's offices; how the doctor sits and how his chair and his person are related to the couch, or, in the preparatory stages of analytic therapy, to the chair in which the patient sits. I even note the placement of the doctor's clock; and to what degree thought, care, tact, and awareness are employed in the major and minor details of the therapeutic atmosphere in which the analytic relationship is going to be developed and understood.

The next question is: How should the candidate report about

the analytic material produced by the patient? Taking notes is imperative, but the true question is how to make note-taking effective and how to use the notes during the hour with the supervisor. The candidate who hides behind his written notes and tries to fill the entire supervisory hour with reading them frequently annoys his supervising analyst to the point of despair. The supervisor feels as if he wishes to stop the candidate from taking notes. This annoyance has caused many a supervisor not to differentiate between the advisability of taking notes and the problem of how to use them. It is established medical practice to keep a record of patients, and analytic notes are a medical demand. It is furthermore a demand of scientific work. It is often of importance, in the analysis of psychosomatic symptoms, to date the appearance and disappearance of a symptom in relation to certain associations or dreams or interpretations. In the course of the treatment questions may arise which can be answered only by a relatively objective note-taking. Often it is advisable not to allow the candidate the use of notes during the supervisory hour so that he may report freely.

Proper reporting of associative material and its interpretation are the best criteria by which to decide whether the candidate is ready for independent analytic work. If he has mastered the art of reporting, he seldom needs further supervision. Then supervised work becomes a pleasure for candidate and supervisor. This then is usually the time in which the supervision can be terminated.

Control work should not be used as a competition with the training analysis. By discussing his patients with the supervising analyst, the candidate can learn many things which have direct bearing on his own character neurosis. Sometimes it is possible that the candidate, caught with his defenses down, may accept interpretations given in relation to his behavior toward the patient which have been given to him many times in his own analysis without result. His differently structured defenses in the supervised situation may enable him to integrate this insight and then make another step toward working it through in his own analysis. I avoid, however, telling the candidate directly: "This is a blind spot of yours; this you have to take up in your analysis." I have found too often that such advice is ineffective. In the first place it is usually warded off by resistance. For instance, the candidate may bring this advice back to the analyst but has forgotten completely what it was all about. More important is the fact that the training analyst often feels that the advice given by the supervising analyst—"Take this up in your analysis"—constitutes an attack on his psychoanalytic alertness. Due to the training analyst's counterresistance, the process of working through as stimulated by supervisory experience may then miscarry in its beginning. If, during supervisory work, I have the feeling that we begin to tread on ground which is better reserved for the candidate's training analyst, I try to activate the hidden emotions in a way that makes me expect the probability that the candidate will bring this emotional experience into his analysis. In other words, problems of countertransference must be raised during the supervision, but as a rule cannot be settled there. The candidate should be considered a colleague who is in the process of becoming an analyst, and not as a patient in analysis who is "acting out."

One more word about the provision that the training psychoanalyst should not supervise the first two cases of his analysands. As Michael Balint once said, this may be a good rule and it may not be a good rule; it has never been tested or even properly discussed. It is probably advisable to follow this rule. There are, however, great and definite advantages in controlling at least one case with one's own training analyst during the late stages of psychoanalytic training.

The student analyst learns a great deal when he turns from

analytic introspection to working with patients. He will recognize his own old problems in a new light. With his analyst, he may make use of such insight. The training analyst, now more distant from the student, may recognize certain blind spots and reaction patterns of his analysand more clearly than he did during the regular course of analytic treatment. He may also talk to his analysand in an atmosphere relatively free of the usual forms of resistance. Finally, the training analyst may utilize information he received from other analysts at meetings of the educational committee or faculty. He may also have gathered some observations concerning the candidate outside the therapeutic situation which he may now feel free to use. At that time, then, the process of working through may take a more realistic turn, but under favorable circumstances it will be quite effective and it will remain within the framework of analytic technique.

Concluding Remark

Looking at present trends in psychoanalytic training, we are probably less confident than Lord Chesterfield when he wrote to his son: ". . . and I am very sure that any man of common understanding may, by proper culture, care, attention, and labor, make himself whatever he pleases, except a good poet." (11)

Perhaps we have to realize that good analysts are neither made nor born—but are developed in a long, tedious, often painful process of analytic maturation in which analysis constitutes an essential part but still only a part. With the discovery of the unconscious, a new dimension in human education was found. So far as matters of training in the widest sense are concerned, we stand at a point of orientation to be compared with the situation of astronomers at the time of Copernicus.

This should make us modest and confident at the same time.

REFERENCES

1. Alexander, Franz. Personal communication, August 18, 1952.

2. Alexander, Franz. The Problem of Psychoanalytic Technique. *Psychoanalyt. Quart.,* 4: 588–611, 1935.

3. Alexander, Franz. Psychoanalytic Training in the Past, the Present and the Future: a Historical Review; address to the Association of Candidates of the Chicago Institute for Psychoanalysis, October 26, 1951.

4. Balint, Michael. On the Psycho-Analytic Training System. *Internat. J. Psycho-Analysis,* 29: 163–173, 1948.

5. Benedek, Therese. Counter-Transference in the Training Analyst. (Panel discussion at the 1950 Annual Meeting of the American Psychoanalytic Association).

6. Berman, Leo. Countertransferences and Attitudes of the Analyst in the Therapeutic Process. *Psychiatry,* 12: 159–166, 1949.

7. Bibring, Edward. Methods and Technique of Control Analysis. (A part of the report of the Four Countries Conference of the International Training Commission.) *Internat. J. Psycho-Analysis,* 18: 369–370, 1937.

8. Binger, Carl. *The Doctor's Job.* New York, W. W. Norton & Co., 1945.

9. Blitzsten, N. Lionel, and Fleming, Joan. What is a "Training Analysis"? (Unpublished paper, Spring 1952).

10. Brosin, Henry W. Psychiatry Experiments with Selection. *Social Service Review,* 22: 461–468, 1948.

11. Chesterfield, Philip Dormer Stanhope, 4th Earl of. *Letters to His Son.* New York, Tudor Publishing Co., 1937. (Letter of Oct. 9, 1746).

12. Cushing, Harvey. Experimentum Periculosum: Judicium Difficile. (Paper presented at New Haven, 1925, on the occasion of the dedication of the Sterling Hall of Medicine, as quoted in *Harvey Cushing, Surgeon, Author, Artist,* by Elizabeth H. Thompson. New York, Henry Schuman, 1950. p. 243).

13. Deutsch, Helene. Remarks on Training and Intuition. Minutes of the 43d Meeting of the American Psychoanalytic Association at Richmond, Virginia. p. 4.

14. Eissler, K. R. The Effect of the Structure of the Ego on Psychoanalytic Technique. *J. Am. Psychoanalyt. Assoc.,* 1: 104–143, 1953.

15. Eitingon, Max. Opening Address by the Chairman, Dr. Eitingon. (Report at the General Meeting of the International Training Commission, Marienbad, August 2, 1936). *Internat. J. Psycho-Analysis*, 18: 350–358, 1937.

16. Eitingon, Max. Reports of the International Training Commission. *Internat. J. Psycho-Analysis*, Vols. 7–20, 1926–1939.

17. Erikson, Erik H. *Childhood and Society*. New York, W. W. Norton & Co., 1950.

18. Freud, Sigmund. Analysis Terminable and Interminable. *Internat. J. Psycho-Analysis*, 18: 373–405, 1937.

19. Freud, Sigmund. *Aus den Anfängen der Psychoanalyse;* Briefe an Wilhelm Fliess, Abhandlungen und Notizen aus den Jahren 1887–1902. London, Imago Publishing Co., 1950.

20. Freud, Sigmund. *An Autobiographical Study*. New York, W. W. Norton & Co., 1952.

21. Freud, Sigmund. Foreword to *Psychoanalyze Yourself*, by E. Pickworth Farrow. New York, International Universities Press, 1942.

22. Grotjahn, Martin. About the "Third Ear" in Psychoanalysis; a review and critical evaluation of Theodor Reik's *Listening with the Third Ear;* the inner experience of a psychoanalyst. *Psychoanalyt. Rev.,* 37: 56–65, 1950.

23. Grotjahn, Martin. From and About Sigmund Freud's Letters to His Friend Wilhelm Fliess During the Years 1887–1902. (Paper read at the 1951 Annual Meeting of the American Psychoanalytic Association on the 95th Anniversary of Sigmund Freud's Birthday).

24. Grotjahn, Martin. A Note About Teaching Psycho-Analysis; illustrated by the example of a seminar on Freud's "Wit and Its Relation to the Unconscious." *Samiksa,* 1: 39–50, 1947.

25. Grotjahn, Martin. Training the Third Ear. A Report on an Experiment with Teaching Conjecture in Psychotherapy. (Accepted for publication as a contribution to the Commemorative Volume on Theodor Reik's 65th Birthday, May 1953).

26. Johnson, Adelaide. Transference and Countertransference Problems in the Working Through of the Late Oedipal Conflict. (Paper read at a meeting of the Society for Psychoanalytic Medicine of Southern California, April 5, 1951).

27. Jones, Ernest. A Valedictory Address. *Internat. J. Psycho-Analysis,* 27: 7–12, 1946.

28. Kardiner, Abram. Report on the Conference on Problems of Psycho-analytic Training, May 1952, Atlantic City.

29. Landauer, Karl. Methods and Technique of Control Analysis. (A part of the report of the Four Countries Conference of the International Training Commission.) *Internat. J. Psycho-Analysis,* 18: 371, 1937.

30. Problems of Psychoanalytic Training. (Group discussion at the Scientific Sessions of the 1949 Annual Meeting of the American Psychoanalytic Association.) *Bull. Am. Psychoanalyt. Assoc.,* 5: no. 3, Sept. 1949, p. 58.

31. Rado, Sandor. Graduate Residency Training in Psychoanalytic Medicine. *Am. J. Psychiat.,* 105: 111–115, 1948.

32. Reik, Theodor. *Listening with the Third Ear;* the inner experience of a psychoanalyst. New York, Farrar, Straus & Co., 1948.

33. Reik, Theodor. The Sublime and the Obscene. (In his *The Secret Self.* New York, Farrar, Straus and Young, 1952. Chap. VII).

34. Sachs, Hanns. Observations of a Training Analyst. *Psychoanalyt. Quart.,* 16: 157–168, 1947.

35. Sterba, Richard. The Abuse of Interpretation. *Psychiatry,* 4: 9–12, 1941.

36. Weigert, Edith. The Importance of Flexibility in Psychoanalytic Technique. (Paper read at the 1952 Mid-Winter Meeting of the American Psychoanalytic Association).

37. Winnicott, D. W. Hate in the Counter-Transference. *Internat. J. Psycho-Analysis,* 30: 69–74, 1949.

ADDITIONAL REFERENCES

Alexander, Franz. The Indications for Psychoanalytic Therapy. *Bull. New York Acad. Med.,* 20: 320–332, 1944.

Alexander, Franz. A Jury Trial of Psychoanalysis. *J. Abnorm. & Social Psychol.,* 35: 305–323, 1940.

Alexander, Franz. Psychoanalysis Revised. *Psychoanalyt. Quart.,* 9: 1–36, 1940.

Alexander, Franz. Recollections of Berggasse 19. *Psychoanalyt. Quart.,* 9: 195–204, 1940.

Bartemeier, Leo H. Presidential Address. *Am. J. Psychiat.,* 109: 1–7, 1952.

Brosin, Henry W. A Review of the Influence of Psychoanalysis on Current

Thought. (In *Dynamic Psychiatry*. Edited by Franz Alexander and Helen Ross. Chicago, University of Chicago Press, 1952. pp. 508–553).

Bulletin of the American Psychoanalytic Association. Meeting of the Board on Professional Standards at the Midwinter Meetings, December 1951. (Vol. 8, No. 1, March 1952, pp. 23–35).

Bulletin of the American Psychoanalytic Association. A Proposed Plan for the Training of Child Analysts. (Vol. 5, No. 1, March 1949, pp. 38–41).

Bulletin of the American Psychoanalytic Association. Special Report of the Committee on the Revision of Standards. (Vol. 8, No. 1, March 1952, pp. 75–107).

Ekstein, Rudolf; Brown, William; Greenbaum, Nathan; Hollingsworth, Irene; Kobler, Arthur; Sargent, Helen. A Method of Supervision for Psychotherapy. *Trans. Kansas Acad. Sci.*, 53: 254–267, 1950.

Fenichel, Otto (with the collaboration of Annie Reich). Theoretical Implications of the Didactic Analysis. (Published as manuscript by the Topeka Institute for Psychoanalysis, 1942).

Ferenczi, Sandor, and Rank, Otto. *The Development of Psycho-Analysis.* New York, Nervous and Mental Disease Publishing Co., 1925.

Freud, Sigmund. Constructions in Analysis. *Internat. J. Psycho-Analysis,* 19: 377–387, 1938.

Freud, Sigmund. Further Recommendations in the Technique of Psycho-Analysis. On Beginning the Treatment. The Question of the First Communications. The Dynamics of the Cure. (In his *Collected Papers,* Vol. II. London, Hogarth Press, 1946. pp. 342–365).

Freud, Sigmund. Postscript to a Discussion on Lay Analysis. (In his *Collected Papers,* Vol. V. London, Hogarth Press, 1950. pp. 205–214, especially pp. 211–212).

Freud, Sigmund. Recommendations for Physicians on the Psycho-Analytic Method of Treatment. (In his *Collected Papers,* Vol. II. London, Hogarth Press, 1946. pp. 323–333, especially p. 332).

Freud, Sigmund. Turnings in the Ways of Psycho-Analytic Therapy. (In his *Collected Papers,* Vol. II. London, Hogarth Press, 1946. pp. 392–402, especially p. 396).

Fromm-Reichmann, Frieda. Notes on the Personal and Professional Requirements of a Psychotherapist. *Psychiatry,* 12: 361–378, 1949.

Frosch, John. Psychoanalytic Training and Practice. (In *The Annual Survey of Psychoanalysis.* Vol. 1, 1950. New York, International Universities Press, 1952. pp. 390–398).

Gitelson, Maxwell. Problems of Psychoanalytic Training. *Psychoanalyt. Quart.*, 17: 198–211, 1948.

Gitelson, Maxwell. Psychoanalysis and Dynamic Psychiatry. *Arch. Neurol. & Psychiat.*, 66: 280–288, 1951.

Gralnick, Alexander. A Postgraduate Psychoanalytic Training Program; its evolution, principles, and operation at the New York Medical College. *Am. J. Psychiat.*, 106: 841–844, 1950.

Gregg, Alan. The Limitations of Psychiatry. *Am. J. Psychiat.*, 104: 513M–522M, 1948.

Grotjahn, Alfred. *Aerzte als Patienten.* Georg Thieme, 1929, p. 274.

Grotjahn, Martin. The Distribution of Training Analysts. *Bull. Am. Psychoanalyt. Assoc.*, 6: No. 4, Dec. 1950, pp. 16–18.

Grotjahn, Martin. The Process of Maturation in Group Psychotherapy and in the Group Therapist. *Psychiatry*, 13: 63–67, 1950.

Grotjahn, Martin. The Role of Identification in Psychiatric and Psychoanalytic Training. *Psychiatry*, 12: 141–151, 1949.

Grotjahn, Martin. Special Problems in the Supervision of Group Psychotherapy. *Group Psychotherapy*, 3: 308–315, 1951.

Institute for Psychoanalysis. *Five-Year Report,* 1932–1937. Chicago, The Institute.

Institute for Psychoanalysis. *Ten-Year Report,* 1932–1942. Chicago, The Institute.

Kaufman, M. Ralph. The Role of Psychoanalysis in American Psychiatry. *Bull. Am. Psychoanalyt. Assoc.*, 6: No. 1, March, 1950, pp. 1–4.

Knight, Robert P. A Critique of the Present Status of the Psychotherapies. *Bull. New York Acad. Med.*, 2nd ser., 25: 100–114, 1949.

Kovacs, Vilma. Training- and Control-Analysis. *Internat. J. Psycho-Analysis*, 17: 346–354, 1936.

Kubie, Lawrence S. The Independent Institute. *Bull. Am. Psychoanalyt. Assoc.*, 8: 205–208, 1952.

Kubie, Lawrence S. *Practical and Theoretical Aspects of Psychoanalysis.* New York, International Universities Press, 1950.

Lee, Harry B. On Supervision of the Transference in Psychiatric Social Work. *Psychiatry*, 3: 421–435, 1940.

Lewin, Bertram. Training in Psychoanalysis. *Am. J. Orthopsychiat.*, 16: 427–429, 1946.

Lewis, Nolan D. C. *A Short History of Psychiatric Achievement.* New York, W. W. Norton & Co., 1941.

Mohr, George J. Present Day Trends in Psychoanalysis. *Psychiatry,* 6: 281–284, 1943.

Murphy, William F., and Weinreb, Joseph. Problems in Teaching Short Term Psychotherapy. *Diseases Nervous System,* 9: 101–105, 1948.

National Conference on Post-War Problems of Psychoanalytic Training. New York, 1946. Proceedings of the Conference. (Reproduced from type-written copy).

Oberndorf, Clarence P. Historical Comments on Psychoanalytic Teaching. *Bull. Am. Psychoanalyt. Assoc.,* 8: 209–213, 1952.

Pinner, Max, and Miller, Benjamin. *When Doctors Are Patients.* New York, W. W. Norton & Co., 1952.

Potter, Howard W., and Klein, Henriette R. Toward Unification of Training in Psychiatry and Psychoanalysis. *Am. J. Psychiat.,* 108: 193–197, 1951.

Redlich, Fredrick C.; Dollard, John; and Newman, Richard. High Fidelity Recording of Psychotherapeutic Interviews. *Am. J. Psychiat.,* 107: 42–48, 1950.

Romano, John. Basic Orientation and Education of the Medical Student. *J.A.M.A.,* 143: 409–412, 1950.

Sharpe, Ella Freeman. The Psycho-Analyst. (In her *Collected Papers on Psycho-Analysis.* London, Hogarth Press, 1950. pp. 109–122).

Sharpe, Ella Freeman. The Technique of Psycho-Analysis. 1. The Analyst. 2. The Analysand. (In her *Collected Papers on Psycho-Analysis.* London, Hogarth Press, 1950. pp. 9–37).

Szurek, S. A. Remarks on Training for Psychotherapy. *Am. J. Orthopsychiat.,* 19: 36–51, 1949.

Teaching Psychotherapeutic Medicine; an experimental course for general physicians. Edited by Helen L. Witmer. New York, Commonwealth Fund, 1947.

Waelder, Robert. Present Trends in Psychoanalytic Theory and Practice. (In *The Yearbook of Psychoanalysis.* Vol. I, 1945. New York, International Universities Press, 1945. pp. 84–89).

Weigert, Edith. Dissent in the Early History of Psychoanalysis. *Psychiatry,* 5: 349–359, 1942.

Weigert, Edith. Die Entwicklung der psychoanalytischen Ausbildung in U.S.A. (To be published in *Psyche*).

Discussion

MILTON ROSENBAUM, M.D.

IN DISCUSSING "training in psychoanalysis," I shall focus on one aspect of the training program which has been emphasized by psychiatric and psychoanalytic educators, namely the relationship of psychiatric training centers and psychoanalytic institutes. The Committee on Medical Education of the Group for the Advancement of Psychiatry has devoted considerable time during the past three years to this problem and I shall draw on those discussions for some of my material.

Historically the responsibility for the teaching of psychodynamics, originally derived from psychoanalytic theory, was assumed by individual psychoanalytic institutes and they continued in this country the European tradition of being separated both from the medical schools and from psychiatry in general. Originally, psychiatrists already trained and experienced went to the analytic institute for training in psychoanalytic theory and practice. As psychoanalytically trained psychiatrists began to play a more important role in medical schools and psychiatric training centers, and as the theory of psychodynamics became increasingly accepted and incorporated into psychiatry, it followed naturally that more and more psychiatrists, together with medical students, medical residents, and medical teachers, were greatly stimulated to know about psychoanalysis, and many began to seek such training. Furthermore, psychiatrists attempted to secure analytic training earlier in their psychiatric experience, with the result that at present the candidates for psychoanalytic training are both younger and less experienced in psychiatry than formerly. In metropolitan areas the majority of psychiatric residents apply to psychoanalytic institutes and since all cannot be admitted, many secure a personal analysis irrespective of future training in psychoanalysis. This in itself has created many problems in training. In this connection an interesting finding gathered from a recent questionnaire sent to every hospital approved for psychiatric residency training showed that of a total of 813 residents, 287 or 34 percent were either undergoing personal analysis or were in formal psychoanalytic training. Another study revealed that almost 50 percent of psychiatric residents in eleven training centers geographically accessible to analytic institutes were in psychoanalytic training or were undergoing a personal analysis. This obviously indicates that many psychiatrists are beginning analysis during their residency training and undoubtedly the percentage would be higher if analytic training were more readily available.

There are many motives which determine the general desire to be enrolled in a psychoanalytic institute. The responsibility to understand and treat the complexities of the human organism increases the resident's search for improved techniques and new systematic knowledge. The analytic institutes were the first to offer intensive individual supervision of psychotherapy, and at present the teaching of psychodynamics is better organized in the institutes. The unavoidable lag in the programs of the residency training centers in the past which were unable to provide this kind of training, and the high prestige value of being a psychoanalyst plus the financial rewards, are other reasons for the increased numbers who seek psychoanalytic training. Obviously a variety of personal psychological factors entered into this quest, but still we must not underestimate the importance of the exposure to psychoanalysis when it became possible for the resident to identify himself with analysts garbed in the respectability of academic medicine. The attitude of the professor and chairman of psychiatric departments toward psychoanalytic training profoundly influences the resident, who, by and large, patterns his own views of emotional illness and its therapy after his residency department in general, and his professor in particular.

It is obvious that a certain amount of inevitable confusion has arisen out of the dichotomy and duplication of training in psychiatry and psychoanalysis. Because of the dichotomy, residents still equate training in psychodynamics and psychoanalytic theory with training in a psychoanalytic institute. Consequently, more demand is made by the resident to be taught the theory of psychodynamics and its application in his psychiatric training. There are some obvious advantages in having didactic courses in psychodynamics taught in a close and appropriate relationship to "on the spot" supervision of residents in their daily activities. The teaching of psychodynamics in a residency training center has the added advantage of exposure to and scrutiny by other medical disciplines. Also, a greater number and variety of cases can be seen, with closer opportunity for recheck on living case material and for re-evaluation through the pooling of experienced opinions. However, many analysts and many analytic training units insist that psychoanalytic training is best given in separated institutes and should be given irrespective of whatever training in psychiatry has preceded it or is going on simultaneously. Others believe that training in psychiatry should go on separately. Many prevalent attitudes about psychoanalytic training remain fixed because of various highly personal opinions. What is needed are more objective investigative studies.

Analytic institutes have always practiced some method of selection of candidates, but very little serious attention was devoted to this important aspect of training until recently. The present methods of selection leave much to be desired. It is to the credit of the training analysts in the Chicago area that they are at present seriously engaged in tackling this problem, and the results of their efforts will be awaited with great interest.

The curriculum in most psychoanalytic institutes as in most teaching institutions jells quickly and resists change. By and large, changes occur by adding rather than altering or dropping established courses. It would be superfluous to list the theoretical and clinical courses in the curriculum which represent the matrix of this part of the program, but the curriculum should be flexible enough to adapt itself to the changes which have occurred and which are occurring in the psychiatric background of the present analytic candidates. Although repeated exposure is one of the axioms of the learning process, undue repetition may lead to a substantial loss of interest. Even though the psychiatric background of the students may vary considerably, more and more students have been exposed to, and undoubtedly have absorbed a good deal of the material covered in, the curriculum of the institute during their residency training. Thus, when such students represent the majority of candidates, the curriculum of the institute should undergo the necessary modifications to insure that the students' needs are met.

This problem is being solved at the present time by closer cooperation between the institutes and those training centers which supply the bulk of the students. Since, as previously mentioned, the present trend is for students to start their analytic training earlier, during the residency period, such coordinated courses must continue despite the warnings of some that the institutes will lose their autonomy. Some would meet this and other problems of training by a more complete integration of psychiatric and psychoanalytic training through the incorporation of the institute into psychoanalytically oriented departments of psychiatry. Steps have already been made in this direction, and although the pro's and con's are many, there is no doubt that the trend is in the direction of such types of integration. Let me cite the situation in Cincinnati as an example of what the future holds. At the present time practically all the members of the senior full-time teaching staff have completed their analytic training. In another five years or so we should have enough qualified analysts to form the nucleus of an institute. When that time arrives it does not seem likely that the same analysts who function as teachers in the department of psychiatry will join hands and form an institute separated from the university department of psychiatry. This situation is not unique for Cincinnati; many other psychiatric departments face a similar future.

Certainly serious problems in training in such an organization can occur, especially when the analyst-analysand relationship is complicated by such factors as personal, professional, and administrative interrelationship in the department. However, with proper understanding and judicious planning, most of these problems can be neutralized and avoided. Will such integrated programs dilute analysis, as some already claim? Rather than acting as an irresponsible and destructive solvent, such a program, truly scientific in spirit and execution, and operating in a milieu of the highest university standards, would become a catalyst for the continuing development of psychoanalysis. In such programs, selected analysts would be encouraged to devote their full time and energy to studying those aspects of analysis for which they are particularly adapted, free from administrative, teaching, and clinical duties and from the grim business of earning a living, which at present impedes the development of research analysts. Indeed in this way psychoanalysis would be enriched much as medicine has been by the combined efforts of the clinician and the research scientist, and although each may be engaged in his own esoteric pursuits, the common goal of increasing knowledge of human behavior will be greatly stimulated.

It is fitting and proper to close with a recent quotation from the man we have come to honor on this day. This is what he said, "My expectation is that in these new university departments of psychiatry, the complete assimilation of the teaching of psychoanalysis both in the psychiatric curriculum and in undergraduate teaching will soon be accomplished, and psychoanalysis as a medical discipline will find its way back to the universities, its birthplace and natural homeland."

Psychoanalysis as a Basic Science

LAWRENCE S. KUBIE, M.D.

THE PLACE of psychoanalysis in Science is determined by its adherence to those fundamental laws which govern all scientific progress and by certain contributions which it has made to scientific techniques. Psychoanalysis has evolved a method by which the subtlest of psychological observations can be made and repeated under conditions in which external variables are reduced to a minimum. This is essential in any scientific discipline. It has developed a technique for introducing a controlled variable into this constant situation, that is, the non-affective interpretation, thus taking an important step toward maturity out of the elementary Naturalistic phase of science.

It has made in addition three basic contributions to scientific methodology: (1) a method for the study of the conscious and unconscious emotional interplay between observer and observed, and of the influence which this interplay exercises upon the observations themselves; (2) a method for assessing the influence of unconscious symbolic values on the study of even inanimate objects; and (3) the first technique for a random sampling of psychological processes, to wit, the technique of free association with all of its implications.

Finally, it has given us a new sophistication about the sources of perceptual, conceptual, and logical error in man the scientist.

But what is Science? A wise religious teacher once said from his pulpit that religion is not Truth but the search for Truth, and that as soon as any religion begins to believe that it has found the Truth it ceases to be a religion. This was a rarely humble statement for a theologian. Certainly a humility no less than this should infuse both the theoretical concepts and the creative efforts of the scientist. As soon as any Science believes that it has found Truth it ceases to be Science. For Science is not merely a body of discovered facts. Once established, these become a part of all human culture, of our general human heritage. Science is rather the effort to approximate Truth, a way of seeking to establish the boundary between fact and fantasy. For Science, when it is honest and humble, is an effort to find ever closer approximations to the facts about ourselves and about the world in which we live. With the gradual elimination of sources of error and the gradual improvement in techniques of self-criticism, it moves ever closer to Truth. Perhaps Science may sometime meet the Absolute face to face to shake it by the hand, but only at some remote point in infinity, which we can extrapolate into the dim future from the grubby chores of today.

In its search for Truth, Science depends upon methods of gathering data, and then of testing with skepticism and constant self-criticism the degree to which these data conform to external realities. This establishes approximate "facts." About these facts the scientist offers interpretations, that is to say hypotheses about causal relationships between these approximate facts. Thereupon, Science tests the accuracy of these theoretical constructions in various ways, the ultimate test always being the ability to predict the events which some future concatenation of circumstances will produce. I repeat that just as Astronomy has often demonstrated that this is the ultimate test, so Science can accept nothing as valid until it is supported by evidence of this nature. Even then it knows that validity is approximate and relative, and that its acceptance is tentative and waits always on more conclusive evidence (6, p. 151).

These are the steps by which any science achieves its goals. Psychoanalysis has contributed both techniques and data for an understanding of how each of these steps can be subjected to distortions. This will be discussed below; but in the meantime the problem of distortion in science is related to a more immedi-- ate question concerning the nature of maturity in science.

A full consideration of psychoanalysis as a basic science would cover many aspects of psychoanalysis and many aspects of science. Some of these topics are covered by other participants in this symposium: as for instance psychoanalysis in relationship to the biological sciences in general, and psychoanalysis in relationship to the social sciences. Another important problem—namely, the ways in which analysis fails to meet the essential requirements of science and needs the criticisms and the techniques which derive from other sciences—will be omitted here, because these points have recently been discussed at length in the Hixon Fund Lectures (8). Therefore, this discussion will be concerned only with the ways in which psychoanalysis fulfills the basic requirements of the scientific process, and has added to them and applied them in new directions.

I. *The Transition from Nature to a Controlled Environment*

We usually say that a science begins to come of age when it emerges from the stage of merely observing and recording data as it occurs in nature: that is, the Naturalist phase. Its next step is always an attempt to reproduce these primary observations in an artificially contrived laboratory setting, where the major variable conditions can be known and controlled or measured, or both. This makes it possible to subject both the primary data and the hypotheses concerning their causal interrelationships to experimental testing and ultimately to mathematical formulations, the precision of which can be tested anew in the laboratory, until at length it becomes possible to estimate the role of each concurrent influence among many variables. In this way Science finally arrives at the point at which events can be predicted before they happen, just as the release of energy through atomic fission was predicted many years before it actually was produced.

Obviously psychoanalysis has not yet reached that stage. We feel, proudly, that we are on the right track, when out of a welter of variables we can predict some fragment of behavior in a patient who is under analysis. Even here we tend tacitly to underplay two facts: (1) We pass over the many inaccurate prophecies which we venture tentatively and in a cautious spirit —our analytic trial balloons. (2) Furthermore, even when we are correct, we overlook the statistical implications of the fact that we have predicted only one out of thousands of activities of the same patient on that same day. These qualifications on our prophetic analytic powers lessen the significance of our isolated successful prophecies. Yet the fact that we can predict even one item of behavior with reasonable accuracy marks a new step in the evolution of man's age-old search for self-knowledge. Maturity greater than this, however, we have no right to claim as yet.

A. THE CONTROL OF EXTERNAL VARIABLES

Yet the fact remains that in certain fundamental ways psychoanalysis is unique among the psychological disciplines in utilizing essential ingredients of a maturing scientific discipline. In the first place, analytic observations are made under reproducible and constant external circumstances. Many components in psychoanalytic technique contribute to this essential scientific

condition by restricting spontaneous changes in *external* variables and at the same time limiting and controlling variations
in the internal emotional milieu in which observations are
made. Thus, when the analyst remains consistently formal and
remote, obscure and unknown, masking his feelings behind a
poker manner and a poker face, wearing the famous beard of
the analytic incognito, he approximates the constancy of the
environment which every experimenter attempts to maintain
in his laboratory. When the laboratory scientist conducts the
same experiment in the same laboratory day after day, whether
on the same animal or on different animals, he strives constantly
to reduce to a minimum the number of uncontrolled variables,
so that when he deliberately introduces one known variable of
his own choosing, at a time of his own choosing, it will intrude
into a constant situation. In analysis, the variable which we
introduce is the interpretation; and under ideal circumstances
it is the only variable introduced. This will be discussed more
fully below (7, 11).

I want to emphasize the fact that I am concerned only with
what is ideal scientifically, dismissing as irrelevant for the moment the question of whether there is a conflict here between
what is ideal scientifically and what is ideal therapeutically. The
existence of such a conflict should surprise no one, since it
arises in every other field of medicine; and there is no reason
why it should not arise in psychoanalysis as well. But there
should be no disagreement that the more scrupulously the analyst adheres to the ancient orthodoxy of the analytic method,
the more objective will be his primary observational data, in
this specific sense, that the less will it have been corrupted by
the intrusion of unintended external or emotional variables
through the observer.

B. THE CONTROL OF EMOTIONAL VARIABLES

A more distinctive contribution of psychoanalysis to scientific methodology is linked to another application of this principle of the limitation of uncontrolled variables. In analysis this principle is for the first time applied effectively to the control of the distorting effects of the interplay of the conscious and unconscious emotional relationship between the object of the investigation and the investigator. It is here that the psychological sciences differ most sharply from such sciences as chemistry, physics, or biology. We gather our data from subjects with whom we establish a two-way affective relationship: observer to the observed and back again. On all levels, conscious, preconscious, and unconscious, feelings of love, hate, fear, and competition play into the relationship between observer and observed while they are in the experimental or observational situation. There are unconscious demands which the scientist makes upon the subject of psychological experiments, and which the subject in turn makes upon the psychological scientist. These can wholly invalidate psychological experiments or distort even beyond recognition the observation and recording of primary data. Unless these emotional forces are carefully controlled they become a continuous source of major error. Psychoanalysis was first among the psychological disciplines to appreciate this source of error, and alone in studying and limiting it.

Many of you will have heard of an example from a superficial piece of research in industrial psychology. A group of women were selected for experiments to show the effects on production of varying light, temperature, the spacing of rest periods, diet, and so on. The experimenters went through a series of changes. Each change increased the output more. Thereupon they went through the same series of changes in reverse, returning step by step to the starting condition; and still each change increased the output. This made it evident that it was not the change in the environment which caused the change in output, but the attention which the girls were receiving, and the gratification of conscious and unconscious needs for whatever such special attention meant to them. This is a banal and simple example; but over the years such influences, unrecognized, have distorted the outcome of psychological investigations in laboratories everywhere. Many an experiment on which some naive young professor of psychology has based his Ph.D., and in which he has used his fellow-students as subjects, has been invalidated by his failure to realize his own unconscious axe-grinding and that of the volunteer student-subjects.

By limiting the freedom of the relationship between the analyst and the patient, under the name of transference and countertransference, analysis makes it possible to scrutinize and to limit this unconscious source of error. This restriction can never eliminate these potent emotional variables entirely: but it limits them and renders them susceptible to more objective evaluation. Inevitably every analyst has his own conscious and unconscious demands. His conscious purposes may be to help, to achieve a therapeutic result, to prove his own analytic capacity, to discover new facts. Underneath these conscious purposes, however, hide his unconscious needs. The extent to which they will influence and distort his observations will depend upon how fully he himself has been freed from their uncontrolled influences through his own training analysis; and also upon how constantly he maintains his own analytic toilet and keeps a watchful eye on his own unconscious. Yet despite even the most meticulous care, a residue of unconscious pressures must inevitably remain; and analytic technique is designed to minimize their influence both on the primary analytic observations and on the secondary process of interpretation. Whenever an analyst emerges from behind the analytic incognito to enter into a personal relationship with the object of his analytic scrutiny, he intrudes into the observational situation the influence of his own fluctuating conscious and unconscious needs, so that these interplay with those of the patient. Again I want to by-pass the issue of whether and when this may be therapeutically advisable, so as to focus exclusively on the question of the effect of this confusion on the value of analytic observations as scientific data. When we intrude such relationships into the observational situation, it is as though we look through a microscope while puffing smoke into the gap between the objective and the slide, so that we study the microscopic preparation through the wavering distortions of swirling streams of smoke particles. Even the most scrupulous maintenance of analytic distance cannot wholly eliminate this source of error; but what it can achieve is nevertheless of critical importance in the ebb and flow of conscious and unconscious affective attitudes. If the analytic incognito and formality are respected, then among the variables which arise in the stream of psychological data to be studied, those which are produced by the *subject's* unconscious processes play a much greater role than do those which are intruded by the *observer's* unconscious. In this way analysis creates a situation in which predominantly one unconscious can be studied at a time instead of two, that one being by intent the unconscious processes of the subject rather than of the observer. This has become a basic principle in all scientific observations of behavior, influencing the design for experimental observations even on lower animal forms. For example, Howard Liddell has reported the influence which this principle has exercised on his studies of conditioned reflex reactions in many animal forms. Some of John Benjamin's students have had like experiences. Frank Beach reports similar observations. Thus, the principle has become one of the guiding rules of laboratory work in the study of the behavior of all living forms. This is one of the basic contributions made by psychoanalysis.

C. THE CONTROL OF SYMBOLIC VARIABLES

I must not leave this topic without referring to one other point: namely, that in a significant way the analyst's unconscious can also influence an observer's relationship to his data on inanimate objects. This occurs whenever the inanimate object is a symbolic representative of some living person.

Patients may dream of stones, trees, boats, wood, the sea, houses, or jewels as representatives of people or bodies or parts and products of bodies. These same inanimate objects may also trigger off neurotic symptoms (phobias, compulsions, mood swings, and the like). Similarly, individuals may work scientifically on inanimate objects which to their unconscious mental processes represent human bodies and their organs and products. Thus a patient once tried to invent a machine which unconsciously and symbolically represented to him his father and parts of his father's body. Scientific work on inanimate objects is not infrequently the screen on which an experimenter acts out his loves and hates of some living person, past or present. What appears superficially to be a piece of simple objective scientific research may because of its unconscious connotations be a pillow that we kick around or hug, an effigy that we may hang or burn, an ikon to which we light incense. What can happen in the dream, in a neurotic symptom, in religious ritual, or in art, also happens in scientific work, in that here too man may live out on inanimate objects his feelings about animate objects: to wit, other human beings and their bodies, and his own as well. This has been recognized only recently and only through psychoanalysis as a source of error in all scientific work. I am describing many examples of these in detail in another study (10). How to control this potent source of fallacy in the training of young scientists and in the supervision and evaluation of research has not been seriously studied as yet.

II. *The Introduction of the Calculated Variable— The Nonaffective Interpretation*

I have already referred to the use of interpretation as the deliberate introduction of a calculated variable. In essence this too is something both new and basic in psychological technique. Psychoanalysis first creates an interpersonal situation in which all controllable externals are maintained constant, and in which those variables which are not directly and completely controllable, such as the interplay of conscious and unconscious feelings, are managed in such a way that the feelings of *A toward B* are allowed free play and free expression while the feelings of *B toward A* are held relatively constant and are deliberately masked. This is the control of the transference-countertransference situation. Into that system of relatively constant forces, a variable is introduced precisely as one introduces a hypothesis into a laboratory. This variable is the interpretation; and every interpretation should be looked upon as a hypothesis which is to be tested.

During the course of every analysis which I personally conduct, before I venture my first interpretation I remind the patient that the scientist who is afraid to be wrong can be right only by accident; and that this is equally true in the experimental laboratory and in psychoanalysis. I explain that every advance in knowledge which experiments achieve comes only as the result of disproving thousands of erroneous hypotheses. For every experiment which proves that some pet theory is true, hundreds are proven to be false. These are the unglamorous, humble yet essential negative results of science: and I end up by pointing out that there is no possibility that the psychoanalytic hypotheses which we call interpretations can be correct with a statistical frequency higher than one has a right to expect for any other type of scientific hypothesis. Indeed, in the forward movement of any science the greater the number of uncontrollable and immeasurable variables, the greater will be the ratio of negative to positive results. In analysis, therefore, where the variables are many, the controls few, and the quantitating devices nonexistent, the proportion of negative hypotheses (that is, of interpretations which are wrong in part or *in toto*) must be higher than in any other field of science. Consequently, over and over again in the course of an analysis I insist to my patients that every interpretation is a working hypothesis to be tested in the psychoanalytic situation, and that I will make thousands of such tentative interpretations which are incorrect for every one which goes directly to the target; but that the disproving or correcting of every incorrect interpretation is as essential to the progress of the analysis as are the thousands of negative results over the corpses of which science makes its progress in the laboratory. Once the analyst understands this, he has turned a corner toward maturity as an analyst. Once the patient understands and accepts it, both intellectually and emotionally, he has taken an indispensable step toward health, and has become a conjoint and active participant in an analysis which is a mature, scientific adventure.

This may seem to be an irrelevant bypath into issues pertaining to therapy; but actually it illustrates a principle which is fundamental for the position of psychoanalytic theory and technique as a legitimate member of the scientific brotherhood. Where this principle is clearly understood and governs the practice of the analyst, the psychoanalytic procedure becomes one with other sciences. Where this fundamental principle is neglected, where an interpretation is looked upon as an intuitive divination, or as automatically true merely because it is derived from the analyst's reactions to the free associations of a patient, the interpretation becomes a fantasy of analytic omniscience.

Moreover, as with all other scientific hypotheses, no one interpretation ever stands alone. The interpretation which is given at any moment is only the current expression of a hierarchy of related interpretations, since in translating any conscious psychological act into its unconscious determinants we always deal with groups of concurrent or sequential determinants operating at different levels.

The methods by which the accuracy of an interpretation can be proved or corrected have been discussed at length in the Hixon Fund Lectures (8). Here, therefore, I will only point out that once it has been communicated, an interpretation can never again be what it was, because the patient reacts to it at once both intellectually and emotionally. It makes a critical difference in the emotional orientation of a patient to an interpretation, however, when he realizes that the psychoanalyst has no vested interest in any interpretation, and that in the search for analytic truth an interpretation can be equally valuable whether it is ultimately proved to be correct or incorrect. This is the critical difference between a scientific and an unscientific use of that calculated variable, the nonaffective interpretation.

III. *Basic Contributions*

I hope that these general considerations may help us to approach more clearly the question of what, if anything, in psychoanalysis deserves to be called *basic* to science in general. The words "a basic science" lead one to think of the mutual interdependence between such sciences as physics and chemistry and mathematics. One cannot conceive of the one without the other, because each feeds to the others facts and techniques without which the others could not operate. Together they form the tripod on which all modern science stands. Certainly physics, chemistry, and mathematics are basic and essential to modern biology and physiology. On the other hand, it is fair to say that although biology brings challenging problems to these more basic sciences, the biological sciences do not feed either methods or data without which this basic trio could not function. In that sense, then, they are the more basic.

The biological disciplines on the other hand are subdivided largely for teaching purposes into subdisciplines (anatomy, histology, physiology, biochemistry, comparative anatomy, embryology, pathology, bacteriology, to mention a few); and although they are segregated into "courses" and "departments" for pedagogical purposes, they use each others' data and techniques interchangeably in the course of their own experimental processes. Even the Chinese Wall that once existed between normal physiology and pathophysiology no longer exists; and the relationship among all these areas of study, teaching, and research forms a circle without a break. Into this intact circle, as we have seen, psychoanalysis has introduced techniques which are vital for the control of the variable forces which arise in all psychological studies. It is here that psychoanalysis has made its contributions to science: (a) The control of the over-all environment in which observations are made has been brought to a new refinement and extended into new areas, particularly with respect to the emotional relationships, conscious and unconscious, between subject and object. (b) It has developed the technique of introducing a calculated variable into this constancy through the nonaffective interpretation. (c) The significance of free associations as a scientific implement is its next major contribution.

A. FREE ASSOCIATIONS

The technique of free association, as it has been developed in psychoanalysis, has broader scientific implications than have been appreciated. That free association is an exploratory instrument is understood. That it is essential specifically for the exploration of relationships between levels of psychological functioning which vary in their accessibility to consciousness is less well understood. *Why* it has this special function, and its consequent place in any systematic understanding of the creative process, is not generally appreciated at all. Yet the reasons are simple; and interestingly enough they are both physiological and statistical.

Physiologically viewed, the technique of free association constitutes a link between psychoanalysis and the psychological sciences in general on the one hand, and the physiology of the nervous system on the other. As has been pointed out elsewhere, the rationale of free associations is a mirror image of the physiological basis of the conditioned reflex (3, 4, 5). Pavlov showed that no two experiences which *impinge* upon the nervous system with a consistent relationship in time can fail to establish a connecting link, the nature of which is dependent in part upon that time relationship. Conversely, the study of free associations in psychoanalysis shows that ideas, feelings, and actions which *emerge from* the nervous system in some consistent time relationship are also bound together in a meaningful pattern, the nature of which is then investigated in the process of analysis itself.

Statistically viewed, free association is our only approximation to a psychological Gallup poll. It is a method of gathering samples of psychological activity which are at least relatively random in the statistical sense. When any two human beings communicate with each other, whether as patient and doctor, as friends, or as a lecturer before an audience, the speaker without being aware of it uses a continuous and automatic process of selecting and rejecting from among multiple simultaneous psychological processes. It is inevitable that any spoken word blocks others which might have been uttered at the same moment. In this way, in the process of orderly thought and orderly speech we eliminate "irrelevancies," as we select those thoughts and ideas which are related to some guiding goal. This is an automatic process, as automatic as walking. We do not have to think out each move as we make our minds walk, any more than we have to think of each muscle that we move as our bodies walk. Obviously this process is essential for the communication of ideas; but the articulate result never gives a true picture of all that is going on in the speaker's head and heart at the time, for the simple reason that communication utilizes weighted samples rather than statistically random samples of a mass of psychological material which can never be expressed *in toto*. It is an ancient scientific principle that where we cannot examine all, we must sample, and that the sample must be both random and adequate. The technique of free association, as used in psychoanalysis, is the first systematic application of this principle to psychological investigations. This fact is basic to an understanding of the scientific significance of psychoanalysis; because the sampling technique which is called "free association" is one of its critical contributions to the scientific process, not only within the psychological sciences, but in others as well.

A word of warning as to the meaning of the word "free" may not be out of place. In the first place it carries no philosophical implication. The word "free" in "free associations" does not imply that such associations are exempt from cause and effect relationships, or from the directing influence of physiological and psychological forces. It implies rather a freedom from any deliberate interference, whether preconscious or conscious, with the spontaneity of the stream of thought itself, that is to say from any deliberate selection and rejection as to which from among the elements of that stream will be communicated.

For this reason the technique of free association throws light on the creative process in the scientist, the artist, and indeed the thinker in all fields of intellectual and cultural endeavor. As has been stated elsewhere (6, pp. 45–47):

It is not always realized that free associations are the natural process by which the mind of the artist and scientist creates. Free associations enable the psychological processes to roam through the mental highways and byways, unhampered by conscious restrictions, gathering up ideas and impressions, putting them together in varying combinations, until new relationships and new patterns come into view. Both in science and in the arts, free association is the essential tool in the process of creative search. Subsequent logical scrutiny subjects these new patterns to a necessary secondary process of retrospective checking and testing. In analysis, the free associations are provided by the patient; the logical scrutiny by the analyst. . . . There are two major psychological levels of linkages, one conscious and the other unconscious. If we allow ourselves consciously to pick and choose from among the thoughts which come freely to mind, it becomes almost impossible to study the role of unconscious links and forces on the stream of psychological events. If, on the other hand, all conscious choices are eliminated, then these unconscious influences come into view. A study of free associations, therefore, constitutes the key to the unconscious, indeed the major key we now possess.

Free associations operate continuously and incessantly; but they are usually masked by the overlay of conscious associations among which we make our primary choices in our daily tasks of communicating our thoughts to one another. It is especially in our fully waking states that preconscious and unconscious linkages are masked by conscious linkages; and at the level of fully conscious alertness it is only with the use of free association as a technique of exploration that we can penetrate the masking action of conscious links. On the other hand the masking overlay of the cloud of conscious relationships is lessened automatically in delirious states, in dreams, in hypnagogic reveries, and in the intuitive, creative, or "inspirational" states of the mathematician, scientist, or artist. Therefore, it is not surprising that so many of the world's great discoveries have been made in what has seemed to be an automatic, intuitive, inspirational flash, or in hypnagogic states, or even in dreams. All of these are moments or states of consciousness during which psychological processes drop back from the most highly evolved level of discrete symbolic thought and imagery and their symbolic representation to levels at which concepts and their symbolic representations and their related feelings roam most freely and fuse and interact and overlap. In addition, these considerations make it clear that some of the energies which infuse speech and thought must at all times derive not from the most highly developed levels of symbolic action alone, but from the deeper, broader, more inclusive and more primitive meanings.

The recent Hixon Fund Lectures (8) developed at some length the implications of this for the exploration of the relationships between various levels of psychological function. Such basic investigations make use of a double technique: (1) induced, controlled alterations in levels or states of conscious organization ("induced, controlled dissociations"); and (2) the technique of free association (using verbal, dance, and art forms, and so on) to provide unweighted samplings of the psychological processes at whatever level is being studied. The application of this principle has already given new insights into psychopathology and normal psychological processes, and into the creative process in science, in all cultural disciplines, and in the arts. These applications of the analytic technique of free association may prove to be more important for her sister sciences than any other analytic contribution, since the study of free associations provides us with a technique for investigating all processes of creative scientific thought.

In its full implications it has also provided us with a necessary tool for our ultimate concern, which is with man himself as a "fallacy-prone instrument of science."

B. MAN AS A FALLACY-PRONE SCIENTIFIC INSTRUMENT

The significance of psychoanalysis among the sciences increases as scientists are becoming increasingly aware that self-knowledge in depth, that ancient Socratic ideal, is the forgotten man in the education of the scientist; and that without self-knowledge in depth, man as the instrument of scientific progress is vulnerable to many fallacies. To the limiting and neutralizing of these fallacies, analysis makes two contributions: (a) an understanding of the intellectual and emotional processes by which the scientist operates; and (b) a corrective for subtle errors which cannot be controlled by the techniques available to its sister sciences alone.

To understand this we must scrutinize again the steps by which every scientific operation proceeds. The initial step involves the observation of phenomena as they occur freely and spontaneously in nature. This step makes two demands which are peculiar to science, with one of which science has long been familiar. We have known that we must not alter phenomena in the very act of observing them, since if the act of observing phenomena distorts them, an artefact is introduced into our primary data. The second precaution deals with a difficulty the importance of which has only recently been appreciated. This is the difficulty of being certain that our ever-present unconscious is not tinting with one hue or another the glasses through which we make even the simplest observations.

Although the full implications of this have been appreciated only through psychoanalysis, it has an interesting pre-history.

Indeed, much of nineteenth century psychology was based on an elementary recognition of the fact that the human observer can himself be a variable source of error, distorting observations which seem to be purely objective. The story dates back to the Greenwich Observatory in 1795, where, in an effort to determine the exact moment at which a star entered the field of a telescope and passed over a vertical hair, the astronomer noted the sound of the stroke of a pendulum while observing at the same time the movement of the star. When certain inconsistencies occurred, an effort was made to eliminate them by having the observer, on hearing the pendulum, press a telegraph key which left an impression on a smoked drum, pressing it again as he observed the transit of the star across the lines of the grid in the telescope. Yet the variations in the observations persisted—in certain instances costing able young astronomers their jobs for "carelessness,"—until it was found that the observations made by the head of the observatory varied quite as widely as did those of his assistants. Ultimately, from this came the concept of "reaction time" and a realization of its variations, then the psychophysiological experiments of Wundt, and much of the psychological experimentation of the turn of the century. Finally, the studies of the time element in word associations brought an awareness of the significant influence of the emotional content of words on reaction time. Thus, these early steps are in line with the later refinements of psychoanalytic knowledge and technique, as applied to the same problem.

Psychoanalysis challenges us to broaden and to deepen our knowledge of the sources of error which are deep in human nature and which influence man's accuracy and judgment as scientists. By tinting the glasses that men wear, man's unconscious begins to play tricks on the primary observations themselves. Consequently it is out of the pastel shades of this faintly colored primary data that he evolves his first scientific theories, which are in essence hypotheses about the possible relationships between his observed data. But these hypotheses are in turn even more vulnerable to distortion by unconscious processes than are the primary observations themselves. Furthermore, as he sets up an experiment to test his primary observations and theories, he no longer observes phenomena as they occur in nature but rather in the milieu which he has created artificially for the purposes of his experiments. About these new data he formulates new hypotheses which again must be tested experimentally. Each successive and alternating step of observation and experimentation tests the previous steps, together with their unavoidable distortions, each time isolating and quantifying the previous variables while at the same time testing the consequences of the derived theories. This familiar sequence of steps serves to balance out the distortions which are introduced by conscious bias; yet the data cannot be free from the distortions of perception and of reasoning whose roots are in our unconscious biases. Thus, the structure of science adds layer upon layer, each layer burdened by subtler and more complex unconscious emotional investments, continually demanding of the scientist an ever greater clarity about the role not of his conscious reasoning alone, but of his unconscious processes as well, as these influence his conscious theories and experiments. Thus each step requires an ever more rigorous correction for the influence of unconscious preconceptions.

Until the advent of psychoanalysis, we had no technique with which to study, much less to modify the unconscious biases which play so important a role in the lives and works of Man the Scientist. Some students of the world of science have recognized their influence: but perhaps because they had no tools with which to deal with such distortions their words evoked little notice. Claude Bernard (1) referred to it in a famous passage in which he compared the experimentalist and the scholastic and the metaphysician, pointing out the fact that "they are all subject to the same internal human laws, plagued by the same emotions, prejudices, and biases, and that these operate equally in the philosopher and the scientist." More recently Richard Tolman (13), the great physicist, referred to "the effects of personal biases on results, the relation between subjective origins and objective outcomes of scientific experiments." He commented also on the fact that the scientist "selects his problem . . . not to attain results . . . but to satisfy his own subjective needs. . . ." And again, "the origin of . . . problems is a subjective one . . ." . . . ". . . that which has objective validity is finally abstracted out from the welter of subjective experience in which scientists as well as other human beings are immersed." Charles Richet (12) recognized this in his spirited volume, *The Natural History of a Savant;* and Alan Gregg (2) has touched on it in his sage volume of lectures, *The Furtherance of Medical Research.*

Evidently a deepening sophistication is slowly developing about Man the Scientist. The father of modern physiology, a great immunologist, our own statesman of medical education, and a great atomic physicist, all recognize the importance of increasing the depth of our understanding of the distorting influence which unconscious psychological processes exercise on the scientific worker. Surely it is time now that this problem be made the focus of an investigation of both the scientific process and the scientist, an investigation in which psychoanalytic technique will be an essential tool and a basic conceptual platform without which such an investigation could not be made.

I could give many concrete examples of the distortions which unconscious processes have produced in the research work of able and gifted scientists whom I have had an opportunity to study: examples in which it can be seen that the creative work of even the most competent of scientists can have the quality of dreams, or of the most banal neurotic symptoms, arising from similar roots, subject to similar symbolic distortions. For lack of time, however, these examples will have to be presented in another study (9, 10).

IV. *Current Limitations on Scientific Techniques and Processes in Psychoanalysis*

No discussion of psychoanalysis as a basic science would be complete without a reference to some of its present limitations. The following list will not attempt to be complete, but only to exemplify some of the important areas in which psychoanalysis still is groping.

A. LIMITATIONS WITH RESPECT TO THE GATHERING OF PRIMARY DATA

To record primary observations in reproducible form is essential for the progress of any science. This necessity confronts psychoanalysis with exceptional difficulties. It is easy enough to take moving pictures, perhaps under infrared light or in color and with sound recording; but to introduce such processes without altering both the observed data and the observing situation is by no means easy. Nor is it easy to evaluate the conscious and unconscious distortions which such devices impose. Furthermore, assembling this data, transcribing it, and restudying it is so heavy a task that the analysis of one hour of work with a patient may require twenty further hours of work by a group of technicians and trained observers. This involves problems of space, of soundproof construction, of finance, and of personnel. These problems are not insoluble; but it would be unwise to minimize the difficulties which they entail.

B. CONCEPTUAL LIMITATIONS

Largely as a consequence of these difficulties, we are not yet in a position to organize even our primary observations into complex abstractions, about whose basic and unitary nature all observers agree. This results in conceptual, terminological, and theoretical ambiguities. As a further consequence, in formulating the relationships between tentative conceptual units, psychoanalysis is still unable to differentiate clearly between description and explanation. Nor is it clear about how and where it is essential to introduce those assumptions about quantitative variations in unprecise units of "force," without which the theoretical superstructure of psychoanalysis remains insecure.

C. PROBLEMS OF VALIDATION

At present tentative validations of psychoanalytic interpretations depend largely on confirmations and corrections which are provided by the free associations which have been evoked by the interpretations themselves. The more precise validations of the future must rest on various types of quantitative measurements which are not now available, on laboratory facsimiles under controlled conditions, and on the accuracy of clinical predictions. It has not yet been possible to establish the ratio of accurate to inaccurate predictions, nor of accurate to inaccurate interpretations. Nor is psychoanalysis as yet in a position to show whether any changes in technique or therapy have altered either of these ratios.

Consequently, although it is not difficult to establish what interpretations may conceivably be *possible,* nor even those which may be *probable,* to determine which interpretations are *uniquely adequate* and therefore *necessary* is still beyond us. In turn this is related to that strange and paradoxical fact that the effects of the impact of unconscious processes on preconscious and conscious processes are more accessible to scrutiny than are the reverse effects of the impact of conscious and preconscious processes on that which goes on behind the iron curtain at an unconscious level.

D. CONTROLS

Wherever we deal with ubiquitous phenomena such as the neurotic process, the problem of controls presents special difficulties. Under these circumstances no group can be selected at random to serve as a control group; and controls depend therefore upon the meticulous comparison of individuals about each of whom every relevant detail must be known.

E. DEFICIENCIES IN SPECIFIC INSTRUMENTS

(1) Psychoanalysis as a science lacks instruments for measuring the relative roles of conscious, preconscious, and unconscious processes in the incessant interplay of forces which determine each moment of psychological activity. (2) It lacks instruments for measuring the relative roles played by biogenetic as opposed to psychogenetic components in behavior, which is instinctually derived and psychogenically shaped. (3) Finally, it lacks instruments for determining the precise point of transition from free to compulsively fixated behavior.

Many of these limitations have been discussed in greater detail in the Hixon Fund Lectures (8). In general they can be summarized by saying that the basic design of the process of analysis has essential scientific validity, but that the difficulties of recording and reproducing primary observations, the consequent difficulty in deriving the basic conceptual structure, the difficulties in examining with equal ease the circular relationship from unconscious to conscious and from conscious to unconscious, the difficulties in appraising quantitatively the multiplicity of variables, and finally the difficulty of estimating those things which increase and those things which decrease the precision of its hypotheses and the validity of its predictions are among the basic scientific problems which remain to be solved.

Conclusion

I hope that these pages have clarified in some measure the position of psychoanalysis among the sciences: its contributions to the standardization of the conditions under which psychological observations are made; its use of interpretations both as a working hypothesis and as a deliberate and controlled variable in an otherwise constant situation; its contribution to the understanding and control of the interplay of unconscious emotional forces in the relationship between observer and observed; its development of the technique of free association as a physiologically and statistically valid method of random sampling in the study of psychological processes; and finally its contribution to our growing maturity and sophistication about the unconscious symbolic forces which make Man the Scientist fallacy-prone. In any final analysis, this constitutes a challenge to our whole educational system. It is my personal conviction that among all the contributions of psychoanalysis to our cultural development, it is this which will continue to be important for many generations, and which in the long view of history will be regarded as the greatest heritage which Freud left to us.

REFERENCES

1. Bernard, Claude. *An Introduction to the Study of Experimental Medicine*. New York, Macmillan Co., 1927.

2. Gregg, Alan. *The Furtherance of Medical Research*. New Haven, Yale University Press, 1941.

3. Kubie, Lawrence S. Relation of the Conditioned Reflex to Psychoanalytic Technic. *Arch. Neurol. & Psychiat.*, 32: 1137–1142, 1934.

4. Kubie, Lawrence S. Review of *Pavlov and His School*, by Y. P. Frolov. *Psychoanalyt. Quart.*, 10: 329–339, 1941.

5. Kubie, Lawrence S. Review of *Lectures on Conditioned Reflexes.* Vol. II: *Conditioned Reflexes and Psychiatry*, by I. P. Pavlov. *Psychoanalyt. Quart.*, 11: 565–570, 1942.

6. Kubie, Lawrence S. *Practical and Theoretical Aspects of Psychoanalysis.* New York, International Universities Press, 1950.

7. Kubie, Lawrence S. Discussion of "The Behavior of the Stomach During Psychoanalysis; a contribution to a method of verifying psychoanalytic data," by Sydney G. Margolin. *Psychoanalyt. Quart.*, 20: 369–373, 1951.

8. Kubie, Lawrence S. Problems and Techniques of Psychoanalytic Validation and Progress. (In *Psychoanalysis as Science.* Edited by E. Pumpian-Mindlin. Stanford, Calif., Stanford University Press, 1952. pp. 46–124).

9. Kubie, Lawrence S. The Problem of Maturity in the Preparation for Psychiatric Research. *J. of Med. Educ.* (in press).

10. Kubie, Lawrence S. Some Unsolved Problems of the Scientific Career. *The American Scientist* (in press).

11. Margolin, Sydney G. The Behavior of the Stomach During Psychoanalysis; a contribution to a method of verifying psychoanalytic data. *Psychoanalyt. Quart.*, 20: 349–373, 1951.

12. Richet, Charles. *Natural History of a Savant.* London, J. M. Dent & Sons, 1927.

13. Tolman, Richard C. Physical Science and Philosophy. *Scient. Month.*, 57: 166–174, 1943.

Discussion

JOHN D. BENJAMIN, M.D.

DOCTOR KUBIE's remarks on psychoanalysis as a basic science offer several avenues of approach for discussion: to comment systematically on those topics covered by him; to concentrate primarily on one of these; or to consider other aspects of the subject, of necessity left untouched by the speaker. In view of the breadth of Kubie's presentation it is with some reluctance that I have decided on the second of these courses as most compatible with the amount of time available.

I turn, then, to the question of prediction, probably because in my own research in psychoanalytic personality theory I am making fairly profuse use of techniques involving various forms of prediction. Kubie's statement that predictability is the most important single criterion of maturity is as little debatable as is his corollary, that since psychoanalysis is as yet far from being a reliably predictive science, it cannot lay claim to real maturity. True as these statements are, they both call for some elaboration. For prediction in science is anything but a simple and unitary affair. There are at least four types commonly met with: (1) The deductive, or theoretical prediction, which validates or invalidates a theory by testing a proposition or hypothesis which is either an integral part of the theory or can be deduced from it. (2) The inductive, or clinical, prediction, which confirms or fails to confirm previously observed antecedent-consequent relationships between two or more variables. (3) The actuarial, or mass statistical prediction, in which the only theory validated is probability theory itself. (All scientific predictions, of course, involve probability considerations. Here I have reference to that special type of empirical prediction represented, for example, by life-insurance tables, and finding application also in other fields on various levels. A differential consideration of probability in relation to prediction in general would involve us too deeply in mathematico-philosophic problems for the purposes of this brief discussion.) (4) The meaningless, or fortunetelling, prediction, which validates or invalidates nothing.

Before discussing further the use of prediction as a validating instrument, I should like to point out that it is also a sign of maturity in science when it is able to demonstrate what it cannot predict, and why. Two contrasting examples from our most mature science, physics, will serve as illustrations. The first is Heisenberg's uncertainty principle, so often misinterpreted as undermining causality. Here, on the basis of theoretical considerations, a limitation is placed on predictability; not a temporary limitation due to the inadequacy of theory, of method, or of mathematical tools; but a permanent limitation due to the nature of the subject matter. Our second example comes from one of the oldest and most mature branches of classical physics, mechanics. Coin tossing is an old pastime in which most of us have, at one time or another, participated. Suppose sometime we should decide to toss thumbtacks instead of pennies. It may seem surprising, but it is nonetheless true, that after all these years mechanics is unable to predict on the basis of dynamical theory alone such an apparently simple thing as the probability that a thumbtack of given dimensions will come to rest on its head or on its side after being thrown against a wall. Here the reasons for failure are quite different from those in our first case; analytic tools adequate to deal with all the variables are simply not available. I mention this trivial example not only to illustrate two different types of nonpredictability, but also to make us feel less self-reproachful at the many predictions in psychoanalysis which are impossible for us to make at the present time, and the others which may conceivably always be impossible to make. Parenthetically, if our frustrated physicist really wants to know the probabilities involved, he can always turn to statistics of the actuarial variety, toss thumbtacks several thousand times, set up a frequency distribution, and predict within well-defined limits of error how these thumbtacks will behave in the future. The same type of prediction is in principle applicable to some aspects of human behavior;

when applied it has the same lack of relationship to motivation and mechanism that our thumbtack example has to the dynamics of classical mechanics.

When we get down to the actual job of trying to make predictions based on psychoanalytic personality theory, we find ourselves confronted with a number of interesting problems. If the predictions are to serve the purpose of testing an hypothesis, there is first of all the not always easy task of stating explicitly the basis on which they are made. For there is nothing easier in our field than to make predictions the success or failure of which has neither validating nor invalidating significance for the particular hypothesis we are attempting to test. This is the case for *successful prediction* whenever we use, consciously or unconsciously, clues which are independent of the hypothesis. Thus we may think we are predicting the development of a childhood psychosis on our appraisal of the nature of the mother-child relationship, whereas in reality we may be using another set of clues, namely certain behavioral phenomena which clinical experience has shown us often precede overt psychotic development. The success of such a prediction may help to make more precise an inductive proposition concerning the antecedent-consequent relationship between two observed variables; and if it does, it is of course of scientific value; but it fails to confirm, refute, or expand the hypothesis it was supposed to test. An *unsuccessful prediction* has no invalidating power when it is applied to conditions which are already known to be at best necessary, but not necessary and sufficient causes. Since this applies demonstrably to some psychoanalytic propositions, and presumably to many of them, it is apparent that there are obstacles to the meaningful use of prediction as a tool for validating psychoanalytic hypotheses. An extreme example of meaningless prediction is the attempt to predict future developments in overt behavior which are already known to be significantly dependent upon unpredictable future environmental variables.

I have discussed elsewhere the problem of surmounting these and other obstacles to the use of prediction in validating or invalidating psychoanalytic propositions. An adequate extension of this discussion would far exceed the limits of these brief remarks. Here I shall mention only one useful way to overcome the difficulties inherent in long-term positive prediction. I call it negative prediction, since it consists essentially of predicting the absence of something on the basis that a condition or series of conditions necessary for its development is absent. The method is applicable over a wide range, and although never as satisfactory as a meaningful positive prediction, seems greatly preferable to no effort at all at the predictive validation of theory.

Since, as stated, I cannot here discuss other aspects of these difficulties and their partial solutions, I should like merely to express my opinion that more can be done with deductive and inductive prediction in psychoanalysis right now, as it stands, than seems likely at first glance, or than has been systematically attempted. Even if this is not true, however, I still would feel that efforts at prediction are very much indicated at the present stage of psychoanalysis. For prediction, if meaningful and explicit, is not only a means of validation: It is also a method of investigation, and equally so whether successful or unsuccessful. Every well-planned experiment involves predictions. Every unsuccessful prediction in psychoanalysis makes us aware of our shortcomings as a science, and demands the discovery of new variables; demands further systematic and semantic clarification of psychoanalytic theory; and demands better communication and operational definition of psychoanalytic facts. Although Kubie is undoubtedly correct in emphasizing that all facts and all theories are only approximations, there is a real and significant difference between the two in what is meant by approximation. The relative truth of a *theory* is given by its usefulness in accounting for all known facts; the relative truth of a *fact* is given by the operations by which it is made known. A third issue to be considered, and one of special pertinence to present-day psychoanalytic research, is the relevance of a fact or a concept for a theory, its explanatory value. In all these areas there is much that can be done right now, with available methods. For the humility and open-mindedness of the scientist, so rightly emphasized by Kubie and Alexander today, need not obscure the fact that we have much to communicate to each other, and to scientists in other fields; nor the other fact that, for a variety of excellent and easily understandable reasons, we have failed rather miserably in communicating this as science rather than as authoritative exhortation. This particular task is, I think, one of several necessary conditions for the productive development of psychoanalytic research at this time. Several encouraging beginnings have been made, here in Chicago as well as elsewhere. One of the many obstacles to better scientific communication lies in the continued tendency, on all sides, to identify motives with values. The motives of scientific criticism and of scientific creation are a legitimate and fascinating subject for the psychoanalyst. But in and of themselves, taken alone, they can never form an adequate basis for a judgment as to the merit of a criticism, the correctness of a finding, or the value of an idea. An unfortunate corollary to this attitude is our tendency toward facile interpretation of the motives of those who disagree with our findings and opinions. What we need most at this time is less exchange of contradictory opinion, and more exchange of the primary data on which, presumably, the opinions are based.

Discussion

THOMAS M. FRENCH, M.D.

DOCTOR KUBIE has discussed interpretation from two points of view. His main point is that, from the point of view of scientific method, making an interpretation to a patient should be looked upon as the introducing of a "calculated variable" into a controlled and standardized situation. The analyst attempts to standardize the situation as much as possible by remaining formal and remote and masking his feelings behind a poker face; and with this controlled situation as a background, he hopes to observe the effects of his interpretation as one might observe the effects of a well-controlled experimental procedure in a laboratory. Kubie makes another very important suggestion: that an interpretation of a patient's behavior should be regarded as an hypothesis to be tested.

In these two statements, Kubie is evidently referring to two different aspects of psychoanalytic interpretation. When he speaks of introducing a calculated variable into a standard situation, he is evidently thinking of an interpretation that is communicated to the patient. But when an interpretation is a hypothesis to be tested, it is really a preliminary scientific formulation which it may or may not be wise to communicate to the patient. It is important to recognize that a psychoanalytic interpretation gets a new significance as soon as the analyst tells the patient about it. From the point of view of scientific method, an interpretation which a psychoanalyst makes only to himself is really a preliminary scientific formulation, a hypothesis to be tested, which may turn out to be either true or false. But when an interpretation is communicated to the patient, it becomes a stimulus which impinges on the patient's emotions, and it will not usually be reacted to on an intellectual plane only, as a scientific hypothesis whose truth or falsity is to be checked in the light of the evidence.

The problem of how patients react to interpretations is a complex one which would be difficult to discuss briefly. Just now, I am interested rather in elaborating further the significance of an interpretation as a hypothesis to be tested.

In my opinion, Freud's discovery of the psychoanalytic interpretive method was his basic contribution to the science of psychology. His new method, like many basic scientific discoveries, was really a very obvious and simple one. It consisted in using the common-sense psychology of everyday life as a key to make intelligible the peculiar behavior of neurotic and psychotic patients. In a lifetime of dealing with other people, all of us build up habits that teach us what to expect of them. These habits of expectation constitute a kind of knowledge of what other people are likely to do. Since this "knowledge" is usually not formulated in words and is often unconscious, we generally call it "intuitive knowledge." It is most trustworthy in situations with which we are familiar. When people behave as we should ordinarily expect them to do, we call their behavior "normal." But Freud discovered that even very irrational behavior becomes intelligible when we succeed in finding out more about it, when we study the circumstances that gave rise to it and learn more about the patient's earlier life experiences.

It is extraordinary how much resistance there has been to accepting this obvious approach to interpretation as a scientific method. Most sciences have their origins in observation from everyday life and then proceed to test and correct the common-sense conclusions arising out of everyday experience and ultimately to refine and extend them greatly. Discerning observation and careful interpretation and analysis of what is observed are necessary and important steps in the development of every science. Our modern experimental approach to physiology was preceded by many years, even centuries, of descriptive anatomical investigation which gave us an understanding of the structure of the mammalian body. If we had never looked underneath the skin of the human body, intelligent experimental or statistical studies of the functions of the internal organs would hardly be possible. But psychology is a young science and, like a small boy, is impatient to grow up, to copy the mannerisms even if it cannot emulate the achievements of older and more mature sciences. This, I believe, is the reason why so many psychologists and even some psychoanalysts today would like to skip over the phase of careful observation and of interpretive exploration of what lies beneath the surface of our overt behavior. When we compare their work with the precision and rigor of some of the experimental and statistical analyses in the physical sciences, we are tempted to repudiate as unscientific those interpretations that are based on the intuitive common-sense knowledge that we all possess. But I think we underestimate the precision and reliability of our interpretive method when it is practiced with good critical judgment.

Kubie warned us, quite properly, that an interpretation should not be looked upon as an "intuitive divination," that it is not "automatically true merely because it is derived from the analyst's reactions to the free associations of the patient." I agree with him that an interpretation is only a hypothesis, but we must ask next how an interpretive hypothesis can best be checked. A good interpretation is more than just a hunch. It should be based on careful evaluation of the evidence; the same intuitive common-sense that we use to arrive at interpretations should also be used critically to evaluate them. Our traditional method of checking psychoanalytic interpretations has been to wait for more facts, for the recovery of actual memories to check our reconstructions, or for behavior that illustrates in less distorted form the dynamic patterns that we have suspected. If our interpretive hypotheses are correct, we expect later events to confirm them. If they are incorrect, we expect later facts to show up their inadequacies.

However, it is easy to become lax and uncritical in our interpretive approach. In order to guard against this tendency, we should try increasingly to examine the criteria upon which we have based our interpretations and to systematize our procedure for checking them against later evidence.

Psychoanalysis and the Biological Sciences

I. ARTHUR MIRSKY, M.D.

ON AN occasion such as this, it is tempting to make global surveys and derive global concepts. It is tempting to review the evidence for the fundamental identity of all forms of life and trace the direction of evolutionary change from the undifferentiated protoplasmic mass to the highly differentiated complex primate. It is tempting to trace the growth of human biology from its origin in philosophy, its development as a natural science, and its maturation as a family of disciplines, as each era brought new techniques and new concepts. It is tempting to describe the adaptive process utilized at each level of organization and contemplate their interactions as they emerge in man's adaptation to changing circumstances. Were I to do so, however, I would be recapitulating that which has been done so well by Gerard (1), Frank (2), Lillie (3), Sinnott (4), Engel (5), and others (6, 7, 8), who have exposed the inadequacies of the purely one-way causal interpretations and have revealed the great promise of the more modern transactional, teleological explanations.

Instead of attempting to understand the complex by means of the simple, of breaking up the whole to deal with the parts, of reconstructing order through statistical manipulation of disorder, of viewing the organism in reaction to environment, today we seek also to understand the part in terms of its dynamic relation to the whole, order in terms of the patterned event, the organism in transaction with its environment, process in terms of goals. No longer do we anticipate that the description of more and more elementary particles in the atom will explain the unit: we now seek insight into the processes responsible for the relatedness of the particles as expressed in organismal, purposeful behavior.

Purpose or goal-directiveness is no longer regarded as some mystic force which transcends the known limits of physical and chemical laws. Goal-directiveness is a property of the organism and a concomitant of the still unknown physical and chemical processes responsible for organization. As Cannon put it, "Since a response in the organism has certain definite consequences . . . we should frankly regard them as being integrated with what has immediately preceded them. The various stages in the response that lead to the consequences may then be looked upon as 'purposive.'" (9)

Bertalanffy (10) makes a distinction between static and dynamic goal-directiveness. By "static teleology" he refers to fitness, that is, to some arrangement which seems to be useful for some specific purpose. "Dynamic teleology," on the other hand, refers to the directiveness of processes which are responsible for the regulations which are peculiar to the organism: its ability continuously to convert the air, soil, and organic constituents of its external environment into the specific compounds of its own protoplasm; its ability to increase in mass and complexity; its potential immortality exhibited in its ability to perpetuate itself in the formation of new units which are like itself; its ability to maintain its own steady state, in other words, to keep from going into equilibrium with its changing environment; and, finally, its response to environmental stimuli with the release of more energy than was contributed by the stimuli, a phenomenon which Gerard (1) has called "adaptive amplification."

The chemical reactions which are responsible for the aforementioned characteristics of the living organism are dependent upon the integrated activity of highly specialized proteins, the enzymes, which catalyze the rates at which energy transformations occur. For practically every chemical reaction or type of reaction, there appears to exist a different enzyme. Consequently, it is the variability in the kind, number, and amounts of the enzymes which determines the individuality of the cell.

Given an adequate amount of enzymes, the cell requires the substrates which serve as sources of energy, the vitamins which form essential parts of the coenzymes, the minerals which act as activators or as coenzymes, water which forms the medium in which the reactions occur, and oxygen which serves to remove the hydrogen or electrons released during the reactions. Consequently, the composition of the extracellular medium largely determines the maintenance of cellular integrity.

In the complex multicellular organism, the composition of the extracellular medium, the "milieu interviews" of Bernard, is determined not only by the availability of food, but also by the adequacy of the mechanisms involved in feeding, digestion, absorption, and the transport of foodstuffs. The rate at which foodstuffs are brought into the circulation, the rate at which they are carried to the cell, the rate at which they pass across the cellular membrane, the rate at which the end products of catabolism are transported and disposed, and so forth, are dependent in large measure upon the integrity of the endocrine and nervous regulatory systems.

A hypophysectomized animal can be kept alive by the administration of appropriate diets. A spinal animal can be kept alive by artificial respiration, intravenous feeding, and incubation at body temperature. Neither the hypophysectomized nor the spinal animal, however, can grow nor can they tolerate a drop in the environmental temperature, the loss of a small amount of blood, or other influences which are innocuous to the intact animal. Although neither the endocrine glands nor the central nervous system is essential for the life of the individual cell or organ, they are essential for those changes in the reaction velocities of the intracellular enzyme systems which enable the organism to grow and develop and to adjust readily and rapidly to environmental influences. It is the integration of the intracellular enzyme systems, the endocrine system, and the nervous system that determines the dynamic stability which characterizes health.

It is pertinent to differentiate the goal-directiveness subsumed under homeostasis from that dynamic stability which is attributable to the fact that all living organisms are open systems, constantly taking in energy, transforming it into form and function, and dissipating the excess. Homeostasis, as described by Bernard and expanded by Cannon, refers only to processes whereby the internal environment fluctuates within fairly narrow limits as the result of *reactions* to disturbances induced from within or without. Such reactions are dependent upon the adequacy of the endocrine and nervous system, that is, structures which are arranged in such a way that a stable state is achieved largely by means of feed-back mechanisms. In other words, homeostasis refers to a closed information system in that variations in output or behavior are "fed back" in order to correct the system's response.

Whereas homeostatic mechanisms can account adequately for the maintenance of the blood-pressure level, the concentration of blood calcium, and other similar phenomena, they cannot account for the continuous breakdown and synthesis of molecules, compounds, and tissues. Whereas homeostasis can account for the maintenance of body temperature, it does not account for such adaptations as hibernation. The steady states responsible for growth, differentiation, propagation, and the other energy transformations which characterize the living organism still await clarification by biological laws now unknown.

To the genius of Freud we owe the recognition of the behavioral manifestations of goal-directiveness in man; the recognition that the organic need subserves symbolic expression. Implicit in his earliest formulations is the concept that behavior is activated by the physiological needs of the organism and is directed toward their fulfillment; that the same forces which are responsible for goal-directiveness on the biochemical and physiological levels of organization also operate to motivate human behavior. Like the modern physicist who measures the electron in terms of particles or in terms of waves, both being necessary, yet mutually exclusive, Freud recognized the complementarity of mind and body. This is revealed in his description of the unconscious as a system which contains "everything that is inherited, that is present at birth, that is fixed in the constitution . . . above all, therefore, the instincts which originate in the somatic organization and which find their first mental expression in the id in forms unknown to us." (11)

Freud conceived the organism to be in a constant state of flux in its effort to maintain a steady state. He envisioned the mental apparatus as a structured system which permits homeostasis through release of tension by satisfaction of instinctual needs and protection from excessive environmental stimulation. This concept, however, could not account for the phenomena associated with growth and development. Recognizing this inadequacy, Alexander (12) introduced the "vector" concept and the principle of "surplus energy," hypotheses which are more in accord with modern physicalchemical ideas about open systems. Subsequently, French's elaboration of the mechanisms involved in the integration of behavior provided a methodology as well as a comprehensive view of the manner in which man maintains his steady state (13). Both Alexander and French have introduced dimensional concepts which are subject to mathematical expression when appropriate measures are developed.

The origin of psychoanalysis as a therapeutic procedure, its development as a method of investigation, and its elaboration as a theory of personality need not be reviewed here. Nor is it necessary to review the evidence that psychoanalysis is a biological science which, together with all other biological sciences, permits clarification of the processes involved in normal and abnormal behavior. Implicit in the modern approach to the study of man is the realization that each biological science provides concepts and techniques relevant to some particular level of organization; that no one level of organization is more or less significant than any other; that disturbances at any level of organization may influence all other levels; and that only through the concomitant investigation of all levels can we obtain some insight into the particular pattern of patterns called man. This is the psychosomatic approach.

Studies emanating from the Chicago Institute for Psychoanalysis during the past twenty years have established the prepotent role of psychic conflict in a variety of physiological disorders which are characterized as the vegetative or organ neuroses. Although the importance of psychological factors in the etiology of various syndromes has been suspected since antiquity, the application of the psychoanalytic technique by Alexander and his colleagues provided more definitive data concerning the processes involved.

After it had been established that the specificity of the personality type is not a determinant in the development of somatic disorders, data were accumulated in support of the concept that a specific dynamic configuration did play such a role in various clinical states (14). The fact that a psychodynamic constellation which appears to be specific for one disorder may occur also in subjects without any somatic disorder or in subjects with some other physiological derangement has led to much controversy. Since there is relatively little disagreement concerning the psychodynamics of patients with duodenal ulcer, this syndrome will be utilized for illustrative purposes.

Patients with peptic ulcer appear to have in common a conflict related to the persistence of strong infantile wishes to be loved and cared for and the repudiation of these wishes by the adult ego or by external circumstances. The resultant frustration is postulated to induce an unconscious desire to be fed, with which is associated the increased gastric activity that normally occurs with the ingestion of food. This hyperactivity of the stomach, through mechanisms that are still unknown, ultimately results in the development of an ulcer.

Utilizing an associative anamnestic or the psychoanalytic technique to evaluate the responses to life-situations, and a biochemical technique, the assay of pepsinogen excretion, to evaluate the responses of the stomach, we confirmed the general conclusion of previous investigators by demonstrating that the mobilization of unconscious oral-receptive and incorporative wishes or the threat to dependent relationships is associated with an increase in the rate of gastric secretion in subjects without ulcer (15).

The rate of gastric secretion of patients with duodenal ulcer is approximately twice that of subjects without gastrointestinal disturbances. Since we found also that the hypersecretion of such patients persists long after the lesions have healed, it became pertinent to inquire whether a hypersecretion can antecede the environmental event which precipitates the clinical syndrome.

During the course of our studies we found that the rate of

gastric secretion of approximately eleven percent of an apparently healthy population is beyond the mean rate of a group of patients with duodenal ulcer. This incidence is similar to that reported for the presence of ulcer in the general population. For practical reasons, we selected for study the two percent of our population whose secretory rates were beyond one standard deviation of the mean of the patients with ulcer (seventeen subjects). Anamnestic interviews revealed the aforementioned typical conflict in nearly all these subjects. One of the patients was followed for about one year, at which time he developed the typical signs and symptoms of a duodenal ulcer which was subsequently demonstrated roentgenologically. Another hypersecretor was studied for about two years before he developed an acute perforation as the first sign of the presence of a duodenal ulcer. In neither subject was the precipitation of the lesion associated with any further significant increase in gastric secretion. In both instances, the signs and symptoms of the lesion followed an environmental event which was very obviously responsible for a mobilization of fears of loss of love and security.

The evidence that is available today indicates that patients with duodenal ulcer have a specific conflict relative to oral-receptive wishes; that patients with ulcer have a hypersecretion of the stomach; that apparently healthy subjects develop a temporary gastric hypersecretion on exposure to an environmental event which mobilizes unconscious wishes similar to those of patients with ulcer; that apparently healthy subjects who are hypersecretors may have conflicts which appear identical with those of the patient with ulcer; and finally, that apparently healthy hypersecretors may develop the typical ulceration in response to a meaningful life-situation which intensifies their conflict.

Although the presence of gastric hypersecretion indicates

that a subject can develop an ulcer, it does not mean that he *will* do so. The data permit only the conclusion that a typical conflict and gastric hypersecretion are concomitants irrespective of the presence or absence of a duodenal lesion. The data, however, do indicate the possibility of an experimental approach to the psychodynamics of the subject who may develop an ulcer at some future date.

Psychoanalytic reconstructions attribute the persistence of infantile dependent wishes to some event during infancy in which a real or fantasied rejection occurred. Such events, however, can be reconstructed from the genetics of many subjects who suffer from a variety of clinical derangements other than ulcer. Consequently, it is pertinent to inquire whether the repressed infantile dependent wishes are responsible for the development of the hypersecretion or whether the hypersecretion preceded the infantile event or whether both are due to some other factor.

In his consideration of the etiologic factors which impede therapeutic progress, Freud stated: "Generally there is a combination of two factors: the constitutional and the accidental. The stronger the constitutional factor the more readily will a trauma lead to fixation, with its sequel in a disturbance of development; the stronger the trauma the more certain is it that it will have injurious effects even when the patient's instinctual life is normal." (16) Thus, as on many occasions, Freud emphasized the necessity for distinguishing the predisposing from the precipitating factors in the etiology of disease.

If it were possible to assay quantitatively the potential capacity of any physiological system of many subjects, the measurements could be expressed in the form of the well-known bell-shaped curve of normal distribution extending between some minimum and maximum limits. Likewise, it is probable that the capacities of different physiological systems will show a similar quantitative variation from subject to subject. It would be futile to describe any part of the distribution curve as more normal than another. The only inference is that every individual has some physiological functions which, relative to others, are quantitatively limited in capacity.

The quantitative limitations of physiological capacity are not static, but are influenced by the adaptive requirements of each age-period. For example, the liver of the infant has a limited capacity which is normal for his age. The same limited capacity to make and store glycogen in the adult would be catastrophic. On the other hand, the rate of wound healing in the child is greater than in the adult, so that given a similar trauma, the adult may be incapacitated for a longer time.

These facts are in accord with the concept that although chronologic aging is constant, physiological aging is quite variable. Different individuals of the same species and different tissues of the same individual change at different rates and consequently have different physiological time or age scales. It may well be that one reason for the important influence of infantile experiences in the etiology of physiological and psychological disorders is related to the much greater rate at which physiological time passes in the younger organism as compared with an older one, so that a traumatization in infancy actually covers a greater physiological span than a similar trauma at a later period. Related to the influence of "physiological time" is the specific vulnerability of different developmental stages, a vulnerability with respect to the physiological capacity as well as to the specificity of the stress.

The mere fact that one system of an individual or that the individual as a whole has a capacity which is poor relative to others does not imply that that system or that individual is necessarily inadequate, since inadequacy can be described only as the resultant of the interaction between the system and the stress to which it is exposed. Any phenomenon, actual or symbolic, which threatens the biological integrity of the organism may be regarded as a stress. Thus, whereas the quantitative limitations of the physiological capacity of a system predict its susceptibility or predisposition to failure, it is the quantity and appropriateness of the stress to which the system is exposed that determines its failure, that is, precipitates the failure.

It is for such reasons that one cannot isolate any specific factor as the "cause" of a disease. As Sir Thomas Lewis emphasized, "when we enquire into the cause of a disease, we are often brought to consider a long chain of relevant circumstances . . . somewhere, however, there is a particular event, which is of cardinal importance to the individual, since it may be said to have set the chain of events in motion in him." (17)

The human organism is most modifiable during the early stages of the prenatal period. For such reasons, the environmental influences which operate on the organism at this earliest and least developed stage have marked and lasting effects on its later development. Since the embryo receives its nourishment from the blood stream of the mother, any condition which affects the chemical state of the mother's blood can influence the structural development of her offspring. Thus, a nutritional inadequacy arising in the mother may affect the developing embryo irrespective of whether the mother's malnutrition is the result of poverty or of a poor appetite attributable to some emotional disturbance. The child that is born from a malnourished mother may not only be smaller at birth but may grow more slowly during the first year of life. Such children may be born with a variety of anatomical and physiological abnormalities which may not become clinically obvious until much later in life (18).

Normal growth of the embryo may be impeded also by bacterial infection, toxins, and other traumata to the mother as well as by the presence of metabolic disorders. The woman with *diabetes mellitus* may give birth to a deformed infant or to one which is so excessive in weight that it may become severely damaged during the birth. The mother who is undergoing a severe emotional stress may carry a fetus which displays a great deal of intrauterine movements and, after birth, the infant may remain irritable and hyperactive for weeks or months. Sontag (19) found that such infants tend to exhibit an intolerance to food and develop various types of gastrointestinal disturbances. Thus, a variety of factors can influence the developing embyro through effects on the mother. These effects, however, cannot be measured until the birth of the infant, and consequently attention must be directed toward the development of techniques which will permit quantitative measurements in the neonate.

In order to attempt an application of the aforementioned familiar quantitative considerations, it is pertinent to present briefly a model of neonatal development. With birth, the newborn must adjust to a sudden and drastic change in those functions which the mother provided. Many of these functions are automatic in that by the time of birth the infant is adequately equipped with the intracellular enzyme systems and their extracellular regulators. For example, the respiratory center quickly responds to the biochemical changes induced by a lack of oxygen because the mechanism essential for the formation and destruction of acetylcholine is quite efficient in that center. The temperature regulating centers, although not quite perfect at birth, are nevertheless sufficiently developed to take over some degree of temperature regulation. The kidneys likewise are not quite perfect but nevertheless are still adequate to excrete the metabolic waste products produced by the infant. On the other hand, there are many other functions which are quite imperfect at birth and require external assistance for their activity. This is the period of the "absolute unconscious," when the infant is in the phase of biological dependence upon his mother (20).

At birth the sensory receptors are suddenly exposed to relatively massive quantities of environmental stimuli. That the receptors are highly responsive to stimulation is suggested by our preliminary studies which show that the thresholds for the perception of olfactory and vibratory stimuli are lower in infants than in any other age group. Since the cortex of the newborn infant is still relatively undeveloped, it may be postulated that, like the decorticated or thalamic animal, he will respond to the sudden bombardment of environmental stimuli as if the stimuli were extremely violent in intensity. Thus, like the decorticated animal which responds to nonspecific external stimuli with the diffuse neuromuscular reaction called "sham rage," the newborn infant responds to environmental stimuli with vasomotor and uncoordinated, muscular activity. Further, like the decorticated animal, the newborn infant responds also in a similar manner to stimuli which are internal in origin. For such reasons, Kubie (21) has proposed these reactions to be the *anlage* of the phenomenon which is recognized subsequently as anxiety.

In spite of the long period of gestation, the newborn child does not have adequate amounts and kinds of enzymes which are essential for the interconversion of certain foodstuffs and for the storage of other foodstuffs. Since the infant has a limited capacity to make and store glycogen, for example, he is limited in his ability to maintain a constant blood-sugar level. Consequently, the blood sugar begins to fall immediately after birth. It may be postulated that the resultant hypoglycemia produces a series of changes in the reaction velocities of the intracellular enzyme systems of the central nervous system with the result that the still relatively uninhibited hypothalamus is stimulated to increased activity. This is reflected in respiratory changes, in an increase in the uncoordinated motor activity, in vasomotor expressions, and in other manifestations of hypothalamic activation. As in the adult after the administration of insulin, activation of the hypothalamus produces an increase in gastric motility and secretion. It is quite probable that other constituents of the blood which are ordinarily provided by the mother during intrauterine life may play a similar role to that exemplified by sugar.

This sequence of events which follows a diminution in the sugar and other constituents of the blood is what we refer to when we speak of an increase in physiological tension. With the ingestion and subsequent absorption of food, the blood sugar returns to normal and the effects of hypothalamic activation subside, so that there is not only a decrease in gastric activity, but also a decrease in the uncoordinated motor activity of the organism as a whole and sleep usually ensues. This is analogous to the response of the hungry decorticated dog which stops its "decorticate activity" after feeding. It is to the *effect* of the ingestion of food rather than to the mere filling of the stomach that we refer when we speak of the gratification of the child's hunger. In accord is the fact that distention of the stomach with a balloon does not inhibit gastric activity.

The postulated repetitive cycle of hypoglycemia, hypothalamic activation, increased motor tonus, ingestion of food, restitution of the blood sugar, and decreased physiological tension gradually leads, as Benedek has described, to the recognition that gratification or the release of tension is the result of a series of events which take origin in the external environment, whereas the source of tension takes origin in the internal environment (22). This recognition is made possible by the association of the responses of all the sensory systems with those that follow the ingestion of food. Thus, the infant who is picked up while being fed begins to associate tactile sensations with the process of eating, that is, with the process which is preliminary to the actual gratification that follows the absorption of the ingested food. The child hears the mother come to him, he sees the mother, he smells the mother, and, consequently, these systems, too, become associated with the process which is preliminary to gratification, that is, with feeding. In some such manner, all sensory systems eventually become integrated into a single unit which is associated with the process which is anticipatory to the release of physiological tension. Instead of tension, the response to sensory stimulation may be like that to the ingestion of food.

When the infant's recurrent physiological needs are gratified by a mother with an adequate "integrative capacity" (13), the infant develops a "sense of confidence" (22, 23) or "trust" (24) which then tends to reduce the tendency for uncoordinated visceral and motor responses to environmental stimuli. Accordingly, "maternal love" refers to the mother's capacity to aid the infant in associating his sensory responses with the process that results in the release of physiological tension; a "sense of confidence" refers to the resultant development of an "integrative field" (13) which permits the child to respond to his environment with greater equanimity in that he feels secure in the adequacy of the mother's integrative capacity. It is during this period that the infant passes from the biological to the psychological phase of dependency (20), that is, when the ego and id have evolved from an undifferentiated phase (25).

Since it is now well established that neonates vary markedly in response to stimulation (26, 27), it can be anticipated that quantitative measurements will reveal variations in the degree of the acuity of different sensory systems, variations in the kind of response to specific stimuli, variations in the degree of response to different kinds of stimuli, and so forth. For the sake of convenience, the acuity of any sensory system may be expressed quantitatively as high, mean, and low. Likewise, the mother's ability to aid the infant in his integration of the various sensory systems—that is, her integrative capacity—may be expressed in similar terms. Then, a minimum of nine mother-child combinations can be postulated for each sensory system; the total number of such combinations becomes infinite. Obviously, the particular combination will determine the degree with which an infant will integrate his responses to environmental stimuli with the tension-reducing effects of the absorption of food.

Ribble (28), Spitz (29), and others have described the devastating effects of severe maternal deprivation during the neonatal period. Such infants cannot develop the ability to withstand the effects of environmental stimuli; instead they utilize such rigid adaptations that normal growth and development are impeded. In accord is the demonstration by Leitch and Escalona (27) that exposure of infants to severe stimulation results in the development of signs and symptoms similar to those described by Spitz as the syndrome of anaclitic depression. It is probable, however, that similar results may ensue from a situation in which the mother-child unit consists of a mother with an average integrative capacity and an infant with supersensitive receptors, or with a limited capacity to respond to food, or with a limitation in the capacity of other physiological systems. In accord are Bergman and Escalona's (30) observations on children who very early in life showed unusual sensitivities and went on to develop psychotic or psychotic-like syndromes. In none of their subjects was there evidence of significant rejecting attitudes on the part of the mothers.

Just as a diminution in adrenal cortical activity results in an avidity for salt, so the child born with a limitation in the potential capacity of the systems responsible for lipogenesis—in other words, with a susceptibility to the development of *diabetes mellitus*—may react as if his requirements were insatiable and seek replenishment through all channels for "incorporation" in his effort to maintain biological integrity.

Furthermore, given a mother who starts with an average degree of integrative capacity and a child with an excessively high sensitivity to environmental stimuli, with increased "incorporative" trends, and so forth, the mother may react to some trait in the child. Then her integrative task may become so excessive that a reduction in her integrative capacity will ensue.

Examination of the psychosomatic literature leads to the inevitable conclusion that almost every physiological disorder is due to some specific type of maternal behavior. Although Spitz may be right in stating that infants with neurodermatitis have anxious mothers with "unusually large amounts of unconscious repressed hostility" (29), it is just as probable that such infants contribute something to their mother's attitude as well as to the pathogenesis of their lesions. Since neurodermatitis occurs in persons with relatively low sebum secretion by the skin, it is possible that an infant with a low rate of sebum secretion may require a different kind and quantity of tactile stimulation. As Erikson (24) put it in his discussion of maternal rejection: "The truism that the original problem is to be found in the mother-child relationship holds only in so far as one considers this relationship an emotional pooling which may multiply well-being in both but will endanger both partners when the communication becomes jammed or weakened." Perhaps every mother is not a "public enemy number one."

In order to delineate the contributions of the infant to the mother-child unit, it is essential to develop methods for the quantitative evaluation of the physiological capacities of infants during the phase of biological dependency. That such is possible is indicated by our studies of the syndrome which was chosen for illustrative purposes, namely peptic ulcer.

After developing a method for the assay of blood pepsinogen (31), and after demonstrating that it is a measure of gastric activity (32), we observed that at all age groups from one day and after, the values for gastric activity distribute themselves normally. Thus, the quantitative measurement of gastric activity reveals the presence of hypersecretors even among infants. In fact, some infants may have values as high as those observed among adult patients with active duodenal ulcers. Our studies have not progressed sufficiently to permit conclusions about the mechanism responsible for the gastric hypersecretion in the newborn, nor about the influence of such an infant on the character of the mother-child relationship. The information that is available, however, does permit some tentative speculations.

In the rather fragmentary model of neonate development, it was postulated that the normal infant develops an increase in gastric secretion as a result of hypothalamic activation and that the absorption of food provides some essential constituents which produce a restitution to the inactive state. It is the rhythmic, repetitive relaxation of physiological tension with which the responses of the sensory receptors become associated. The infant with gastric hypersecretion has a stomach which is behaving constantly as that of the hungry normosecreting infant. Therefore, it is questionable whether such a hypersecreting infant can respond to feeding with the same degree of relaxation as does the normosecretor. It may be that in such instances, even the mother with an excellent integrative capacity will be only partially successful in her efforts to provide that satiation which permits the infant to pass successfully through the biological and into the psychological phases of dependency. As a result, infantile dependent needs will persist. The degree with which the infantile dependent wishes persist will depend upon the quantitative aspects of the mother's integrative capacity as well as upon the rate of gastric secretion. Thus even a relatively minor degree of maternal deprivation may serve to intensify the infantile wish. Fear of future deprivation—that is, fear of loss of love—and all the factors which are responsible for superego formation will influence the extent to which the persistent infantile wish is repressed.

Subsequently, environmental events will be perceived in terms of the persistent infantile wish, so that events which are innocuous to most become noxious to the hypersecretor. A threat to established dependent relationships, or a failure in defenses, will tend to intensify the infantile wish. The tension thus produced will decrease the integrative capacity and be discharged in the nonspecific reaction of anxiety with its physiological concomitants. Since pyloro-duodenal spasm is a component of the anxiety reaction, the normosecretor may develop the signs and symptoms of pyloro-spasm whereas the hypersecretor will develop a peptic ulcer.

Thus, it is postulated that the presence of gastric hypersecretion not only serves as a predisposing factor but also plays a role in the persistence of infantile oral-receptive wishes which then act as precipitating factors when mobilized by meaningful environmental events.

In accord with these speculations are the observations that peptic ulcer is much more frequent among children than was hitherto suspected. Girdany (33) now has a fairly large group of children in whom the duodenal lesion was discovered by roentgen examination. Preliminary evaluation of his data suggests that environmental events as well as the tensions associated with major developmental stages may serve to intensify the infantile dependent wishes and precipitate the duodenal ulcer.

Given the knowledge that an infant is a hypersecretor and given the knowledge of the degree of the mother's integrative capacity, it should be possible to predict the specific type of circumstances which may prove so stressful as to result in the physiological disintegration we recognize as peptic ulcer. Thus, prophylactic measures may ensue.

With the preceding we have emphasized that goal-directed behavior is the resultant of biochemical and physiological factors in transaction with the human environment. The proper application of psychoanalysis as an investigative tool will yield a measure of the subject's integrative capacity and will reveal the specific psychodynamic constellation which tells us what factors can intensify the persistent infantile wish. The proper application of biochemical, physiological, and pharmacological techniques will yield a measure of the particular physiological system that has played a role in preventing the development of an adequate integrative capacity as well as the system which is predisposed to failure. The proper application of psychoanalysis as a therapeutic procedure will make it unnecessary for the patient to view the environment through the screen of his infantile wishes.

The logical extension of the studies initiated by Bernard and Freud, and extended by Cannon and the investigators of the Chicago Institute for Psychoanalysis, leads us to recognize that it is the multidimensional approach to the study of man that Freud must have had reference to when he said: "for in the psychical field, the biological is really the rock-bottom" (16).

REFERENCES

1. Gerard, R. W. Organism, Society and Science. *Scient. Month.*, 50: 340, 1940.

2. Frank, L. K. Teleological Mechanisms. *Ann. New York Acad. Sci.*, 50: 189, 1948.

3. Lillie, R. S. *General Biology and Philosophy of Organism.* Chicago, University of Chicago Press, 1945.

4. Sinnott, P. W. *Cell and Psyche.* Chapel Hill, University of North Carolina Press, 1950.

5. Engel, G. Homeostasis, Behavioral Adjustment and the Concept of Health and Disease. (In *Mid-Century Psychiatry.* Edited by R. R. Grinker.) Springfield, Ill., C. C. Thomas, 1953.

6. von Bertalanffy, L. The Theory of Open Systems in Physics and Biology. *Science,* 111: 23, 1950.

7. Cannon, W. B. *The Wisdom of the Body.* New York, W. W. Norton & Co., 1932.

8. Bentley, A. F. Kennetic Inquiry. *Science,* 112: 775, 1950.

9. Cannon, W. B. *The Way of an Investigator.* New York, W. W. Norton & Co., 1945.

10. von Bertalanffy, L. An Outline of General System Theory. *Brit. J. Philos. Sci.,* 1: 134, 1950.

11. Freud, S. *An Outline of Psychoanalysis.* New York, W. W. Norton & Co., 1949.

12. Alexander, F. *Fundamentals of Psychoanalysis.* New York, W. W. Norton & Co., 1948.

13. French, T. M. *The Integration of Behavior.* Chicago, University of Chicago Press, 1952.

14. Alexander, F., and French, T. M., et al. *Studies in Psychosomatic Medicine.* New York, Ronald Press, 1948.

15. Mirsky, I. A.; Kaplan, S.; and Broh-Kahn, R. H. Pepsinogen Excretion (Uropepsin) as an Index of the Influence of Various Life Situations on Gastric Secretion. In *Life Stress and Bodily Disease.* Res. Pub. Assoc. Research Nervous Mental Disease, 29: 628, 1950.

16. Freud, S. Analysis Terminable and Interminable. *Internat. J. Psycho-Analysis,* 18: 373, 1937.

17. Lewis, T. *Clinical Science Illustrated by Personal Experiences.* London, Shaw & Sons, 1934.

18. Warkany, J., and Mitchell, A. G. Relation of Endocrine Disturbances to Certain Heredodegenerative Symptoms. *Am. J. Diseases Children,* 55: 231, 1938.

19. Sontag, L. W. Determinants of Predisposition to Psychosomatic Dysfunction and Disease. Problem of Proneness to Psychosomatic Disorder. Chapter 2 in *Synopsis of Psychosomatic Diagnosis and Treatment,* by F. Dunbar. St. Louis, C. V. Mosby Co., 1948.

20. French, T. M. Personal communication.

21. Kubie, L. S. A Physiological Approach to the Concept of Anxiety. *Psychosom. Med.*, 3: 263, 1941.

22. Benedek, T. Adaptation to Reality in Early Infancy. *Psychoanalyt. Quart.*, 7: 200, 1938.

23. Benedek, T. The Psychosomatic Implications of the Primary Unit: Mother-Child. *Am. J. Orthopsychiat.*, 19: 642, 1949.

24. Erikson, E. H. *Childhood and Society*. New York, W. W. Norton & Co., 1950.

25. Hartmann, H.; Kris, E.; and Loewenstein, R. M. Comments on the Formation of Psychic Structure. *Psychoanalytic Study of the Child*, 2: 11, 1946.

26. Fries, M. E. Psychosomatic Relationships Between Mother and Infant. *Psychosom. Med.*, 6: 159, 1944.

27. Leitch, M., and Escalona, S. K. The Reaction of Infants to Stress. *Psychoanalytic Study of the Child*, 3/4: 121, 1949.

28. Ribble, M. A. Clinical Studies of Instinctive Reactions in Newborn Babies. *Am. J. Psychiat.*, 95: 149, 1938.

29. Spitz, R. A. The Psychogenic Diseases in Infancy; an attempt at their etiologic classification. *Psychoanalytic Study of the Child*, 6: 255, 1951.

30. Bergman, P., and Escalona, S. K. Unusual Sensitivities in Very Young Children. *Psychoanalytic Study of the Child*, 3/4: 333, 1949.

31. Mirsky, I. A.; Futterman, P.; Kaplan, S.; and Broh-Kahn, R. H. Blood Plasma Pepsinogen. I. The Source, Properties, and Assay of the Proteolytic Activity of Plasma at Acid Reactions. *J. Lab. & Clin. Med.*, 40: 17, 1952.

32. Mirsky, I. A.; Futterman, P.; and Kaplan, S. Blood Plasma Pepsinogen. II. The Activity of the Plasma from "Normal" Subjects, Patients with Duodenal Ulcer, and Patients with Pernicious Anemia. *J. Lab. & Clin. Med.*, 40: 188, 1952.

33. Girdany, B. R. Personal communication.

Discussion

GEORGE C. HAM, M.D.

THE SCIENCE of psychoanalysis has clearly demonstrated that, at least during our postnatal existence, our behavior and our emotions are overdetermined. In fact, our total operation at any given moment is the resultant of multiple stimuli from foci extending both backward and forward in time as well as laterally in terms of space.

The importance of this to the biological sciences far exceeds its present apparent impact. Even though now in clinical medicine the fact of psychodynamic influence in the causal chain and therapy of disease has become a daily consideration, the ramifications and full exploitation of this investigative approach are in their infancy.

And now in the wise words of French, as we have all heard many times, "We must discover what is in focus here." From an evaluation of the manifest content of the program and the material that we have heard I would formulate that a discussion of biological science and psychoanalysis is indicated.

The scope of psychoanalysis in the biological sciences is tremendous. One might, for example, discuss in detail:

(1) Hypotheses pertinent to biological science derived from the insight of psychoanalytic investigation into bodily processes and their validation; or

(2) The sharper definition of techniques of multidisciplinary evaluation of biological integration now in ripening and maturing accuracy; or

(3) The place of psychoanalysis, as it has affected, and is affecting, the understanding of the natural history of disease and of prevention, and its applications in the broadening scope of social factors and responsibility. Psychoanalysis has assisted in these areas through its emphasis on the importance of time and space to an organism.

Rather, I find my interest turning backward over twenty years, to speculation about the next twenty years, using one aspect of biology as an example.

I should like first to turn our attention for a few moments to the "X" factor of Alexander as it pertains to psychosomatic response and disease. It is now common knowledge and accepted fact that in certain vegetative diseases there is a chronic physiologic disturbance associated in a meaningful way to psychodynamic constellations. Increasingly it is becoming evident that specific disease entities are the final result of specific chronic bodily concomitants of specific personality conflicts in a specific constellation of pressures and techniques of integration. Yet no constant 1:1 relationships exist. The particular somatic abnormality does not always follow even though the typical psychodynamic *Gestalt* is present. An "X" factor, a difference in organ responsivity or organ or tissue sensitivity or resistance, has been postulated. This concept is historically a safe one and biologically tenable, but we do not know why this is so—if true —or how such tissue, organ, or system variation comes about.

Arthur Mirsky has pointed his usual facile cerebral microscope in this direction. He has aimed directly at the area of biological integration that the work of the Institute and others has now made imperative to understand. Alexander and his coworkers have through the application of psychoanalytic investigation of biological adaptation brought us to the point where it has become necessary to include in our field of vision the prenatal aspects of man if we are to understand his postnatal, ego-directed, and ego-influenced existence.

We now see, if we stand back far enough to have an adequate field and perspective, that biologic-psychodynamic inter-responsivity, to be understood, must include not only the vicissitudes of the ego but also basic biologic limitations, hypo- and hyper-reactivity, not limited to the postnatal biologic development and reaction. Our concept of biologic-environmental ecology must be extended backward in time into an accurate evaluation of the factors pertinent to the biologic adaptations of the foetus to its changing environment, commonly considered to be constant, of the biochemical-hormonologic, physiologic milieu of the mother.

Increasing evidence of the gross disturbance of foetal development in relationship to gross biologic stress of the mother increases the importance of developing techniques to study more subtle aspects of this symbiotic biologic microcosm. A moment's reflection on the striking rate of growth that occurs during the nine-month gestation as compared with the rate of growth during the postnatal life indicates the immense importance of this biologic period to development. The fact that there are periods in embryologic development when emphasis is on the rapid growth and differentiation not only of special tissues, but also of special systems, one after another, suggests that the milieu at these periods would be of special importance in determining the nature of the response of the cells, enzymes, and neurological components of that group of cells or system. From this postulate and with our knowledge of the changing foetal environment that follows the mother's fluctuating response to her own environment, the changing cortico-thalamic-pituitary adrenal response—to mention only one system—it becomes imperative to develop techniques which will make possible detailed measurement of the changes in the biology of the mother and thus of the foetus and to relate this to the critical growth and development periods of the foetal organism. It does not seem too far off to think of understanding, in a predictive way, what response to expect of a newborn and later in his growth, if we are given the psychodynamic facts of the mother during pregnancy, her biologic response, and the related time chart of foetal growth and development. It may be that the "X" factor mentioned above will become a predictable and therefore understandable expectation rather than a concept of necessary logic. We could postulate that a given foetus is exposed to a high level of adrenergic substances due to the mother's psychosomatic response to an external or intrapsychic conflict during the period of intense growth of the hypothalamic structures of her foetus, that this then might be the normal level of biochemical stimulus for this foetus for this tissue, in contrast to some other foetus whose hypothalamic structure developed in a mother and uterine environment of lower or higher concentration. What will be the situation and response or the required biochemical milieu for this particular foetus postnatally? Will this organism have to produce a higher level of such adrenergic substances to maintain operation in a standard environment, or will he be excessively sensitive to these factors produced in conjunction with his integrative tasks? Will this, for example, lead to chronically hyperactive function in this area, possibly stimulating thyroid function and an ever-increasing vicious circle of stimulation—over-response—stimulation and the clinical syndrome of thyrotoxicosis. We do not know, but we will; and it will come because the frontier of understanding of human adaptation has been pushed back to the point where the logic of an "X" factor, arrived at by psychoanalytic investigation of biologic processes, makes imperative the exploration of this new frontier.

A moment more of crystal gazing suggests an even further

extension of our understanding and predictions of man in the future. May it not be possible, despite Lysenko's present and total discreditation among geneticists, that the long-term symbolic adaptive pressures of an individual, affecting his somatic response in the terms discussed just previously, can subtly affect germ plasm? Are the genes and chromosomes so inviolate and uninfluenced by their chronic and immediate biodynamic environment? May not the biologic *anlage* at this level carry not only the biologic fixed heritage but subtle, temporary alterations reflecting the psychodynamic biologic pressures of the organism which produces the germ plasm and harbors it? To go even further, can one escape the interpretation of being evaluated as afflicted with pseudologia fantastica if one suggests that even mutation may not be merely coincidence but an understandable event in a continuum of biodynamic integration? Again only fragmentary evidence appears, but I wish to emphasize that psychoanalytic understanding and investigation have brought us to this point of question and are an essential ingredient of progress in understanding, in a teleologic and biodynamic way, these possible extensions of our knowledge of life and its vicissitudes.

Discussion

JOHN ROMANO, M.D.

DOCTOR MIRSKY has dealt with his assignment in logical and economic terms. In discussing modern transactional teleological concepts of organismal behavior, he has drawn our attention to purpose or goal-directiveness, to the significant distinction between static and dynamic teleology, and to the limits of theoretical and applied usefulness of the conventional concept of homeostasis. He approaches goal-directiveness in refreshing naturalistic terms, avoids mystical treatment of the unknown, and with Sinnott (1) frankly states that goal-directiveness is a property of the organism and a concomitant of the still unknown physical and chemical processes responsible for organization.

Mirsky acknowledges our indebtedness to Freud for his recognition of the manifestations of goal-directiveness in man. The evolution of a hedonic motivational psychology derived from primary clinical data has, in the minds of many of us, constituted a significant if not the major contribution to human biology in the twentieth century. Mirsky does not choose to pursue in detail the historical evolution of the instinct or drive hypotheses, but jumps in time to the contributions of Alexander as they relate to surplus energy and to French's elaborations of the mechanisms of goal-directive behavior. Both, he believes, lend themselves eventually to quantitative treatment and both avoid the fundamental error of utilizing equilibrium concepts not applicable to living organisms.

It is precisely this section of the paper from which I gained most and for which I am deeply grateful. As one whose major interests and experience have been the study, treatment, and care of the sick, the teaching of students, and in a more limited way, the systematic clinical investigation of human behavior, I believe that the distinctions made between equilibrium, stability, and dynamic steady states will prove most useful in producing more appropriate analogic models which in turn can be used for teaching and for the pursuit of new knowledge. In this regard I recommend to you an editorial by DeWitt Stetten entitled "Thermodynamic, Kinetic, and Biologic Stability," recently published in the *American Journal of Medicine* (2). Like Mirsky and the authors whom he quotes, Stetten distinguishes between thermodynamic equilibrium, kinetic stability, and dynamic steady states. In a concluding sentence Stetten stated, "The stabilizing factor which is more or less peculiar to living systems is the dynamic steady state in which energy linked synthetic processes offset spontaneous degradative processes to maintain, in the normal animal, the required degree of constancy of chemical composition."

In his concern with causality, Mirsky charts the constant transactional nature of events which occur between genotype and life experience (intrauterine, birth, extrauterine) leading to phenotypic expression. From his detailed and painstaking studies of gastric secretion he illustrates vividly the multiple factors which lead in turn to individual differences. What is not clear to me is the nature of the point-to-point relationship between blood pepsinogen and gastric activity.

I was pleased to learn the very wise statement of Sir Thomas Lewis concerning multiple causality of disease. As a teacher and a clinician, I have accumulated considerable evidence to demonstrate the difficulties in attempting to teach concepts of multiple causality to medical students (3). Further, I am reasonably convinced that the concept is poorly recognized and used sparingly in the practice of medicine. My sample is limited in number and restricted to medicine, and it may be that similar difficulties are found in the teaching of other sciences. It may also be, as Tolstoy warned in *War and Peace* (4), that this is a universal problem and that man's search for the single cause is innate. However, those of us who are engaged constantly in teaching wonder whether the unique social ethic of the immediate responsibility of the physician as he deals with the repetitive urgencies of comforting and relieving patients of pain and fear forces him toward a single cause. This appears even more evident when one considers the inexperience and concomitant anxiety of the medical student in his initial perception of his patient. Another factor may be related to the learning process.

of the medical student, who naturally has to restrict his attention in order to achieve certain goals in the learning process. We have learned to be more patient in our teaching as we have found that it is impossible for students to keep multiple factors in mind if they have not in the meantime obtained knowledge of the significance of the more immediate factors involved.

In the model which he presents of neonatal development, Mirsky outlines a sequence of events initiated by a fall in blood sugar immediately after birth. He states, "The postulated repetitive cycle of hypoglycemia, hypothalamic activation, increased motor tonus, ingestion of food, restitution of the blood sugar, and decreased physiologic tension gradually leads, as Benedek has described, to the recognition that gratification or the release of tension is the result of a series of events which take origin in the external environment, whereas the source of tension takes origin in the internal environment." Immediately previous to this he stated, "It is to the *effect* of the ingestion of food rather than to the mere filling of the stomach that we refer when we speak of the gratification of the child's hunger." From my reading of his paper I was not sure whether he was using this example of a servomechanism to illustrate one of perhaps many similar physiologic tensions experienced by the infant (cold, wetness, distended viscera, change in position), or whether he was endowing this specific mechanism with primal significance. Furthermore, I would appreciate knowing the primary data which he has accumulated which leads him to the inferential statement concerning the effect of the ingestion of food rather than of the filling of the stomach in gratifying the infant's hunger.

I must admit to uncertainty in my mind with propositions which deal with the violent response of the neonate to stimuli; and of inferences drawn from such observations. There appears to be little question that the tool kit of the infant is significantly different from that of the adult organism. However, have we tended to oversimplify our observations or failed to relate the infant's behavior to the state of his organization as an infant? Have we tended to project onto the infant our own model of the adult organism with its greater repertory of adaptive devices? The point, I believe, is more than academic, as it relates itself to a key assumption of psychoanalytic psychology, namely the critical vulnerability of the early life experience of the organism. Mirsky's explanation of the inconstancy of physiologic aging may have its counterpart in psychologic aging. Does the young organism have strengths as well as weaknesses? Have we tended to apply slavishly and with stereotype a railroad time-table of psychologic aging when factors, genic and experiential, may modify considerably the rate and intensity of learning?

REFERENCES

1. Sinnott, Edmund W. The Biology of Purpose. *Am. J. Orthopsychiat.*, 22: 457–468, 1952.

2. Stetten, D. Thermodynamic, Kinetic, and Biologic Stability. *Am. J. Med.*, 13: 251–254, 1952.

3. Romano, John. Basic Orientation and Education of the Medical Student. *J.A.M.A.*, 143: 409–412, 1950.

4. Tolstoy, Leo. *War and Peace.* New York, Modern Library. p. 918.

Psychoanalysis and Social Science

With Special Reference to the
Oedipus Problem

TALCOTT PARSONS, PH.D.

I AM PARTICULARLY happy and feel greatly honored to have the privilege of talking to the members of the Chicago Institute for Psychoanalysis and your guests on this happy occasion and on this subject. We social scientists are well aware of the outstanding role which in the twenty years of your existence has been played by this Institute in developing the borderline field between our disciplines, not only in the work of Franz Alexander himself, but throughout a whole series of the other members of the Institute.

For my own part I wish to outline briefly a view of the more general theoretical relations between psychoanalysis and social science, particularly that of psychoanalytic theory to my own discipline of sociology, and then to illustrate this concretely with a few suggestions about the integration of their respective contributions to that very central problem area of psychoanalytic theory, the analysis of the Oedipus complex. This will consist essentially in the attempt to relate some aspects of the sociological analysis of the family to the psychoanalytic theory of the development of the personality of the child more systematically than has previously been done.

With respect to the more general problem, my starting point

is the conviction that all the sciences of human behavior—or as some of us tend to call it, action, particularly on the socio-cultural levels—share a common frame of reference and, in certain broad outlines, a common conceptual scheme for analysis. Though there is complete continuity with the biological sciences, the focus of interest of the sciences of action is not on the internal structure and processes of the organism, not, that is, on its anatomy and physiology, but on its "behavior," which essentially means its *relations* to objects in its environment or situation. It is indeed the fact that of all branches of psychology, psychoanalytic theory, from the early phases of the development of the libido theory by Freud, has been strongly dominated by this perspective, which above all has paved the way for its fruitful integration with social science. Freud of course wished to get as much help from biology as possible, but the distinctive ideas of psychoanalysis, it is perhaps not too much to say, center on the relations of instinctual drive and ego organization to objects of different kinds.

These relations of the organism to objects, which I like to formulate as the modes of "orientation" of an "actor," are not isolated and discrete, but come to be organized in systems. Besides the suggestion that psychology, including psychoanalysis, and the social sciences share the common frame of reference of focusing on orientations to objects, perhaps the most important basic point I wish to make is that the systems in which behavior or the orientation of action are organized are not of a single fundamental type but of *two*, both interdependent and interpenetrating, but nevertheless analytically distinct, so that in the development of theory they cannot be assimilated to each other in the sense of "reduction" in either direction (1). These I would like to call personality as a system, and the social system. Personality is the action or behavior system which is organized about one specific living organism. It is not itself the organism, but the system of action *of* the organism; it cannot be abstracted from the object relations of the organism, but is *constituted by them*. Put a little differently, it is not "that which" is related *to* objects, but is the *system of relations* to objects, having no existence apart from this. Particular relations to particular objects of course change, just as the specific biochemical content of body organs changes, but the system of relations persists. This is perhaps an unfamiliar way of looking at the concept of personality, but whatever merits or demerits it may have in other respects, it is extremely useful in defining the relations of psychology, as the theory of personality, to social science.

A social system, as distinguished from a personality, is the system constituted by a plurality of organisms—or "actors"— in *interaction* with each other. It is constituted by the same concrete behaviors or orientations as are personality systems, but there are two crucial differences: on the one hand it involves a different mode of abstraction in terms of system-reference, and on the other a different basis of inclusion and exclusion of empirical facts as relevant. The central key to these differences lies in the fact that only in the limiting case of the "total society" as a social system, does the participation of a personality in a system of social interaction, that is, a social system, comprehend even as much of his personality as can be said to constitute "memberships" in social groups. It is not the personality of the individual which is the unit of a social system, but his *role*. Thus in the case of the family the father as personality is at the same time, let us say, a lawyer, and also a Presbyterian; all three are constitutive of his personality, but they constitute three independent though also interdependent roles.

Nevertheless the specific family as a system, in abstraction from the extrafamilial roles of its members, has all the classic properties of systems in a scientific sense. Its units interact with each other; they are interdependent in the sense that changes in the state of any one result in changes in the others and thus in the "state of the system"; and the system can be analyzed in terms of the concept of equilibrium in that a given change sets up tendencies to restore the state which would otherwise have existed, though these may be more than counteracted by tendencies to disequilibrium and the state of the system may thus be permanently changed. It is this analytic independence of social systems as systems from the personality which justifies treating social science from a theoretical point of view as independent and not simply as a field of "applied psychology."

This extremely broad orientation to our problem will be made more meaningful if one further fundamental complex of considerations is added to it. Both biologists and social scientists are increasingly aware of the continuity of the social aspect of life from the subhuman to the human worlds; for example, it is quite clear that the system of reference for analyzing the processes of natural selection is by no means only the individual organism and its survival. But equally there seems to be agreement that what is sometimes called symbolic process has reached a level of elaboration in the human species which makes it, for most purposes though not all, qualitatively different from anything in the behavior of the lower organisms. However, symbolic process is precisely an aspect of the mode of relation of the organism to the world of objects; it is thus central to all the sciences of behavior.

We may cut through many steps of analysis and simply say that by symbolic process objects acquire significance for action which extends beyond their directly physiological functions for the organism, for example, oxygen in the atmosphere for respiration. Symbolic meaning-complexes for the human adult come to be constitutive of all the major orientation and behavior patterns which are of interest to the psychologist and social scientist, including the definition of goals of the individual's action, his cognition of his environment, his choice of instrumental means to his goals, his attachments to objects, especially other human beings, and most obviously his "cultural" interests, his ideals and values.

Symbol-meaning patterns are furthermore created in the processes of action themselves, especially though not exclusively the processes of interaction on social levels. They are learned by the individual and not given in the genetic constitution of the organism. Above all, and this is crucial, they are not only something "possessed" *by* the human personality as objects external to but somehow controlled by it, they are directly *constitutive of* the human personality. Freud, with his theory of the superego, was one of the first to understand this fundamental fact, for he held that moral values, introjected or internalized as the superego, may be interpreted to be a particular class of the meaning-patterns of symbols.

The symbol-meaning patterns which become internalized in personalities and in a parallel sense institutionalized in social systems constitute, in my opinion, the core of what our anthropological friends call the "patterns of culture." Culture in this sense is both an aspect of and a precipitate from the processes of human action. It is not itself an empirical system of action in the same sense as a personality or social system, and it thus constitutes a system in a slightly different sense, in that imperatives of pattern consistency are imposed on any personality or social system which is to be organized about and through cultural symbol-meanings to any high degree, which is clearly the case with any which are distinctively human. Culture then is to be considered an essential *component* of any concrete system of human action, whether it be personality or social system. Freud's insight was entirely correct on this point, but I have argued elsewhere (2) that it should be extended beyond moral values as such to include all the major components of the culture common to the major interaction systems in which the individual is involved.

On the high level of abstraction on which the preceding sketch has been held, a few important inferences for the relations of psychoanalytic and social theory may be drawn.

The first of these is that unless the view stated above of the analytic independence of personalities and social systems should prove to be fundamentally wrong, there can be no neat "one-to-one" correspondence between the two classes of systems with respect to structure or to the mechanisms involved in their processes. We cannot, that is to say, neatly "match" personality or character structure and social structure or the patterns of its institutionalized culture; this has become, to my mind, abundantly evident empirically through the difficulties which so many attempts to state simple relations between "culture and personality" have encountered (1).

The basic type of relationship is unfortunately much more complex. There must be common pattern components, but these fit into the organization of the respective systems in different ways, because, first, though the *role* in a social system is actually *part* of the personality of the member—this is what we meant above by interpenetration—it is only part. The *rest* of the personality system of any given member will be different from those of the others. Secondly, the roles in the given social system of two or more members are also differentiated from each other. I am therefore most emphatically not denying that the interrelations are fundamental; I simply say that there is every indication that they are far more complex than certain schools of thought have suggested, and that recognition of this complexity is the first step toward better understanding. Put in technical terms, every problem of such interrelations involves the complexity of handling at least two different system-references at the same time.

A second broad inference is that the analysis of symbolic process constitutes one of the principal bridges between the analysis of personalities and of social systems. Indeed it hardly seems to be too much to say that every important advance in the understanding of human action within the frame of reference I have sketched, has by implication, if not directly, involved a better understanding of symbols, their relation to motivation, and the organization of their meanings in systems. It is mainly in this sense that I should like, in the interests of fruitful cooperation with the social sciences, to enter a plea against certain tendencies toward the "biologizing" of psychoanalytic theory. Certainly, as Mirsky has emphasized, every addition to our knowledge of the relation of internal processes of the organism on physiological levels to its behavior is welcome and important. But unless it can be directly related to the distinctively human levels of symbolic process it seems to me such knowledge is unlikely to contribute very directly to the crucial problem area of the relations of the personality to social systems and to culture.

A third inference concerns the differences in the relations between personality and social systems, not only in different societies but in different *parts* of the same social structure. Much earlier thought has attempted to establish a global relation between personality and "American Culture," or the "Russian Character" and the structure of Russian Society as a whole. Of course, whether on the cultural or the social system level, there must be a degree of integration if any system of human relations is to retain stability and distinctive properties over time; otherwise it would simply fall apart or explode. Hence such attempts are far from fruitless. But the integration of a society is *always* very far from complete. Furthermore, the scientifically important problem of personality and social system is very frequently not the "total" problem but some partial problem, for example, of the relation of an individual or class to his family, to his occupational situation, to his partners on the golf links, and so on. The psychoanalyst often quite rightly tends to see and emphasize consistent trends running through several of these contexts, such as a general tendency to be submissive to authority yet secretly resentful of it. But in the broad perspective of the social sciences the current trend is, I think, on the cultural level to see a network of "dominant *and variant*" patterns (3) and on the social system level to think of a society as though it were a social system composed of a complex network of interlocking and overlapping sub-systems which are partially independent of and differentiated from each other. A personality is never, beyond infancy, related to only one of these sub-systems, but always to a plurality, and his relations to different ones are different. Only, therefore, for certain specific purposes is it fruitful to talk about his general relations to "society"; for many if not most purposes it is more important and more fruitful to talk about his involvement in one or a few specific subsystems of the society. One of the most important lessons we sociologists have had to learn, and relearn again and again in the use of the theory in empirical work, is the extreme importance of being clear to *what system* as a point of reference any given statement of fact or of analytical interpretation applies. And, as noted above, this becomes doubly important when more than one system must be included in the analysis.

Rather than dwelling further on these generalities, however, it will be more fruitful to outline an approach to the more specific problem area of the Oedipus complex within the framework outlined above. Essentially what I wish to do is to try to bring forward a few considerations about the family as a social system and about the interaction process in which the developing child participates as a member, which seem to bear on the Oedipus problem as it has been dealt with in psychoanalytic thinking. It will not be possible to do more than very broadly suggest an approach.

In sketching the setting for a few empirical suggestions about the Oedipus complex I wish to discuss briefly three main topical areas which at first sight may seem to have relatively little relation to each other but all of which bear on the larger problem. These are: first, some findings of research in the field of small group interaction with respect to the phases of group process and to the role structure of small groups; second, the relation of these findings to certain features of the human family treated as a social system; third, certain parallel features of two important cases of intimate social interaction, namely, (a) the process of psychotherapy regarded as a system of social interaction between therapist and patient, and (b) the process of social development of the child as a member of the family— again regarded as a system of dynamic social interaction.

The first consideration to report is that careful study (4) of the processes of interaction in small groups, where the group is set a task to accomplish as a group, has shown that the process tends to follow a relatively definite patterned sequence of phases. Four of these have been distinguished; they are: first, the "adaptive" phase of mobilizing information and other facilities and evaluating them in relation to the group goal; second, the "goal-attainment" phase of actually working out commitments of the group to the decisions which constitute fulfillment of its task; third, the "integrative" phase of adjusting the internal relations of the members of the group to each other in order to establish or re-establish its solidarity as a group; and, fourth, (often overlapping with the third) phenomena interpreted as constituting mainly release of emotional tensions, joking and laughter, and expression of "relief" that the job has been successfully accomplished. With the many variations of detail which inevitably enter in, and over a considerable range of different kinds of tasks, this pattern holds up in its broad outlines as "typical." Moreover, since the groups have been chosen without regard to specific personality composition, the pattern seems to have something to do with the exigencies of the process of interaction in a system as such.

A second broad empirical finding about small groups has come out of the same work. In groups lacking in any clear initial basis of differentiation of role and status between the members —they have been of about the same age, of the same sex, and of about the same class status—there appears in the course of group interaction a clear and uniform differentiation of role between the members with respect to two "axes" of differentiation. The first is the "hierarchical" axis of difference of influence on the group goal-decisions, which coincides with "prestige" in certain respects; the second is the "qualitative" distinction between "leadership" in what Bales calls the "task-oriented" area and the "social-emotional" area. The latter differentiation involves greater activity for the "task leader" in the first two phases mentioned above, for the "social-emotional" leader in the last two.

It has proved possible to interpret these two sets of findings of research in the processes of small group interaction in terms of the most general theory of social systems, and through this to show that the differentiation of phases over time, and patterns of differentiation of roles within the group which tend to remain stable through time, can *both* be derived from the same fundamental features of the process of interaction in a small group if it is regarded as an equilibrating system (5).

Without a discussion of additional evidence it may seem quite a jump to infer from this second finding anything at all

about our second main problem area, namely the social structure of the human conjugal family and its significance. Here it
is only possible to point out that most sociological discussions
of what is distinctive about the family among social structures
have centered about biological points of reference, notably age
—or more specifically generation difference as somehow related
to superiority-inferiority—and sex. I should like here to suggest the importance of a somewhat different perspective. The
types of differentiation which on an extremely simple and elementary level emerge in the course of interaction in small
groups having no previous bases of differentiation are, as stated
in general theoretical terms, essentially the same types which
are institutionalized in family structure throughout the world.
Though total kinship structures vary greatly in different societies, the basic structure of the conjugal family unit of man,
wife, and their dependent children, is much more nearly constant. My suggestion here is that the major axes of differentiation of family structures are of generic significance in the broad
total picture, not simply because they are biologically grounded
—though that is certainly important in certain connections—
but because they are the bases of differentiation which appear
in *any* system of social interaction of a small number of inter-
acting units, when it is sufficiently "shaken down" to have developed a certain degree of stability as a system, even when these
biological points of reference are not present. Very broadly
the differentiation of the role of the father as "task leader,"
of the mother as "social-emotional leader," and of the children
as less preeminent in either respect is a common feature of family structures everywhere.

There is, of course, a whole range of problems of interpretation in detail of such an extremely broad set of statements. For
example, in the American urban family the "task-leadership"
of the husband-father must be interpreted particularly in the

light of the importance in our society precisely to the family as a group, of his occupational role and the income earned through it which is the foundation of the "style of life" of the family. The fact that the man may do much less in the internal management of family affairs than does his wife therefore need not mean that, in terms of the total adaptation of the family to its situation, his *instrumental* role is strategically the less important of the two; indeed, the contrary is generally the case.

My interest in the broad outline of the structure of the family is at present confined to its contribution to understanding the process of child development. Perhaps the most important point to emphasize here is not that the child is simply exposed to several discrete human objects in his family who "happen" to have the characteristics of belonging to two sexes, and to be differentiated by age, thus to be his mother and his father and his siblings; but that these objects constitute a definite type of *system,* and a system the properties of which are of far broader *sociological* significance than any particular collection of biological characteristics of its members, properties which are found in the *many* kinds of groups, and are by no means confined to groups the members of which are biologically differentiated in this way. I thus wish to argue that certain cardinal features of the differentiation of the *roles* of the sexes in the strict social-system sense is of generic significance in the structural differentiation of social systems; it is not simply a function of the biological composition of the family group.

To turn now to the third problem area mentioned above, the phase pattern of group process was not introduced just for its general interest, but because it seems to furnish a most important clue to the process of development of personality. Let me try to make this clear by describing a process of developing theoretical insight. As previously reported (6, 7) it has for some time seemed to me possible to state four principal conditions of successful psychotherapy (in the broad sense which includes psychoanalysis) which pertain to the orientations of the therapist to his patient. These I have called permissiveness, support, denial of reciprocity, and manipulation of rewards. It furthermore appeared that these same basic components were to be found, not only in the therapeutic process, but more generally in what sociologists call the "mechanisms of social control," for example, religious ritual.

Only in very recent work (5), however, has it been possible to relate the succession of *relative* importance of these orientation components (which define the institutionalized role of the therapist) to the *temporal* order of the therapeutic process. A rough order has, however, emerged. This may be stated schematically as follows: First, permissiveness for the expression of the patient's preoccupations, however shameful or trivial, is necessary to get the process started; this after all is the "fundamental rule" of psychoanalytic procedure. Second, there soon develops the transference which is possible only because, though carefully regulated, there is a supportive element in the attitude of the therapist which enables the patient to come to "depend on" him. The therapist's support in particular is then put to the test by the negative elements of the patient's transference and used as a most important point of reference for analysis. Third, however, once transference is established, the patient puts forward "overtures," most of which the therapist should not reciprocate; if he is tempted to do so it is interpreted as countertransference which he must try to control; these overtures are of course both positive and negative; the therapist may be "seduced" either into illegitimate support or gratification, or into illegitimate anger and hostility. Finally, the therapist eventually comes to deal with his patient on a mature level of mutual interaction, in which interpretations are offered and the patient is rewarded by approval and esteem for his capacity to achieve insight and to handle his problems. It is significant how frequently in discussions of therapy there is reference to the "work" that the therapist and the patient are doing together, to their cooperative endeavor.

It should be emphasized again that this is a temporal order only in a rough sense. By no means do the earlier orientations of the therapist suddenly disappear, but broadly each of these phases having been "worked through" is a precondition of the next emerging into the central place. Thus support is not a primary problem until transference is well developed, and it is only with well-developed transference that denial of reciprocity becomes of central significance; finally the importance of not introducing certain interpretations until the patient is "ready" for them is widely recognized.

It must be remembered that the therapeutic process is a process of social interaction. The phases I have just outlined are phases of change not simply of therapist or patient as individuals, but of the therapist-patient system as a system. When seen in that light it seems logical that there should be some relation between the pattern of phases of change in this system and in other systems of social interaction. Looking at the problem in this way led to the insight that what we have here is exactly the phase pattern of "normal" task-oriented group process, but *with the order of the phases in reverse*. In therapy, that is, tension release for the patient comes first, not last. This leads on through transference and support to the consolidation of the integration of the system. Only when the transference problem in this aspect has been to some extent dealt with is it possible to deal with what the patient "wants"—particularly in the transference relation—and thus with the decisions which are to be made by them together as a system, while the final phase is primarily concerned with adaptation of the system to the social environment outside itself, that is, to the establishment of "mature" patterns of behavior on the part of the patient and the breaking of the transference dependency. The essential process here is the shift from fulfillment of the patient's pathological wishes, which after the establishment of the transference he hopes to gratify in partnership with the therapist, to the fulfillment of the mature goal of recovery which involves renunciation of the pathological wishes.

It seemed to us at the time—a conclusion confirmed by other evidence—that this reversal of phase order had to do with the fact that this was primarily a process of *learning* for the patient, of change in the state of his personality as a system. This suggestion then led on to the insight that the classic Freudian pattern of the stages of child development could be fitted into the same pattern of analysis with remarkable exactitude; with this statement I at last come around to my announced empirical subject of discussion.

Again put very schematically, the earliest stabilized phase of childhood may be spoken of as one of permissiveness for tension-release centering above all about oral gratifications, not only of hunger needs but the "erotic" generalization of these to associated pleasurable experiences; the "plateau" of relative stability is the state of "oral dependency." The next major phase centers in the development of the love attachment to the mother, and thus the transition from oral dependency to love dependency in what Freud called the first "true object relationship." We may then treat the anal phase, including the prominence of aggression in it, as the phase of transition between the two "plateaus." The predominance of mutual "supportive" attitudes between mother and child at this time is nearly obvious. The next major transition of course is through the Oedipal crisis, in the broad sense applicable to both sexes, to the latency phase in Freud's sense, and finally through adolescence as the last phase of transition to "genitality" or maturity. It does in-

deed seem that the pattern of unfolding of the psychotherapeutic process, most clearly visible *in extenso* in the case of full
psychoanalysis, constitutes a kind of a repetition of the development of personality itself; there is, along with the obvious difference, a striking congruence of pattern.

This is the broad framework within which I wish to put forward a few very tentative ideas about the Oedipus problem.
I should like to suggest that this provides a perspective in which
the phases of personality development of the child may fruit-
fully be analyzed in terms of their interdependence with and
interpenetration in the phases of change of a system of social
interaction, the family, in such a way that the changing character of the *role* of the child is an integral part of the process
of the system partly determined by, partly determining com-
plementary changes in, the roles of all the other members of
the family.

The next step, then, is to sketch out the main sequence of the
roles of the child in the family which correspond to the phases
of his personality development. The infant, we may say, is primarily in the passive role of an object of care: his needs are
provided for and his wishes within certain limits are gratified;
it is only gradually that he assumes an active role of participation in interaction. This, as we know, centers most directly
on his relation to the mother, the two coming to form what
sociologically speaking may be called a solidary subsystem of
the family system. By the time this stage is reached the role
of the mother has also changed; it is not so much to take care
of the child as to care *for* him; the focus is on the *reciprocal*
love relationship. The child's primary goal in life, superseding
primary organic gratifications, comes to be both to be loved
by his mother, and, it must not be forgotten, to love in return.
It is not only his need for her love, but also his capacity to
love and his need to express it in his action which form the

foundation for the acceptance of higher disciplines in the transition to the next phase. There has, I am convinced, had to occur by this time not only the formation of the "attachment" to the mother in the more narrowly emotional sense, but also a complex process of cognitive symbolization by which the mother and her attitudes become a coherent object of orientation. Furthermore, the element of dependency here reflects the hierarchical structure of the family as a system; the relationship of mother and child is reciprocal in some respects but not in others. Above all the mother has another love attachment—to the father and of course to older siblings if any—in which the small child does not share. This structural asymmetry in the relationship is fundamental to the dynamics of the socialization process.

The third major phase brings the child into a role where this exclusiveness of solidarity with, hence dependency on, the mother is broken through and the child becomes more a responsible participant in the interaction of the larger family system. He is expected to "do his share" in relation to family functions, to act like a "big boy" (or girl), and in general to "be a credit" to both his parents, that is, to the family. It is the transition to this new role which is directly relevant to the Oedipal problem. We suggest that the assumption of sex role is a particularly crucial aspect of this. But before entering on these problems it may be remarked that the fourth phase signalizes "emancipation" from the family of orientation with both the capacity and the permission to form erotic attachments again, but this time outside the family, and connected with that, autonomous orientation to the social world outside the family, to a greater degree than heretofore. When this stage is reached he is no longer a "dependent" member of the family but is entitled to autonomy—his participation is in terms of his own "voluntary cooperation." The general principle then of development of the child's role is that of a series of steps from participation centered in a narrower subsystem of social interaction into the next wider one; thus from mother-child as main system, to family as a whole, and then to outside society.

What must the child "learn" in the course of this process? Of course he must acquire knowledge of himself and of the world about him, and he must acquire specific skills of a variety of sorts. But with considerable confidence it is possible to say that the most important learning process is the internalization of the patterns of the culture, particularly the value-orientations appropriate to his roles. These, we know, are not merely something he comes to "know about" but they become constitutive parts of his personality.

It is as a critical phase of this process, transitional between two stages of relative stabilization, that I wish to see the Oedipus complex. If the above analysis is correct, then the child must emerge from his special relation to his mother, his dependency on her, to full participation in the family as a system. In so doing he must for the first time play a role which is differentiated in respects other than that he is a "little child." The focus of this differentiation is clearly the assumption of his sex role, the shift from being just "child" to being boy *or* girl, but clearly not both. Naturally, given the structure of the family and his place in it, the prototypes of the sex roles are his two parents, and equally naturally, their relation to each other, as well as his relation to each in turn, comes to be a focal center of his preoccupations.

It must be remembered that a central aspect of growing up is to be expected to take increasing responsibilities, to *do* many things on increasingly high levels of performance. It is therefore understandable that the problem of *adequacy* should be particularly central to the child. While he is in the pre-Oedipal dependency phase his anxieties center on the problem of security (can he count on his mother's love?); with the transition, the question is more and more, "Can I *do* what is expected of a big boy, and will my parents, who are both judges and executioners, be satisfied with my *performance?*" Looked at in terms of the internal structuring of anxiety, this preoccupation with adequacy seems to be one main point of genesis of the problem of guilt. Guilt, in this connection, is the subjective sense of having done—or wanted to do—things which are felt to be wrong. However important ambivalence toward the mother as a love object may be in the background, this aspect also seems to be of great significance, particularly in American society with its strong emphasis on individual achievement.

A final question of assumption may be raised. The relations between biological and other determinants of human action involve questions which will not be settled for a long time. But much of the thought of our time has tended to treat the personality characteristics and attitudes of the two sexes as primarily "emanations" of their genetic constitutions. The tendency of the analysis I am presenting here is the contrary, to explore as fully as possible the hypothesis that a large part of sex-role-determination, including the categorization by the individual *of himself* as belonging to one sex, is learned in the processes of social interaction, using the anatomical differences of the sexes as points of reference, but only in this sense is it "determined" by them. Freud spoke of the "constitutional bisexuality" of the child. I should like to suggest that the question of its importance is in need of further investigation, and further, to put forward the hypothesis that a much greater part of sex-categorization is learned, and not biologically given, than psychoanalysis tends to assume. The fact that the spontaneous lines of the differentiation of roles in groups which are homogeneous in sex composition coincide so closely with the lines of sex-role differentiation in the family, seems to me to be cogent evidence in favor of this view.

Seen within the framework outlined above, a number of features of the emotional dynamics of the Oedipus complex seem to take on a somewhat new and clearer pattern of meaning. Naturally, however, the suggestions put forward here are tentative and in need of systematic verification. The first keynote I wish to suggest is the importance of the situation of *social* strain in which the Oedipal child is placed. Here it becomes necessary to distinguish clearly between the negative and the positive aspects. The child is in course of being "pried" out of the security of a stable love relationship to his mother. This is a situation of strain on *both* sides and is met with the typical reactions to strain; there is ambivalence: compulsive clinging to the relationship (by both parents) and the development of hostile reactions. There are high levels of anxiety, and much production of fantasy. This is the negative aspect. At the same time the child is being taught something new. He is expected to assume new patterns of behavior and is rewarded for it when successful—but learning is difficult. His mother is committed to these values and will be rewarded by her child's progress. By deeply institutionalized patterns of the culture, this system of new expectations is centered about the child's sex; if a boy, his identification in this sense with his father; he must learn to be a boy and to be clearly distinguished both from his mother and from his sisters.

At the same time this process is going on in a definitely structural setting. As a child, he is in an inferior status relative to adults, though this inferiority is gradually decreasing; we have reason for believing that in a situation of decreasing *actual* disadvantage his sense of *relative deprivation* (8, 9) may well be expected to increase (relative that is to the father and other adult males). Moreover, he (the boy) finds that his mother is not altogether a free agent in things that matter most to him; she is bound by her special love relationship to her husband; indeed this is the keystone of the structure of the family as a system in which the boy now comes to participate so much more fully. Whereas on the earlier lower level of participation his love relationship to his mother could fit into a protected niche, now that he becomes much more active, it tends to come into conflict with the rights of the father who, it must be remembered, is not only an "intruder" but *also* the boy's role-model.

We presume that the pressure thus to restructure roles comes partly from the sheer biological maturation of the boy, including of course the phallic phase of sexual development. But the consequences of maturation are implemented by expectations of the culture through the actions and attitudes of the parents. These are expectations of what a big boy should and should not do.

In making a few suggestions as to how the process works out, I should like to emphasize in particular the interrelations between the emotional constellations in which reactions to strain are so prominent and the processes of symbolization. Let us start with the erotic component. It was suggested above that one primary aspect of the significance of eroticism in child development lies in the fact that it can serve as a vehicle of the *generalization* of cathexis from the primary organic sources of gratification to wider contexts, so that an attitude system is built up of which erotic gratification comes to be a primary *symbolic* expression. In other words, I am suggesting that instead of being purely constitutional in significance, the child's erotic development may be treated as an integral part of the process of learning through social interaction, that is, as both determinant *and* consequence of this process. Of course the organic capacity for pleasure must be present—just as the child must have suf-

ficiently developed organs of speech in order to learn to talk—
but this constitutional basis does not determine either whether
he will learn to speak. Above all I wish to suggest that the
development of infantile eroticism is more nearly comparable
to the learning of language than it is, let us say, to the growth
of the hair. Erotic gratification comes to be a primary symbolic
focus of the love attachment to the mother, since tender physical contact with her had played such an important part in their
relationship.

The primary reason why pre-Oedipal eroticism is a barrier
to further development seems to lie in its connection with dependency, which would keep the boy "tied to his mother's apron
strings"; it is thus a prominent symbolic focus of what he must
overcome in order to become a big boy. In such a situation it
is understandable that there should be a duality of aspects in
the structure of the anxiety which is associated with eroticism.
On the one hand, it is anxiety that it will be necessary to re-
nounce dependency on the mother; on the other hand and at
the same time, anxiety about not being able to accomplish what
is expected, including this renunciation, but also including the
many positive performances expected.

In this context it seems possible to suggest certain interpretations of the significance of the penis, or castration fear, and
of certain related phenomena. I would tend to put it that it is
not so much that having a penis *makes* the boy masculine, but
that the penis is a *symbol* of his masculinity, and it is crucial
that this is a masculinity not yet achieved. Then masturbation,
which so often tends to be a focus of guilt at this stage, may be
interpreted, at least in part, as a symbolic act which is guilt-
provoking largely because it means directly a perversion of
masculinity; it is regressing to erotic gratification and doing
so precisely with the aid of the symbolic focus of the struggle
for emancipation from erotic dependency. It is true that secret

masturbation is a partial step of emancipation, because it dispenses with the presence of the mother. But *any* erotic gratification is deeply bound up with the connotation of dependency and hence, in this stage, inadequacy, that is, incapacity to stop being a little child.

Again from this point of view the fear of castration may be regarded as involving an element of projection, on the father as role-model, of the boy's own feelings of guilt about his regressive acts and wishes and his feelings of inadequacy. In this context it seems to be a way of saying, at least to himself, that he does not *deserve* to be considered a big boy, he should have this symbol of his masculinity taken away from him. The state of conflict, however, is presumably so acute that he cannot directly express his sense of guilt and turns it into anxiety of being mutilated from outside. This would seem to help explain the point Freud so strongly emphasized that in castration fear the danger is felt as coming from outside.

Perhaps, too, it is legitimate to suggest that the prominence of castration fear at this stage is evidence in favor of the hypothesis that sex-categorization must be learned in the cognitive sense, that it is not simply a question of the boy's "accepting" his sex but of his internalizing it as a role-definition and expectation. We are in general familiar with the extent to which children fuse together matters of fact and of sentiment. Is it not attributing undue intellectual sophistication to the four-year-old to think he knows that the penis is anatomically his by biological inheritance, that it cannot be given and taken away? Is it not possible that castration to him means primarily taking away the *symbol* that he has a right to be considered and treated as a big boy?

More generally the view that sex role is learned and that the anatomical differentiae of the sexes play a part as symbols and not merely as "facts" may have an important bearing on the problem of homosexuality. The classical formula is that the homosexual, if he plays the role of a member of the opposite sex, has been unable to *accept* his sex role, in the sense that cognitively he "knows" he is male or female but "emotionally" he *wishes* he belonged to the opposite sex. I would suggest the possibility that, unconsciously of course, since it is in such drastic conflict with the culture, he may often *believe* that he belongs to the opposite sex. Thus, for instance in paranoia, it may well be the belief (and not only the aggression associated with such a radically unacceptable wish) which is projected in hallucinations. This is in accord with the view which I have developed elsewhere (2) that cognitive categorization is internalized just as much as moral values are.

A few words may also be said about problems concerning the structuring of aggression in the Oedipus situation. It is of course well established that the boy's aggression is directed mainly against his father. Freud, it will be remembered, strongly emphasized the parallel structure, that the girl's aggression is directed mainly against her mother. This parallel strongly suggests that the pressure of expectations for assumption of the *new role* constitutes a primary focus of the system of strain; the resentment is against being *forced* to grow up. In each case the primary target is the role-model who embodies the goal about which there is so much ambivalence and anxiety. This to me is evidence of the importance of pressures impinging on the child from the expectation systems of his parents rather than from the physiological processes of sexual maturation alone, though of course these are essential ingredients of the process.

In the case of the boy it would seem to be almost obvious that the scapegoat mechanism is also operating. Since it is the attachment to his mother which is threatened, he naturally finds it difficult if not impossible to believe that she has any part in doing such things to him; the path of least resistance seems most obviously displacement on the father. Again, when combined with the factors of anxiety and guilt, the intensity of the projected castration fear is understandable.

At this point the direct parallel as between the sexes breaks down in what may well be one of the focal points of the dynamics of differentiation of sex roles. The critical fact is that although both sexes go through the early attachment to the mother, the boy may retain the same sex of erotic object in later life, but the girl must change the sex of her object. This is doubtless related to the duality in the girl's accusations against her mother; on the one hand she allegedly deprived her of a penis, on the other she did not give her enough milk, that is, was not a loving mother. But for the girl to displace too much of this aggression upon her father jeopardizes the only recourse she has in a situation of strain with her mother and would "contaminate" her later directions of erotic object attachment. This necessity to repress aggression more drastically and thoroughly may well have something to do with the tendency to a more passive and conformist orientation on the part of girls than of boys.

There seems to be sound ground for assuming that, in processes of action, over time there tends to be a balancing out of advantages and cost. If the girl has to accept a heavier burden of repression of aggression than her brother, it seems reasonable to suggest that there is somewhere a compensating motivational advantage. This probably lies in the opportunity which is denied to her brother for full indentification (in the sense of role-internalization) with the primary love object. The suggestion is that the feminine role is not in this more fundamental sense a disadvantaged one but that rather the boy's exclusion from this solidarity of feminine succession is one of the sources of the disturbance he undergoes in the Oedipus period.

For him the balancing compensation seems to lie in the privilege of being allowed again, much later and under stringent conditions, to love and be loved by a mother, this time not his own mother but the mother of his children.

There is one final topic on which the framework of analysis sketched here can, I think, throw considerable light. The Oedipus situation has here been interpreted to be a "crisis of transition" in the development of a system of social interaction which produces severe strain on the child and is one of the major points at which later pathological processes may take root. Indeed it is probably not too much to say that *normally* it produces a mild or incipient neurosis. But there is a "normal" outcome which is at least relatively free of neurosis, and the question thus arises of whether anything can be said within our framework which bears on the process by which the Oedipal crisis can be successfully overcome.

The suggestion is that this can be considered as in certain respects analogous to a process of "group therapy" in which the two parents constitute essentially a "therapeutic team." (It is of course a central difference from therapy that the parents also have been agents of bringing on the crisis.) First let us take up the broad outline of the process and then the division of labor between the parents.

Permissiveness takes essentially the form of toleration of "childishness"—which of course as in the therapeutic care has its relatively clearly defined limits. There is a delicate balance between this permissiveness for expression above all of dependency needs and of aggression, and their restraint. In particular it may be suggested that there is an analogy between good parental discipline in this respect and the therapist's control of "acting out." Permissiveness should in general be restricted to expression in *symbolic* form—in fantasies, dreams, and preoccupations. Similarly the child is given stories—in our day "comics," radio programs, and so forth—but is restrained from too much overt performance.

The second aspect is support. Here the important point is that in the Oedipal phase, the support should not be in continuing the love dependency with the mother, but acceptance in full membership in the *family* as a larger system. The focus of the support then is not found in the parents distributively as individuals but *collectively* as a team. One may perhaps say that the parental couple as *married* become an object of transference, both positive and negative. Hence their erotic relationship to each other becomes a critical focus of symbolic preoccupation; the central meaning reference presumably concerns the privileges of maturity. This must surely be one of the reasons for the child's preoccupation with sex. It also has much to do with problems of the incest taboo which cannot be taken up here.

Denial of reciprocity and manipulation of rewards then have to do with what are generally treated as the problems of "discipline" of the growing child. Above all, it seems to follow from the whole situation that the child tends to seek reciprocation for two types of illegitimate wishes, those expressing his dependency needs and his aggression. Here certainly the proper parental attitude bears a close resemblance to that of a good therapist in that refusal to reciprocate is essential but at the same time is not allowed to destroy the supportive attitude. Here again the importance of the solidarity of the parents with each other is evident. Perhaps the commonest source of trouble is a situation where the child can "play them off against each other." Much the same is to be said about the manipulation of rewards, especially by attitudes of approval and disapproval. The most important point is that only sufficiently mature performance should be rewarded but equally the reward should be generously forthcoming when earned. The importance of the solidarity of the parents is again evident.

What then is the significance of a team of two parents with differentiated roles in place of one therapist? It must be remembered that the adult patient has, however imperfectly, already been socialized—he has a "mature self" with which the therapist can deal. This is not true of the child, who must be motivated to undertake and carry through the difficult process of acquiring a strong ego and superego.

It is suggested that differentiation of function between two agents makes it possible both to mitigate the inevitable strains of the process and to provide more strategic vantage points for the application of leverage. In the first place, the love dependency on the mother is so crucial that too abrupt discontinuance would be seriously traumatic. In order to minimize abrupt disturbance of this, it is a great advantage to have the father available as an object on which to *displace* both aggression and some elements of exaggerated dependency, for example, romantic idealization of his "omnipotence." His greater "distance" from the child has its positive functions. By the same token the imposition of demands by the "authority" of the father also has its functions. In general, we may suggest that the permissive-supportive aspect of control of the child is more concentrated in the mother role, the symbolic focus of the disciplinary aspect more in that of the father. The critical point is the *symbolic* focus in each respect. Its relation to actual implementation is very complex.

It is further clear, however, how important is the fact that the role-differentiation between the parents should be a genuine differentiation within an integrated system. The solidarity of the parental couple is the keystone of the integration of the family as a social system, in this as in other respects.

Only a few words need to be said in conclusion. Essentially what I have attempted to do in this paper is to show in one particular field how some of the most important findings of psychoanalysis can be fitted together with some of the findings of social science. This fitting together may necessitate modification of some specific interpretations previously current in psychoanalysis, and some of the perspectives of psychoanalysis, just as psychoanalysis has influenced social science.

This problem of adjustment of the frames of reference, terminologies, and foci of interest in problems always exists when two relatively independently originating traditions of thought attempt to come together—the difficulties should not be underestimated, but given good will and competent work, they are probably not insuperable. To me the overwhelming impression is not that of difference and difficulty of understanding, but the striking closeness of fit of the results of the two scientific traditions.

The psychoanalytic procedure has immensely widened our observational knowledge of the subtle dynamics of human motivation, and psychoanalytic theory has given us what so far is our most sophisticated conceptual scheme for the analysis of personality as a system. Now that part of social science which I may call the theory of social systems proves, largely independently, to have produced results which directly complement those of psychoanalysis (and of course other branches of psychology).

When the two traditions are put together the range of theoretical reasoning which becomes possible is immensely wider than before, with correspondingly greater scientific resources for tackling empirical problems than could have been commanded so long as the two traditions remained separate.

My hope is that this paper, by showing this fit of psychoanalytic and sociological analysis in some detail for the problem area of the Oedipus complex, will have caught the imagination of some of the psychoanalytic group. What is important is not that what has here been said should constitute a finished product—as such it is small and fragmentary indeed. It is rather the promise of increased understanding and control of human action through mobilizing together the intellectual resources of two great bodies of thought toward a common scientific goal.

REFERENCES

1. Parsons, Talcott, and Shils, Edward A., with the assistance of James Olds. Values, Motives, and Systems of Action. (In *Toward a General Theory of Action*. Edited by Talcott Parsons and Edward A. Shils. Cambridge, Mass., Harvard University Press, 1952, pp. 47–275).

2. Parsons, Talcott. The Superego and the Theory of Social Systems. *Psychiatry*, 15: 15–25, 1952.

3. Kluckhohn, Florence R. Dominant and Substitute Profiles of Cultural Orientations: Their Significance for the Analysis of Social Stratification. *Social Forces*, 28: 376–393, 1950.

4. Bales, Robert F. *Interaction Process Analysis;* a method for the study of small groups. Cambridge, Mass., Addison-Wesley Press, 1950.

5. Parsons, Talcott; Bales, Robert F.; and Shils, Edward A. *Working Papers in the Theory of Action*. Glencoe, Ill., Free Press, 1953. Chap. IV.

6. Parsons, Talcott. Illness and the Role of the Physician: A Sociological Perspective. *Am. J. Orthopsychiat.*, 21: 452–460, 1951.

7. Parsons, Talcott. *The Social System*. Glencoe, Ill., Free Press, 1951. Chaps. VII and X.

8. Stouffer, Samuel A., and Others. *The American Soldier*. Princeton, N.J., Princeton University Press, 1949. (*Studies in Social Psychology in World War II*, Vols. 1–2.)

9. Merton, Robert K., and Lazarsfeld, Paul F., Editors. *Continuities in Social Research;* studies in the scope and method of "The American Soldier." Glencoe, Ill., Free Press, 1950.

Discussion

DAVID SHAKOW, PH.D.

WITH THE kind permission of Doctor Parsons, I shall not consider further the points he has made nor deal with the theoretical relations of psychoanalysis and general psychology. Instead, I wish to raise with you problems connected with some aspects of these relationships. In some ways, my comments tie in with both parts of the program, since they relate to both training and research.

This vigentennial celebration of an Institute that has been in the forefront of many advances in psychoanalysis, though perhaps not so great a landmark in the development of the field as the meeting at Clark University in 1909, is still significant, for it comes at a period when psychoanalysis appears to be entering a new era of security and maturity growing out of the recognition of the significant contribution it has made to many fields. Psychoanalysis is at a point where its choice of direction for the future can be deliberate, and determined by the objective needs of the situation. The evidences for this status are many and are too well known to require recounting.

With respect to the social sciences, the area of especial interest at the moment, it is no longer necessary to marshal the evidence of the tremendous impact that psychoanalysis has had upon them and particularly upon psychology. The skeptics that remain should read Brosin's (2) recent survey and Boring's (1) history of psychology. In 1924, when the first edition of his *History of Experimental Psychology* was published, Boring, the historian of psychology, had not even reached the stage of being skeptical about psychoanalysis. In this volume there are only four passing references to Freud and one to psychoanalysis. In the second edition, published a quarter of a century later, Boring finds that Freud can no longer be ignored, a condition which for the historian, he points out, is the test of greatness. There are eight pages on Freud and four more on psychoanalysis, as well as some thirty other references elsewhere in the text. Although Wundt's still remains the portrait of the frontispiece, Freud has in other ways replaced him in importance—and even gone beyond him. For Helmholtz, Darwin, James, and Freud are now recognized as the great men of psychology's history—a status never given to Wundt. This evaluation, it must be pointed out, occurs in a history of *experimental* psychology, in which the psychology of personality and motivation necessarily takes a decidedly secondary role. I have on another occasion (4) discussed the present predominating interest in the field of motivation and the increasing tendency to view other areas in psychology from the motivational point of view, both genetically and dynamically. These influences stemming largely from Freud are reflected in the content of much of today's experiment as well as in contemporary theory.

If we ask what the major tasks before psychoanalysis now are, I believe that students of the field would be in fairly general agreement that one such task is the consolidation of psychoanalytic contributions about personality within the scientific framework. This calls, on the one hand, for facing up to the many difficulties that all social, and even biological, scientists have in different degrees to meet. I refer to such problems as the markedly heterogeneous universe from which samples must be drawn, the difficulties of translating concepts into testable hypotheses, the especially difficult problem of repeating observations, and the especially difficult problem of the effect of the observer upon the observed. Of all research, the last is perhaps most prominent in psychoanalytic research, for in no other area is the dependence upon the individual observer as instrument so great, the investigatory processes so clandestine, and the identification of the investigator with his theory so profound. Because of this, there is especial danger of ending up with what J. Robert Oppenheimer has called a "self-sealing system."

On the other hand, the achievement of consolidation requires psychoanalysis to make its determinism explicit, to identify and make public the data on which its predictions are made, and to test these predictions by relevant methods.

In this connection, you may be interested to hear of the reactions of some basic scientists to the problem. A few years ago a group of outstanding physical scientists, responsible for the organization of intensive conferences in different areas of science, considered seriously the advisability of having a week-long symposium concerned with the assessment and evaluation of the scientific evidence in psychoanalysis. In order to make a decision, the group met with persons in various ways interested in the area. The kinds of questions that came up repeatedly were of this nature: What is the "evidence" for the validity of the theories? What basic changes of theory have taken place since Freud? What data have influenced the changes? What are the raw data on which psychoanalytic theory is based? What standard of scientific rigor is represented in the collection of data? The committee, though generally sympathetic, finally decided against holding the symposium at the time because of the belief that there was not enough "evidence" of the kind that roughly met their own criteria of evidence to make worth while a five-day meeting.

What I have indicated as a present need seems self-evident. Why has there been so much delay in psychoanalysis becoming a part of the family of sciences?

Some of the factors are clear. They are manifestly an outgrowth of the marked opposition both in medicine and in psychology which the presentation of psychoanalytic data and hypotheses aroused. (It might be pointed out that in the earlier days psychology was perhaps more accepting of psychoanalysis than medicine.) Both directly and defensively this attitude resulted in a separation from the sciences and from medicine. In this atmosphere, too, it is not surprising that a sense of isolation developed, an attitude resulting in a reluctance for integration with other fields.

Another factor appears to have played a most important part —the fact that psychoanalysis is a therapeutic device as well as an investigative method leading to a certain body of theory. It was this practical aspect of psychoanalysis which, working against the previously mentioned forces, inevitably tied it closely, through psychiatry, to medicine. In time, with the gradual conquest over prejudice, the affiliation with medicine became increasingly close. There was, however, no parallel affiliation with university science and psychology, where with respect to theory at least, it logically belonged. Psychology would have profited from such an association, and psychoanalysis, too, might have reciprocally benefited. The affiliation with medicine has certainly led to distinct gains in range of activity and in power. Whether it has had some negative effects, one cannot say with certainty; my conjecture is that it had.

The integral relationship of therapy and theory in psychoanalysis has had many advantages. The almost constant contact with the raw material and the facilitation of movement back and forth from the field of the study are duplicated almost nowhere else. Unfortunately, such a close relationship also carries with it certain disadvantages. One of these is the tendency for the practical to take precedence, both because of its direct demand value and because of the greater monetary and immediate social rewards. Another disadvantage is the almost total limitation of participation in the field to persons with medical training. Such a policy results in the exclusion of classes of persons whose fundamental interests are more apt to be on the investigative and theoretical side. Both of these factors have, I believe, handicapped the development of psychoanalysis and the achievement of its full promise.

So much for a glimpse of historical aspects. Psychoanalysis, having achieved high status and security, should now be able to reduce some of its preoccupations with the past and with the present, and plan more systematically for the future.

Psychoanalysis, as has so clearly been recognized in the program of this Conference, has to plan ahead in two major areas: (1) in relation to training of both psychoanalytic and other therapists; (2) in relation to the development of psychoanalysis through research. Relatively more effort will, I believe, have to be directed to the latter goal than has been the case in the past. This is so for two reasons. First, because therapeutic activity is much more likely to draw support. Besides requiring less nurture, considerable outside pressure to meet immediate needs in this area is likely to be exerted. Second, because the research goal is ultimately the more important. I should like to devote my final remarks to the consideration of this area, not as relates to content, but rather in relation to training.

I make a plea not only for greater recognition by institutes of the importance of research in psychoanalysis, but for emphasis on training programs that are oriented toward the development of persons who can contribute effectively to research. This will necessarily involve institutes in giving to research a status and a proportion of staff time and resources that has not been possible in the past.

It appears to many who examine the present scene, including myself, that if such aims are to be accomplished, a change in certain policies of psychoanalytic institutes, particularly policies relating to the recruitment of students, is called for.

Psychoanalysis too rarely attracts from medicine persons with a research outlook and motivation. On the other hand, as I pointed out earlier, psychoanalysis has, because of its therapeutic emphasis, almost entirely cut itself off from recruiting nonmedically trained persons. In fact, such persons have generally had to break down quite formidable barriers in order to be able to work at all in psychoanalysis.

When we consider the predominant social science aspects of psychoanalysis, and for the present, speaking non-reductively, the importance of this aspect cannot be denied, one wonders if psychoanalysis has not been remiss in not actively seeking out young social scientists for training to supplement its recruits with medical training. Psychoanalysis has a great need for social scientists who have shown promise in their own specialties and who are strongly motivated to continue in the investigative area related to psychoanalysis. The need of social science for psychoanalysis does not require emphasis and is, I trust, implicit in everything I say.*

There are many reasons why such action seems called for. In fact, it appears the only reasonably practical measure to achieve the stated goal. The constriction of the population from which psychoanalysis has permitted itself to draw has led not only to an artificial limitation of the number of research workers, but has also resulted in a narrowing of the base of the field, effects that one cannot help believing have hindered the more rapid scientific advance of psychoanalysis.

Both of these points are perhaps obvious, but I should like to develop at least the second briefly. Alan Gregg (3) has com-

* Many of the points I make hold for biological science investigators as well; it is my assignment that leads me to limit my remarks to the social science area.

mented in relation to medicine generally that the problem of the recruitment of persons for research is made particularly difficult. The student at the end of his training period has open to him not only a research career but also a career of practice which offers substantially greater financial rewards. In the particular branch of medicine of greatest interest to us at this Conference, psychiatry, a field where the training investment is even greater, the competition from practice will inevitably be keener. For the nonmedical student, on the contrary, such competition is practically nonexistent. And what is perhaps even more important, these students, especially the ablest of the group, have already gone through a process of selection of field of interest which does a great deal to ensure a life devoted to scholarship or research in the academy.

Such considerations raise a problem that has, I am sure, troubled many of you for a long time. I refer to the handicaps under which independent psychoanalytic institutes with a serious interest in research, but carrying a heavy burden of therapy training programs, have to struggle in our present-day culture. Can the superego supports so necessary for perseverance in research be made available in such institutions? It is, indeed, an unusual person who can in these days maintain himself against the pressures to redeem the many hostages he has had to give to fortune because of his long period of preparation for a career. When to this load is added that of keeping up with the Worldly Joneses, the person who bears up is even more unusual. In the semi-protected environment of the university, where one's associates feel less of this pressure to redeem, and where the goals of the Academic Joneses are somewhat different from that of their worldly cousins, goals organized in a pattern more consonant with the values of a life oriented to teaching, research, and scholarship, one is more likely to get the community support for one's superego that most of us, with very few exceptions, need. Outside of the academy, I am sure you will agree, such conditions are much more difficult to attain.

For these reasons, if we are interested in meeting the research needs of psychoanalysis, we must consider whether ultimately a much closer relationship of institutes and universities is not called for, perhaps even to the extent of actual integration of the institute into the university. Such a step would not only have reciprocal benefits for psychoanalysis and the university fields but also would result in an increase of the number of both medically trained and nonmedically trained investigators. Whitehorn, in the appropriately entitled "Academic Lecture" (5) at the 1952 meeting of the American Psychiatric Association, has presented some major arguments for this point of view.

What shall we say about the program of training to be provided for such social science students? I do not believe that any of us is prepared to be very specific. On several general points I am, however, convinced, first, that the program must be *experimental;* and second, that the training must be determined by the *needs* of the situation and not by irrelevant factors. My own present view with regard to specifics is that a personal psychoanalysis is *sine-qua-nonical,* and some form of supervised analytic work almost so. In addition, a considerable part of the present program of training is probably valuable—some of it less so. In any case, experimentation and individualization are necessary. Whatever is done, however, should be determined by the needs of the training and not by irrelevant factors such as fears that the student may eventually go into the practice of therapy, or the *fach*-symbolic emotional investment in the "control" case.

On several occasions recently I have had to try to see psychologists as they are perceived by different groups of psychiatrists. Being visually minded, these "empathies" tend to come to me in the form of visual images. In relation to certain psychiatrists, two images pretty consistently come to mind: One is that of a big pre-Soviet Russian moujik (you know the stereotype) with a scratch across his face; the second is that of a couch with somebody hidden underneath. If these were my own images, I would, for an audience such as the present, just take a chance and let you make your own interpretations. But since these images really belong to these groups of psychiatrists, I must not hazard misinterpretation. I shall therefore tell you what they really stand for. In some psychiatric circles, the prevalent notion appears to be that one has only to scratch the surface of a psychologist to uncover a "hell-bent-for-therapy" Tartar. And in some less symbolically minded psychiatric circles there is a notion that a psychologist is hidden under every therapeutic couch, ready to pop out any minute to take over the therapeutic armchair.

May I suggest that these images are both based on definite sampling errors? Undoubtedly, they are correct for some persons. For the great majority of psychologists, however, it would take quite deep surgery rather than a scratch to get at the Tartar, surgery at a depth that discloses the universal projective Tartar. As for our friend under the couch, I have a suspicion that most frequently he prefers to remain right where he is during the session, left alone to manipulate the levers he has attached to the springs and to change the disks on the turntable, and when the session is over, to be able to study the records he has collected. Most psychologists, you know, sublimate their impulses pretty well at the level of finding out.

A psychoanalysis primarily interested in the advancement of knowledge will discard the narrowness and the defensiveness revealed by these and similar images. We are *not* discussing here the training of students from the social sciences as practicing therapists—this is an entirely different problem not at all relevant. We are discussing a much more important problem—that of the preparation of promising nonmedical investigators about whom this issue does not arise. Their designation as competent and ready for such a program defines them as persons aware of the goals as well as the limitations and range of their training and needs. The only legitimate question here, given the right person, is: What is the very best training he should have to help him in making a contribution to the advancement of the field?

The combination *within* persons of theoretical knowledge both in their own field—whether it be sociology or anthropology or one of several branches of academic psychology—and in psychoanalysis, to which are added scientific discipline and a direct and deep contact with the psychological complexities of the human organism, and the combination of such social science investigators *with* medically trained investigators who have gone through a parallel but different program should do much for the effective integration of psychoanalysis into the behavioral sciences. It should do a great deal, too, to increase the potential contribution of these sciences. I am not implying that a miraculous advance is likely to result. I am certain that seminal notions such as those of a Freud are most unlikely to come from such training or such associations. They come rather from the persons who walk alone. I have elsewhere (4) expressed myself on the need for accepting the relatively slow tempo of development in the social sciences. This program may be recommended as one means of possible speeding up this slow process.

REFERENCES

1. Boring, E. G. *A History of Experimental Psychology*. Second Edition. New York, Appleton-Century-Crofts, 1950.
2. Brosin, Henry W. A Review of the Influence of Psychoanalysis on Current Thought. (In *Dynamic Psychiatry*. Edited by Franz Alexander

and Helen Ross. Chicago, University of Chicago Press, 1950. pp. 508–553).

3. Gregg, Alan. *The Furtherance of Medical Research.* New Haven, Yale University Press, 1941.

4. Shakow, David. Some Aspects of Mid-Century Psychiatry: Experimental Psychology. (In *Mid-Century Psychiatry.* Edited by Roy R. Grinker. Springfield, Ill., C. C. Thomas, 1953. pp. 76–103).

5. Whitehorn, John C. The Meaning of Medical Education in Our Society. *Am. J. Psychiat.,* 109: 81–88, 1952.

Discussion

JOHN P. SPIEGEL, M.D.

PROFESSOR PARSONS is one of those remarkable persons who seem to be at home with the vocabulary and concepts of practically any scientific discipline. In fact, he stimulates in me exactly the same kind of admiration and envy I experience whenever I listen to someone who has mastered three or four foreign languages. Undoubtedly, it is this breadth of interest which has made it possible for him to do creative work in the borderlands between various professions. I am also sure, on the basis of much experience, that for this reason a study of his work is richly rewarding. For he is one of a small band of valiant scientists who have attempted to bring order into the vast and untidy field of the theory of human behavior. This effort has been all the more exacting because of the resistance put up by the highly specialized disciplines, such as psychoanalysis, to being broadened, reinterpreted, or synthesized with the social sciences.

This exposition is typical of Parsons' effort to develop psychological theory and sociological theory in such a fashion that they can both be brought into the same frame of reference. I shall not discuss the details of this paper because the range of its content is too broad and too specific—at least where the Oedipus complex is concerned—to be handled briefly. I shall rather deal with one or two aspects of Parsons' methodological approach which seem to me significant to the possibilities of integration between psychoanalysis and the social sciences.

The framework of my discussion is the question of the position of the scientific observer relative to his data. It is coming to be increasingly evident that much of the confusion at the theoretical level of the behavioral sciences is due to the fact that the theoretician has not bothered to define the nature and position of the human observer—who is, after all, the only operational instrument we have in this area. Such questions as the possibility of reducing psychology to biology, on the one hand, or of explaining it entirely on the basis of social theory, on the other, are entirely the result of omitting to specify the observer and the way he collects his data.

Before I become too abstract, let me present, by way of illustration, a fragment of a concrete observation from a psychoanalytical situation. A highly intelligent young female patient was in treatment because of unhappiness in her marriage, and because she was blocked in her desire for a professional career. She was deeply ashamed of her multiple failures in life. On the other hand, she vigorously denied having any feeling of guilt about her promiscuous heterosexual fantasies which were occasionally expressed in brief affairs with married men. She explained these actions to herself as simply pleasurable episodes completely in harmony with her moral code. The problem of the analysis centered about the repressed sense of guilt and its denial through the mechanism of shame in the interplay of forces so lucidly described by Gerhart Piers.* On one occasion

* Piers, Gerhart, and Singer, Milton B. *Guilt and Shame.* Springfield, Ill., C. C. Thomas (in press).

she was calmly telling me of an incident of the previous day involving her efforts to captivate the husband of a friend. She was very jealous of the professional achievements of this friend, and as she was describing her envy, I thought she was very close to perceiving the revengeful motive behind her efforts to capture the husband, but I said nothing. At this point she suddenly broke off her account, turned around and stared at me for a moment, and then asked me if I liked her. When the question went unanswered, she began to reproach me for being unsympathetic and indifferent to her.

Now let us see what happens if we apply Parsons' method of approach to this commonplace process of events occurring between psychoanalyst and patient. Parsons, if I understand him correctly, states that social roles contain elements that are common both to the personality as a system and to social groups as a system. Thus social roles are the common link to the parallel and correlative analysis of the psychological structure of the individual and the dynamic structure of a social group. Furthermore, he points out that the situation which obtains between analyst and patient is a microscopic social system with all the definable properties of a system such as the tendency to maintain a steady state, to react to disturbances with compensatory mechanisms, and so forth.

Proceeding on the basis of these concepts, if we inspect the situation I have just described for its role determinants and its system properties, what do we see? In the beginning both patient and analyst are playing what Parsons would probably call instrumental roles. In other words they are both working in harmony on the solution of a problem, namely, the cause of the patient's unhappiness. The role of each complements and satisfies the expectations of the other and the microscopic social system which they form is in obvious equilibrium. Suddenly the homeostatic mechanisms of this diminutive social group are disturbed. Now it is well known that the mechanisms under-lying any system of transaction or equilibrium are most clearly evident at the critical points of strain or transition—a point repeatedly made today by Parsons. It behooves us, therefore, to examine closely the change in the role determinants. The patient initiates the change by switching to an expressive, affect-oriented role. She wants to know if the therapist likes her. This is a good place to remark on a point previously made by Jurgen Ruesch.* What we describe in psychoanalytic terms as trans-ference manifestations can be described in role terms as the tendency on the patient's part to manipulate the role relations. Without consulting with the analyst as to his role preferences, and without appearing to perceive the strain introduced into the interaction situation by sudden switches and reversals of roles, the patient changes the role assigned to the analyst. The analyst is thus faced with a choice which has the deepest im-plications. If he refuses the new role assignment, then the pa-tient is frustrated, and the strain in the system of interaction becomes increasingly evident. If, on the other hand, he accepts the new role assignment, the steady state in the system is re-stored, often at the cost of ignoring the factors responsible for the strain. It is this latter solution which I suspect is the under-lying process in what is called supportive therapy.

At this point it might be well to take stock of this method of analysis. Is there any particular advantage in specifying the nature of the roles played by analyst and patient and in de-scribing the state of the interaction system they compose? I think there are two points to be made. The first is that role behavior is the immediately presenting aspect of any type of behavior and we have previously lacked a systematic way of describing it. Parsons is quite correct, it seems to me, when

* Ruesch, Jurgen, and Bateson, Gregory. *Communication; the social ma-trix of psychiatry.* New York, W. W. Norton & Co., 1951.

he describes it as the link between personality systems and social systems. For we cannot hope to be able to classify roles in our work as analysts, even though we and our patients are always playing one role or another. It constitutes the data that are closest to our observation. Yet we have been unable to apprehend it because the classification of roles and their properties can only be derived from observations made by many observers in many different social situations. Lacking any cognitive or symbolic system for describing roles, we have had to rely, as analysts, on our intuitive knowledge derived from breadth of experience. This is the quality which French has named the common-sense grasp of experience, and which others have described as the "definition of the situation." It is certainly the only way in which we can grasp the meaning of any personal or social situation. If we can develop, with the help of the social scientist, a way of systematizing and standardizing our description of social roles in interaction situations we shall have immensely improved our ability to standardize our operations—and it is this facility which is most seriously lacking in all the behavioral sciences.

The second point concerns the normative aspect of social roles. There is a right way and a wrong way to act in a social situation, and this rightness or wrongness is specified with various degrees of rigor for practically every situation. When an individual's behavior departs from the standard role, it is not lost, generally speaking, in meaninglessness, but becomes a variant or deviant role. Furthermore, any variant or deviant role can be characterized with reference to two different perspectives: the motivation behind it and the degree of its conformity with or departure from moral and cultural standards. It is precisely because of this that, in my view, the Parsons method contributes an effective operational tool to our analytical procedures. On the one hand almost all our judgments about the motivation of behavior are based on inferences concerned with variant or deviant roles. As the patient I described above was telling me her story, I was concerned with the variant *femme fatale* role she intended to play toward her friend's husband. Certainly it was incompatible with the friendship role toward the wife. Therefore, I was moved to speculate about its cause. Similarly, when she switched roles and asked me to play an expressive role more suitable for a friendship or a courtship situation, I was again driven to wonder about the motive force behind it.

On the other hand, the degree of dominance, variance, or deviance in the selection and playing of a role must take place with reference to moral and cultural standards which the social scientists are coming, more and more, to call value orientations. The judgments serve as guides to the propriety of action both for the social group and for the individual. They form, so to speak, the cognitive map of the superego, although they tell us little about its underlying dynamic structure. Nevertheless, they are attached, in ways that are known to all of us, to the strongest emotional currents and are thus always operative in any interaction situation. For example, they form on both sides part of the data of observation I reported in the above analytic fragment. The patient claimed moral approval of her behavior while I inferred that she had very strong but unconscious value orientations in conflict with her seductive role. For my part, I had to be aware of the influence on my behavior of my own value orientations. I did not remain silent to her question because I morally disapproved of her role. Still I had to be aware of the probability of the patient's putting this interpretation on it. The discrepancies in the patient's role behavior made me aware of the existence of both conflict and discontinuities in her value judgments. Indeed, the whole confusion in her mind over the nature of the feminine role was conditioned by the serious conflict between her emphasis on achievement values —which require for their success equal emphasis on loyalty to groups—and the desperateness with which she pursued private and individualistic goals.

The perspectives that are implicit in the role—both the motivational forces of instinctive drives (plus the defenses against them) and the value orientations that oppose or approve the drives—refer to systems that are remote from our observation. As psychoanalysts we are provided through our training, through the observations of many other analysts, and through our own experiences in participant-observation with many clues for the systematic understanding of motivational processes. No matter how remote from our immediate data are the inferences we draw about the intervening variables, we can reach a high degree of probability regarding them because of the operational tools provided by our genetic, topographical, and dynamic concepts. This is not the case, however, where value orientations are concerned. These are based on data which are only feebly accessible to us in the ordinary course of our work. Values can be systematized only by reference to social systems and subsystems. They are abstractions from the class, occupational, family, regional, or ethnic behavior of large groups or whole civilizations. We are dependent upon the help and cooperation of social scientists for systematic training in this area. Unless we receive such help we will have to depend on the accidental cultural broadness and social experience of the individual analyst. With it, we shall be able immensely to increase the range of our effectiveness both in research and therapy. It is because of these interrelations that, to my mind, Parsons' theoretical approach offers such direct stimulation to the possibilities of cooperative and fruitful interplay between psychoanalysis and the social sciences.

PART TWO

Training and Research at the Chicago Institute for Psychoanalysis

NOTE

Staff publications cited are
listed under author's name in
PUBLICATIONS, 1932–1952, page 281.

Psychoanalytic Training

GEORGE J. MOHR, M.D.

IN 1932, five students were being trained in psychoanalysis at the Chicago Institute for Psychoanalysis. In 1952, the students numbered 150. During the twenty-year span, certain changes have been noted in the composition of the student body. The first candidates were largely practitioners of psychiatry who had completed their medical training some years earlier, who may or may not have qualified for the Board of Psychiatry, but who were eager to take advantage of the increased facilities for training in psychoanalysis. At that time, psychiatric training in medical schools and psychiatric hospital residency programs offered little or no psychoanalytic orientation.

Immediately following World War II, all psychoanalytic institutes were flooded with applicants returning from military service. The tremendous impetus given to the development of psychiatry by the experiences in World War II with psychiatric disturbances among military personnel is well known. Many military physicians untrained in psychiatry were given short-term periods of intensive psychiatric training and placed in responsible positions requiring psychiatric knowledge and skill. These so-called "ninety-day wonders" actually carried heavy burdens in providing care for the emotionally disturbed men during the war period. As a result of this experience many physicians not previously interested in psychiatry were strongly attracted to the field. Many sought psychiatric training. This enthusiasm brought to the Institute physicians somewhat younger than the earlier candidates, but fairly mature and seasoned personalities with considerable clinical experience behind them.

Recent years, particularly with the establishment of the Associated Psychiatric Faculties of Chicago, have seen a still further change in the student body, with respect to background and training. Many students now decide, during their medical school period, to turn to psychiatry as a specialty. Since qualification for the Psychiatric Board requires three years of psychiatric residency, the candidate seeks psychoanalytic training during this period. This has advantages in that the greatly needed psychoanalyst is enabled to begin his period of service and practice at an earlier age.

While there has been great change in the student body, the Institute staff has remained quite stable. A large part of the original staff still teaches our students, and a number of others have been on the staff for ten to fifteen years. Some of our faculty members have moved to other parts of the country, and now participate in the training programs of other psychoanalytic institutes. Additions to our faculty have been made from our own students, so that an increasing proportion of the teaching is being done by graduates of our own Institute. Every effort is made to have the more capable and promising of the students participate in the research and teaching, in the expectation that youthful energy and perspective will help maintain the vigor and breadth characteristic of the Institute and essential to its growth.

A great discrepancy lies between the demand for psychoanalytic training on the part of the medical profession and the available teaching resources. The amount of time required for the training of a teacher in itself constitutes a formidable obstacle. Aside from premedical college years, the student in psychiatry requires four years in medical school, one year of general internship, and three years of psychiatric residency for psychoanalytic training. The preparatory analysis required of each student takes at least two years, but this period to some degree overlaps the residency years and in its later phases, the didactic part of the training. A minimum period for training in psychoanalysis is three years, but it is the rare student who actually completes his training within this time. Most students need from four to five years. The American Psychoanalytic Association requires five years of active membership as one qualification for the prospective training analyst. Roughly speaking, then, approximately ten years will elapse, beginning with entrance to medical school, before a physician will qualify as an accredited psychoanalyst, and a period of fifteen years before he is accredited as a training analyst, prepared to conduct the analyses of prospective candidates. Add to this the two to four years of premedical college training, and the figures begin to be astronomical. This time factor, however, has much to do with the chronic deficit of adequate facilities for the physician seeking training in psychoanalysis. To be sure, appointments to the faculty include younger psychoanalysts, known to be gifted, who may not have had the five years of Association membership requisite for the so-called training analyst. These younger staff members contribute greatly to the teaching program, but cannot be of immediate help with respect to the preparatory analyses and the supervision of students in their own analytical work with patients.

THE CURRICULUM

The general approach of the Institute to the teaching of its students might be characterized as a historical critical approach rather than one of indoctrination. The basic theory and principles of psychoanalysis are taught in historical perspective, with emphasis upon the evolution and development of psychoanalysis. Emphasis has been placed upon early exposure of the student to first-hand observation and experience with patients. Theory has been taught on the basis of exposure to such opportunity for observation and direct study of patients. Demonstration courses, covering psychopathology and diagnostic studies, are introduced at the beginning of the course. Case seminars are started as early as feasible for the given student. It is our conviction that this consistent and early exposure of the student to the patient vitalizes the student's understanding of the formal courses and teaching, which can be interpreted in the light of this experience.

The course of training requires of every prospective candidate a preparatory personal analysis. The major purpose of this analysis is to further the emotional growth and development of the candidate, freeing him from neurotic character traits or disturbances that might interfere with his freedom to understand adequately and respond appropriately to the emotional reactions, attitudes, and responses of the psychoanalytic patient. The insight the candidate gains thereby about himself and his experience sensitizes him to better understanding of the psychoanalytic experience of his prospective patients. The personal analysis also provides opportunity for the establishment of the suitability of the applicant as a candidate for training in psychoanalysis. Only after a period of personal analysis is the candidate finally accepted as a student at the Institute.

With the emphasis placed upon first-hand experience with patients, the Institute is organized about its outpatient clinic. Patients are selected on the basis of their suitability for the training program and the research programs of the Institute. The selection of patients from the outpatient clinic, rather than from the private practice of physician-students, has the great advantage of ensuring a better selection of patients for this important phase of training.

Since 1948 the Institute has participated in a joint program of residency training in psychiatry and training in psychoanalysis with three cooperating psychiatric teaching centers: the University of Chicago Medical School, the University of Illinois College of Medicine, and the Institute for Psychosomatic and Psychiatric Research and Training of Michael Reese Hospital. A program which integrates the psychiatric residency program with that of the Institute has been established. Trainees in psychiatry accepted for this program are selected jointly by the Institute and the participating psychiatric centers.

The teaching structure developed with the establishment of the Associated Psychiatric Faculties represents a distinct advance in the basic program of the teaching of psychoanalysis. It breaks down the relative isolation in which psychoanalytic institutes have operated. The historic early resistance of medical schools and the medical profession to the teaching of psychoanalysis made it necessary, for many years, that independent institutes carry the full responsibility for this teaching and training. By the time the Chicago Institute was established, a basic pattern for such institutes had been laid down in the development of the Berlin Institute, which flourished in pre-Hitlerian days. Our own Institute has sought to develop a curriculum and to establish methods of teaching representative of the best academic standards.

During the past two decades, postgraduate teaching of psychiatry has come more and more under the influence of psychoanalytic thought. The integration of postgraduate psychiatric teaching with psychoanalytic training, as represented in the Associated Psychiatric Faculties, is a logical outcome of the belated rapprochement between medical teaching and training and psychoanalytic training. Medical schools today, not merely in their departments of psychiatry, but in the teaching of pediatrics, internal medicine, and other specialities, increasingly take cognizance of the significance of psychoanalysis and psychoanalytic thought to the development of medicine and to the training of the physician. There is indication that before many years major responsibility for the teaching of psychoanalysis as a medical specialty will be assumed by medical schools as a part of their postgraduate programs. At several universities, full integration of psychoanalytic teaching into programs of psychiatric residency training under medical school auspices already has been achieved.

Until the many problems inherent in the assumption of responsibility for psychoanalytic training by medical schools can be worked out, it is essential that institutes such as our own continue to develop superior standards of teaching and training, and the construction of curricula that interpret the increasing impact of psychoanalysis upon the field of medicine in particular, and upon the social disciplines as these contribute to the understanding of human behavior.

PSYCHOANALYSIS IN THE UNITED STATES

World War II and the disruptive conditions in Europe preceding the war have had a profound effect upon the development of psychoanalysis in America and abroad. Many established teaching centers in Europe were completely destroyed, or seriously curtailed in their activities. For a considerable number of years, the countries overrun by Germany, and now those behind the Iron Curtain, were isolated from the continuing stream of medical and psychological development. The United States gained many experienced and competent teachers of psychoanalysis as a result of the exodus from Europe. The impact of these psychoanalysts upon American psychoanalysis has greatly enriched the teaching of psychoanalysis in this country.

The American scene has been particularly favorable to the expansion and development of psychoanalysis as a medical specialty and as a basic psychology. Using as a rough measuring stick the "census" statistics provided by records of the International Psychoanalytic Association, it is clear that psychoanalysis has flourished in America in an encouraging manner. In 1931, 216 active members of the International Psychoanalytic Association were resident on the European continent and in Great Britain, 68 in North America, and 6 in Asia. The 1952 membership list of the International Psychoanalytic Association shows 202 active members in Europe and Great Britain, 516 in North America, 31 in South America, and 51 in Asia.

During the twenty years of its existence, the Chicago Institute has played a considerable part in this great expansion of psychoanalysis in the United States through its program of training leaders, now active throughout the country.

Psychoanalytic Therapy

ADELAIDE M. JOHNSON, M.D.

A VITAL part of the research program of the Chicago Institute for Psychoanalysis has been a study of psychoanalytic techniques.

We proceeded with the empirical knowledge that all psychologic diseases arrange themselves along a spectrum of therapeutic challenge. Those at the extreme right might react best to dynamic, highly supportive therapy. Those far to the left might be best helped by an extensive uncovering treatment as defined by Freud for the transference neuroses.

Psychoanalytic Therapy * (Ronald Press Company, New York) published in 1946, presents a report of a systematic study of therapeutic techniques which covered approximately ten years.

In general the research of the Institute resolved itself into an exploration of the following:

(1) What is a diagnostic dynamic formulation of the problems and assets of every individual patient?

(2) What diagnostic criteria are valid in determining the treatment choice?

(3) What are the treatment methods from which to choose, and may they be interwoven as the necessity arises?

* Staff publications cited are listed under the author's name in Publications, 1932–1952, page 281. This book is the first under Joint Publications.

(4) What are the essential psychodynamic factors in any psychotherapeutic process?

(5) Is there a qualitative distinction observable in those psychotherapeutic factors from case to case?

(6) If we can objectively decide the foregoing, can we, and have we the right and responsibility to anticipate certain goals in the treatment process?

These research questions in time appeared to be subsumed under two major categories:

(1) What is the best dynamic procedure for masses of cases along the spectrum that are not suitable for the classical analytic approach or do not require such extensive therapeutic management?

(2) What reformulations might emerge in our experimental approach of postulates and beliefs purported to be sound which we have accepted as the best means of conducting classical analysis?

The possibility suggested itself that this exploration might reveal such additional knowledge as would make an uncovering therapy effective more often than Freud and many of us had experienced.

DIAGNOSTIC FORMULATION OF ASSETS AND PROBLEMS

Alexander and French and others of the Chicago group wrote explicitly and in detail about the need for careful diagnostic formulations and tentatively planned therapy—the need for some semblance of a grand strategy, an idea of the main goals and approaches necessary for treatment with the tactics always subject to change, with complications dictating a profound modification of the original comprehensive plan.

We were aware of the possibility that a great deal of the judgment which enters into a diagnostic formulation, as well as the decisions about what might be best for the patient, was subject to the personality of the physician. Awareness of this danger undoubtedly was one factor fostering the violent criticism of the Chicago group for attempting a careful diagnostic formulation and planning a therapy with certain reasonable goals before commencing therapy. The criticism was: "How can you presume to decide how far this patient should go in achieving mental health?" The criticism continued: "Any diagnostic exploration tampers with and distorts the potentials of the transference neurosis."

The alternative to such a preliminary determination of goals was a trial analysis. Many of us thought that trial analysis for all nonpsychotic patients smacked of the old shotgun prescriptions in medicine: give the patient "the works" for a time and see what happens. If the trial analysis (artificial as it is) is unfavorable after three or four months, and is abandoned, has no damage been done? Is it worse to interfere with the natural evolution of the transference by such careful diagnostic study as we advocate, or is it more injurious to tell a patient at the end of three or four months that he should not be analyzed? Have follow-ups been made on the ultimate outcome in such patients? Who treated them later and how?

Many of the group felt that it was not possible to plan or undertake a therapy without a thorough diagnostic formulation. The Chicago members believed that in the past psychoanalysts had not been willing to assume the responsibility of making a careful diagnostic evaluation initially because of their limited experience. Greater experience and knowledge today make it possible to define more clearly what might be safest and best for a patient. In fact, advanced knowledge makes us responsible for such a preliminary appraisal of each case. We have been keenly aware of the difficulty of this task. We readily admitted that the original appraisal must be subject to continuous re-evaluation as the treatment progresses. On the other hand, to encourage every patient to engage in a trial analysis constitutes an unwarranted failure to assume our responsibility as physicians.

DIAGNOSTIC CRITERIA FOR DETERMINATION OF CHOICE OF TREATMENT

Our next concern logically was what diagnostic criteria, if any, are valid in determining the treatment choice. Such extrinsic factors as limitations in time, money, distance, and personnel available become matters of consideration in planning therapy. These, however, are not nearly so difficult to judge as dynamic criteria for treatment choice. The dynamic treatments to be considered consist of varying degrees of support and uncovering. Also the intensity of the treatment and particularly of the optimal transference must be considered. Each case must be evaluated individually from many points of view: is this an acute neurotic disturbance in a patient heretofore well stabilized; is this an acute neurotic decompensation in a patient suffering from chronic neurosis; is this a mild or severe chronic neurosis; was the childhood background malignantly distorted although the present acute disturbance appears relatively well encapsulated and mild; have the work and social relationships previously been relatively gratifying and productive regardless of the apparent seriousness of the acute picture; is the current external life-situation seriously collapsing or is it relatively stabilized; is it compatible with an improvement of the neurosis; do the patient's assets provide a significant counterbalance to the pathologic features in a given case?

Most of the members of the Chicago group became increasingly alert to sensing the assets in a patient, so that the focus of consideration was as much or more on the assets as on the pathology. Other considerations must be defined and evaluated in each case to decide a plan of therapy. Even if for extrinsic reasons the patient can come for treatment only once or twice a week, the choice of therapy may well be a long, searching, largely uncovering analytic therapy. It would seem there is no end to the necessity for continual exploration and clarification of this subject of criteria for judging treatment of choice. Many more studies by groups should be undertaken to find out how to minimize or eliminate the unconscious uncommunicable subjective factors operating in the physicians' evaluations.

Every effort was made initially to gain a broad perspective of the total terrain of the patient's personality so that the analyst might decide what limitations of goal, if any, should be exercised in treatment. French felt in all cases that this view from the mountaintop was necessary at the beginning lest the participants (analyst and patient) in treatment soon become lost in the gulleys and ravines.

GOALS IN TREATMENT

In planning treatment it was easier in some cases than in others to decide that the analysis of some relatively circumscribed problem might lead to restabilization of the patient; that a complete working through of the infantile neurosis seemed uncalled for in a patient heretofore productive and relatively happy in his relationships. In other cases the experimenter decided a fairly thorough analysis of the infantile problems seemed necessary, but attempted to use new and more flexible techniques to achieve a healthy ego expansion.

Goals of treatment might be far reaching in one patient and very limited in another; decisions were based on evaluation of the strength and structure of the patient's personality, on extrinsic factors, and on the special skills and limitations of the therapist. Evaluation of the correctness of certain diagnostic hypotheses and predictions could be made in some cases. Other cases were evaluated retrospectively—this made them less valuable in the actual experimental part of the program, but invaluable in furnishing data for further experimentation.

Of course, today, much more is known about dynamic supportive (anaclitic) therapy in phases of such illnesses as serious organic conditions with psychogenic etiologic factors, of schizophrenia, and during some periods in the treatment of adolescents.

In the Chicago work, and all over the country today, many therapists highly trained and experienced in the methodology of classical analysis begin their treatment with careful dynamic formulations and some tentative strategy for achieving certain goals which in their judgment the patient can achieve. The analysts so concerned in this work feel that they not only achieve more for more patients but also at times arrive at better results in the cases treated long and intensively but more flexibly.

THE ESSENTIALS OF THE THERAPEUTIC PROCESS

With regard to the essentials of the therapeutic process, a number of fundamental principles in analytic therapy were considerably clarified. In general, it is a sound basic analytic rule that no important changes in the life-situation should occur until after the completion of treatment. There were excellent reasons for such a view; especially the fear that a patient would "act out." However, such a rule can become nothing but sabotage in treatment of certain cases where the patient really should marry or make some important job change as part of his growth in treatment. Alexander has formulated this by saying that there probably should be no important basic change in the life-situation of the patient "unless both the therapist and patient agree."

It is clear that the goal of any uncovering therapy is to make irrational attitudes conscious and recognized by the patient as irrational through increased reality testing by the ego. Even in dynamic supportive therapy the aim is to help the ego of the patient to some such equanimity. In purely supportive therapy one cannot avoid development of the transference neurosis; and it must be analyzed. Certain technical devices are known, however, for obviating as much as possible resistance resulting from intensive transference involvements.

In all uncovering therapy the main instrument is analysis of the resistances arising through the development of the transference neurosis. Believing we had a considerable knowledge of psychodynamics, the Chicago group experimented with controlling the intensity of the transference. It was found that the therapist can consciously direct the intensity and depth of the transference in order to achieve a projected goal. What is interpreted, and the timing and form of such interpretation provide a potent instrument in determining, in part, direction and range of transference feelings. Also the frequency of contact, the distribution between the emotional changes in daily life and transference are means of raising or lowering the intensity of the transference involvement.

These important therapeutic instruments were the subject of a great deal of scrutiny in the Chicago research, and no other part of the study created more violent criticism. This seemed like a real befogging of the one sure pilot light of rational therapy. While insisting on the validity and possibility of such management, it may be admitted that the fears and doubts of many of our colleagues were understandable in some measure because at the time we conducted our research, analysts were not nearly so aware of and frank about countertransference problems as is true today. However, a physician who has little bias *consciously* controls the depth of the transference and restricts its range and direction to achieve the projected goal earlier.

The Chicago group thought that this was a justifiable experimental procedure, that it became the responsibility of the therapist to use it consciously in maintaining the optimal transference level for the best progress in each particular case, no matter whether we dealt with psychoneuroses, organic cases with psychogenic factors, small or adolescent children, or near psychotics.

To be experimental and to avoid the hazard of the therapist's "acting out," the total dynamics of the treatment situation must be consciously managed. Retrospective rationalization of what was done is not in keeping with the scientific spirit of investigation or experimentation.

During our work it became well established that the intensity of the transference and the regression can be increased or minimized by use of certain technical devices such as frequency of interviews, use of the couch or not, the regularity of interpretation of transference resistance and of dreams. How well these devices can be utilized depends much on the flexibility of the well-trained, highly experienced analyst. In anaclitic therapy the therapist consciously chooses to "act with the patient's unconscious needs" if you will, but this is quite different from unconsciously allowing oneself to be maneuvered by the patient into "acting out."

The classical thesis that the emotional experience is the main factor of therapeutic change was re-examined. Formerly the emphasis was on the fact that a transference experience is a less intensive repetition of early pathogenic experiences (Freud). Also it was stressed by Freud that in adult analysis the mature ego is exposed to conflicts which the child's ego could not solve. According to the classical theory, these two factors are primarily responsible for the therapeutic effect of the transference experience.

In our formulation we added a third factor, namely that the

therapist does not respond as the original father or mother did. It was not assumed that parents never react to their children in a healthy manner, but that they are always to some degree emotionally involved in their children and therefore not completely objective. The patient's discovery of this difference was called "the corrective emotional experience." The aim to foster this experience was consistently maintained throughout our work. Alexander stresses that every analysis has an emotional climate, depending on the patient's transference and the analyst's countertransference. He proposed that this emotional climate should become a conscious concern of the analyst and not be left to chance. The traditional aloof psychoanalytic attitude is by no means spontaneous but is highly studied. "The blank screen" can never be realized and the patients often complained of the artificiality. When a therapist has become aware that a patient needs warmth or firmness, the therapist can respond appropriately, qualitatively and quantitatively as seems wise. This is very different from any studied, unspontaneous so-called objectivity or artificial "role playing."

Many patients, such as adolescents and the very ill, may need support, educational procedures, and guidance to avoid breaks. The analyst who has an unconscious need to make the patient in his own image and the analyst who cannot give up the rigid technique of the so-called classical analysis are both unqualified to treat patients who need supportive advice and educational information. Such therapists would be guilty of "acting out" because of their own unconscious conflicts.

In attempting to distinguish between analitic psychotherapy and classical analysis some have maintained that the distinction rests on two points: (1) The classical analyst works with the infantile neurosis entirely as it unfolds in the transference neurosis. (2) The classical analyst is passive, whereas the psychotherapist is more active, at times interfering with the evolution of this process and its potential.

This is an oversimplification of the problem. The terms "passivity" and "activity" need clarification. Actually either behavior, if unconscious, may constitute an "acting out" on the part of the therapist and interfere with the transference potential in an unsuspected way. Certainly, ground rules laid down at the beginning of classical analysis immediately distort the direction and intensity of the transference potential. Transference is one expression of regression, and every analysis of the resistance in the transference leads to deeper regression and greater dependence on the analyst. The analyst with his knowledge and experience exposes the meaning of the resistance, so that the patient consciously makes a new choice.

In analyzing the resistance and exposing new feelings to the patient, the classical analyst does not make the choice for the patient, but only reads or translates the road signs for the patient, who then chooses his direction. We do recognize, however, that the analyst may omit or include mention of certain road signs depending upon his judgment or timing, and so forth. A dynamic psychotherapist, in judging what goal might be possible of achievement by the patient, should, when the ego is working safely, function similarly. That is, he should analyze the resistances that arise in the enterprise and leave it to the patient to make his choice. However, the choice of what part of the resistance he interprets and the form and the timing rest with the therapist seeing his patient two or three or six times a week. Every analyst influences the direction and depth of the transference in this way. When he does it unconsciously, then he is in danger of "leading" or "acting" for his own sake rather than the patient's. Likewise, any good analyst, whether seeing patients two times or five or six times a week, becomes active, supportive, and educational and intervenes with a decision when that patient is dangerously confused and frantic.

Classical analysis as clearly defined by Freud for psychoneuroses is unnecessarily limiting. Anaclytic therapy in the severe organ neuroses, schizophrenia, and the many disturbances of children operates according to rational psychoanalytic principles about human behavior. However, in such therapy, the same degree of passivity by the analyst as is usual in the analysis of psychoneuroses would be nontherapeutic. Likewise, insight achieved by interpretation is virtually useless in certain phases. Analysis of some of these profoundly sick people may be prolonged and extremely intensive. Literal distinctions of "passivity" versus "activity" or interpreting versus not interpreting are spurious criteria of whether or not the therapist is employing rational psychoanalytic concepts and principles.

Some people consider psychotherapy as merely preparatory for classical analysis. That may be the case, sometimes. In many instances therapy may initially be one or two hours a week, without tampering with the transference potential; after a year the intensity of the transference may become so great as to be unbearable without more frequent interviews. This sequence does not constitute a preview followed by a full performance; it is a continuum. Qualitatively there is no distinction whatsoever in the successive phases. Many patients in deep depressions, able to verbalize almost nothing, are only made more guilty by frequent interviews. They may begin far better on one or two hours a week with no qualitative distinction in the two phases. Over-simplified concepts such as "activity" and "passivity" in such treatments have little validity in defining dynamically what transpires. *Is there a qualitative and quantitative distinction in content and affect in dynamic therapies?*

Many physicians who are experienced in classical analysis but have not treated patients one or two hours a week maintain

(1) that such infrequent hours will not expose pregenital conflicts or (2) that anything short of classical analysis *should not* penetrate such pregenital areas: that if such material does appear, the ego defenses are probably weak and it may be dangerous to proceed, or that the therapist has made a mistake in the direction of "wild analysis."

The Chicago group found in many patients, treated one or two hours a week over a long period, that much pregenital conflictual material did appear, but not because of unpredictable wild analysis or enfeebled egos. Others have since found the same to be true and have agreed that the distinction is not qualitative but quantitative in those cases where the therapist in no way interfered with the evolution of the transference. Some of the classical analysts, inexperienced in dynamic psychotherapy, have felt that the appearance of pregenital material was evidence that the therapist had made a mistake. It seems logical to us that in focusing on current relationships and analyzing resistances at the genital level the patient will move in one of two directions; either toward facing some new phase of the Oedipal conflict or toward regression to some safer pregenital atmosphere. If he does the latter because of unbearable tension, it would seem necessary to follow his lead and deal with such fundamental difficulties as arise, to provide a firmer foundation from which he may finally return to face the genital conflicts with less fear. This concept refers to those cases where the original plan was to effect as thorough a reintegration as the patient could master. Throughout, the number of necessary hours per week will vary.

Our research group conceived of no sharp lines between levels of the personality to be explored, but consciously restricted the extent of the analysis depending upon what seemed necessary for a given patient, whether by long, short, profound, or superficial psychotherapy.

The Chicago group maintained that the plan of treatment in many cases may constantly change; that is, with supportive psychotherapy initially, transference complications may so develop that the whole therapy moves into a much more uncovering type of analysis with varying degrees of emphasis in dealing with the transference neurosis. Classical analysts who have no experience in dynamic uncovering psychotherapy often maintain that one can never achieve the intensity or depth of the transference neurosis in psychotherapy if hours are varied during different phases. On the contrary, those of us doing psychotherapy two hours a week have frequently had the experience that the transference neurosis may become so intense as to be unwieldy, that progress could be made only if the hours were increased greatly to "work through" the transference neurosis. It depends upon the patient and upon what is happening in him as well as in the therapist, whether decrease or increase of hours will modify the intensity of the transference reactions. For instance, patients with strong dependent needs, knowing that they can remain in analysis for a long period, five hours a week regularly, certainly will procrastinate about facing the anxiety connected with the dependency conflicts. Decreasing the frequency of the sessions may facilitate awareness of the tension connected with these conflicts and force the ego into greater effort at exploring this problem. We know that regression and indulgence at levels where the patient was formerly greatly deprived is of therapeutic value and often must be granted. Later or concomitantly, however, and with proper timing, the early repressed hatred must be brought to consciousness in an atmosphere of relative frustration.

THE VALUE OF FOCUS ON THE CURRENT SITUATION

We all know how important genetic material is for the therapist's understanding of what is happening in the treatment.

But we know also that treatment becomes much more significant to the patient when he is continuously made aware of what goes on in current relationships, especially in the transference, because that is the proving ground for reality, past and present.

Since our purpose in treatment is to strengthen reality testing, we focus more on the actual problems and turn to the past only to reveal motives for the present irrational reactions. This search into the past is not only necessary for the therapist's understanding but at times is essential for clarifying the behavior of the patient.

Since the best results are achieved when the ego is working optimally, there seems no point in the analyst's overburdening an ego in its reality testing by being so "mysterious" that the transference neurosis becomes far too intense.

GROWTH OUTSIDE TREATMENT HOURS

It is common to conceive of analytic hours as oases of progress in a desert otherwise inert. The assumption that only in treatment interviews will problems be solved can become a dead end. It may constitute an effective defense against facing anxiety which may be painful. Freud himself came to the conclusion that in some cases, such as phobias, a point is reached when the analyst must encourage the patient to engage in activities formerly avoided. Many of the group in Chicago emphasized that the therapist should be aware that a great part of the patient's experience in working through an understanding of his problem transpires outside the therapeutic hour. These relationships therefore should be scrutinized continuously in the interview. This is *not* to say that feelings which should be worked through in the transference should be allowed free drainage into outside channels. This alone will never resolve the conflicts with the therapist. However, what happens outside the hours provides clues and constitutes a proving ground for what is developing with the therapist.

INTERRUPTIONS IN THERAPY

Alexander and some other members of the group have been particularly interested in experimenting with interruptions (other than vacations) to facilitate mobilization of conflicts and testing of the patient's growth, especially in the later phases of treatment. Alexander has emphasized the plateau on which a patient may rest as a defense against the anxiety of moving on into exploration of other problems. It certainly is true that interruptions over a long period will mobilize conflicts in some cases, whereas in others this procedure may serve as proof to the patient that he can now manage many new situations. This technical device, as indeed all techniques, useful in experienced hands, can be misused. It certainly should not be employed to cover up the therapist's shortcomings.

CONTINUING STUDIES OF THE PROBLEM

The Chicago group chose to define its research with the view of (1) modifying the plan of classical analysis so that it was employed as a highly flexible approach to cases across the total spectrum, and (2) re-examining certain "accepted" classical analytic techniques in those specific cases where we definitely had decided upon thoroughgoing resolution of the infantile neurosis.

Another point of departure for research in this subject was elected by the standing committee on Psychotherapy and Psychoanalysis of the American Psychoanalytic Association whose work has been proceeding for the last five years. The view of many of the panel members is that analytic psychotherapy involves a different terrain from classical psychoanalysis, a terrain to be explored and mapped, using the wealth of psychoanalytic concepts as a compass to facilitate exploration and as a blueprint to construct some rational communicable frame of reference for treatment of masses of cases not suitable, extrinsically or dynamically, for classical analysis. The research is proceeding with the hypothesis that dynamic psychotherapy may be an approach as effective as classical analysis with increasingly greater range of applicability, and that it is more inclusive theoretically and practically than classical analysis as literally conceived for the psychoneuroses.

It is apparent that many of the views of members of the Chicago group are gaining wide acceptance. The need for a diagnostic formulation, a flexible plan of therapy, and the dynamic essentials of the therapeutic process in analytic psychotherapy and classical analysis is becoming more clear. The enthusiastic re-exploration of certain concepts previously taken for granted in Freud's original copyright proceeds comfortably in the search for dynamic principles of therapy. It is noteworthy that the American Psychoanalytic Association appointed the standing study committee to explore the therapeutic process because of the national interest and concern emerging from the Chicago research.

Psychoanalytic Psychology

IN THE field of psychosomatic medicine the Chicago Institute has made significant contributions not only through its findings but perhaps as much through the methods used to arrive at them. Scientific teamwork has been achieved here in spite of the very intimate analytic material and the highly developed individualism of analysts. This sort of teamwork has in itself made a novel contribution to the practical *methodology* of psychoanalytic research. In this subspecialty, of application of psychoanalytic findings and thinking to organic medicine, psychoanalysis has caught up with the general trend in modern research which finds a carefully coordinated team of specialists replacing the isolated savant.

Theory of Psychoanalytic Psychology

This phenomenon, of analysts working closely together and arriving at their conclusions in a more or less concerted fashion, is less in evidence when we consider the contributions of the individual members of the Staff toward formulation and reformulation of psychoanalytic *theory*.

To state that most of the theoretical work was done by individuals rather than by the group as such, is not to say that it is devoid of mutual influence, since every formulation has been subject to group discussion and criticism before and after publication. We do not consider that this individualistic approach to psychoanalytic theory constitutes a defect. On the contrary, it reflects a general atmosphere of freedom from indoctrination or conformism, and a spirit of independent critical inquiry.

This state of affairs in psychological theory makes a survey of the Institute's contributions in this field necessarily sketchy and incomplete. There is no clear-cut historical development, nor are there many common predilections. But to report only on the researchers' individual contributions would do injustice to the spirit of the Chicago Institute, which is clearly perceptible yet hard to define. To show the mosaiclike picture of this evasive group spirit, the following is an attempt to point out the "philosophy" behind each inquiry or theory rather than to be too explicit about either method or content.

When Alexander came to this country, he brought with him an attitude toward psychoanalysis which he has documented in his *Psychoanalysis of the Total Personality*. This attitude did two things at once. First, by elaborating and even dramatizing the dynamic interplay between ego and superego, he made both intrapsychic tension and character formation more understandable. The new formulation opened the way for easier application to allied fields of research. Second, the ego was established as the core of the self in understanding psychic structure. From then on psychoanalytic investigation has never left the ego out of sight. These two formulations in Alexander's first book presented a fresh approach, abandoning the overemphasis on the id which led to what Freud himself had called metapsychological speculation. This approach facilitated a fruitful return of psychoanalysis to the two fields from which it had increasingly isolated itself: somatic medicine and biology on the one hand, and psychology on the other.

The next step on this road is marked by the formulation of Alexander's so-called vector psychology, stated in concise form in "The Logic of Emotions." This paper established the close relationship between the psychologic tendencies of incorporation, elimination, and retention and their biologic basis. These concepts, together with the emphasis on polarity in biology and behavior, establish the principles for a "syntax" of emotional life which presents a distinct advance beyond the classic ideas of oral, anal, and sexual drives, the dualism of the life and death instincts, and the concept of the ego as merely a sum of defense mechanisms. (Freud's *Todestrieb* has been thoroughly discussed as a corollary to nineteenth century thermodynamic concepts by Szasz in "On the Psychoanalytic Theory of Instincts.") Later on Alexander added the principle of "surplus energy" to his conceptual system. According to this, all instinctual expressions begin as erotic playful activities which are gradually absorbed into useful functions of mastery and self-preservation. The amount of instinctual energy not utilized for these purposes remains sexual. The emphasis here is on regarding sexuality as a quantitative factor, a kind of discharge, and not as a special form of life energy qualitatively different from others. (See Alexander: *Fundamentals of Psychoanalysis*, and also the statements in a brief article, "Three Fundamental Dynamic Principles of the Mental Apparatus and of the Behavior of Living Organisms.")

Another contribution of Alexander to psychoanalytic theory which proved fruitful is a sharper differentiation between structural and instinctual conflicts. A structural conflict is between an instinctual drive and the superego; an instinctual conflict is between two irreconcilable drives. An important clarification of the structure of the superego is contained in Alexander's "Remarks About the Relation of Inferiority Feelings to Guilt Feelings," and was recently taken up again by Piers in his study of "Guilt and Shame." *

Dream research, too, was greatly enhanced by the first attempt

* Read at meeting of Chicago Psychoanalytic Society, November 1950.

to quantify results from dream interpretation (Wilson: "Quantitative Dream Studies"). This was later highly elaborated by French in his study of the so-called "sequestration dreams." In the latter, the neurotic part of the personality, or the basic conflict, is represented by a figure separate from the ego of the dreamer, thus frequently heralding a successful objectivation and resolution of the neurosis. (See Alexander: "The Voice of the Intellect is Soft. . . .")

The research by French represents a logical and organic continuation of Alexander's attitudes which paved the way for psychoanalysis to become a true basic science rather than a sum of hypotheses related to a clinical epistemology. French's interest centered very early on the functioning of the ego proper rather than on the repressed id drives or the repressing superego forces. He became interested in the normal functioning of the mind as well as in its performance in situations of stress. He made it even clearer that the ego cannot be understood as merely a bundle of defenses but has to be viewed as that "organ" which has the all-important task of synthesis and integration. This line of research brought psychoanalysis into close contact with fruitful trends in modern "normal" psychology, like Pavlov's conditioned-reflex experiments, Köhler's and Koffka's *Gestalt* psychology, Lewin's topological or vector psychology and various concepts of the psychological field, and Tolman's learning theories. French's approach implies more careful attention to the phenomenology of both normal and abnormal mental processes, which in turn facilitates and enriches the analysis of the underlying dynamics.

His research methods include a new approach to the study of dreams as efforts to solve problems and tasks rather than as attempts to express inadmissible "latent dream thoughts." He investigates the way in which the dream process deals with reality factors. French's work is now in the process of publication under the title of *The Integration of Behavior*. The first of the five planned volumes is on *Basic Postulates*.

Benedek's field of research interest encompasses the border line between biology and psychology in human development, as well as the psychology of woman. Her research on the ovarian cycle points out new findings on the parallelism between the hormonal and the emotional cycle in woman. Benedek drew attention to the biopsychological phenomenon of the early "symbiotic" mother-child unit. She was one of the first to inveigh against the rigid feeding schedules and the otherwise "sterilized" early mother-child relationship which endangers the establishment of an optimum degree of confidence in the growing individual. In her concept, human development evolves as a continuous process of adaptation and integration, and not in distant stages characterized by newly emerging drives.

Gerard, Mohr, Ross, and Sylvester work along similar lines, and have furthermore contributed to the better dynamic understanding of various clinical syndromes such as anorexia, enuresis, tic, and delinquency. Josselyn and Johnson have been particularly interested in the developmental phase of adolescence.

Weiss' main object of investigation has been the basic function of the ego in its relation to reality, usually referred to as identification and projection. Weiss is influenced in his approach by Paul Federn's theories of ego states, ego cathexis, and ego boundaries.

Application of Psychoanalytic Psychology

PROBLEMS OF ANALYTIC TECHNIQUES

The Institute has always been interested in problems of therapeutic technique. Since the general attitude of the group tended to view analysis as a basic science of human behavior, analytic treatment became just one of its many applications. Although deep analysis remains one of the most important research tools, analysis as treatment is open to experimentation.

There is probably a widespread impression that the Institute has been predominantly interested in *brief* therapy. It is true that the increasing demand of the public, particularly because of the great number of psychiatric war casualties, created a natural pressure in this direction. The fact that the Institute sponsored the Brief Psychotherapy Council tended to confirm this impression. However, the prime interest all along has been in a *more effective* therapy.

Two different yet convergent factors tend to encourage an advance in this direction, one theoretical and the other experiential. The earlier detailed analysis of the interplay between ego and superego, and the study of transference and countertransference made it seem possible that the therapist could better establish an emotionally significant relationship by deliberately emphasizing one of these two aspects of the therapist's attitude toward the patient. This possibility was probably first implicitly suggested in Benedek's paper, "Defense Mechanisms and Structure of the Total Personality."

The other guiding factor in the entire research in therapy was the repeated experience, shared by every successful psychotherapist, that even cases which at first seem to be intricate and difficult react quickly and dramatically to a comparatively short therapeutic contact and can show not only a so-called symptom cure but also changes in structure and outlook. The group felt that the analyst's traditional disdain for such events as "mere transference successes," "flight into health," and the like, was begging the question. They felt it important to gain analytic understanding of the dynamics involved in such cures.

The results of seven years' investigation are recounted in the joint publication *Psychoanalytic Therapy*. The main theoretical gain here is probably the description and structural analysis

of the role of the "corrective emotional experience" for successful analytic treatment. This book with its perhaps too vigorous
advocacy of certain manipulations in the transference-countertransference situation, aroused sharp antagonism, particularly
among those analysts who tend to regard the analytic procedure as an unchangeable ritual and psychoanalytic theory as
its exegesis. This antagonism contributed to a frequent mis-
understanding of the term "corrective emotional experience."
A corrective emotional experience is not meant as a sudden
dramatic relief of emotions or catharsis, such as a "good cry."
Nor is it a sudden dramatic insight or "change of heart," like a
religious conversion experience. It is simply the growing—conscious or unconscious—awareness of the fact that the present
environment is not a continuation of the infantile world, that
emotionally significant persons are not replicas of parental images, and that this experience has been gained in the immediate emotional relationship to the therapist. In the process of
partial and temporary identification with ego and superego of
the therapist, faulty superego and ego-ideal structures can be
abandoned.

Changes in frequency of analytic sessions and therapeutic
interruptions at certain stages in an analysis were recommended
when they would tend to keep the resistance tension at optimum, when they would prevent an unproductive dependency
or, on the contrary, mobilize repressed dependency claims.

Psychoanalytic Therapy does not contain the only contribution of the group to analytic technique. All clinical or theoretical papers offer generalizations on therapeutic handling, and
most theoretical theses have immediate applicability to therapeutics, or at least must be tested in practice. We mention especially French's study of the analytic process as a phenomenon
of learning ("A Clinical Study of Learning in the Course of a
Psychoanalytic Treatment") and his attention to progressive

ego integration as guideposts in the course of treatment ("Ego Analysis as a Guide to Therapy"). Johnson has made ample use of concomitant treatment of children and parents, not only as an effective means of dealing with the "family neurosis," but also as a research tool. Child analysis proper as a specific modification of the classic approach has been dealt with by Gerard, Ross, Sylvester, and Mohr. Psychoanalytic observations on the treatment of psychoses have been presented by Grinker and McLean, Grotjahn, French, and Piers.

SOCIAL SCIENCES AND THE ARTS

From this outline of the psychological orientation of the Chicago group, it follows logically that the social environment is considered as the other end of a bio-psycho-social continuum. Alexander's interest has set the pace. It is significant that in his earlier study of delinquency (with the brilliant jurist, Hugo Staub) he considered both the psychology of the criminal and his immediate "environment," that is, his judge and the public's attitude toward law (*The Criminal, the Judge, and the Public*). Only in a later study encouraged by Healy did he go into an analysis of the individual criminal character (*Roots of Crime*). Further insights into the psychological genesis of delinquency were provided much later by Johnson and Sylvester.

More than a score of Alexander's publications apply psychological insights to problems of the social sciences. His *Our Age of Unreason* has found widespread recognition as an attempt to look through the psychoanalyst's glasses at history, political philosophy, and sociology.

In our troubled times, it is only natural that extensive treatment has been given to the problem of democracy and the kind of maturity it requires. French has contributed to this discussion, Moellenhoff has studied the Nazi character with its mechanisms of projection, and French, Gerard, and Alexander joined in a discussion about problems of a war society and the tasks of peace immediately following the cataclysm. Alexander pointed out in "The Price of Peace" how expression and channelizing of aggression is possible within the societal structure of a democracy, whereas a totalitarian society which represses the internal struggle leads by necessity to outside aggression. He also devoted a paper to the problems of an atomic age and the possibilities of abundance of leisure for which the present compulsive generation is ill prepared.

Helen McLean has interested herself in the problems of prejudice and racial discrimination and has studied several aspects of Negro psychology. The material for this and similar studies is derived from the personal analyses of members of various racial and cultural groups.

In the first years of the Institute, there were a number of interdisciplinary seminars on an advanced level. Several outstanding social scientists participated and were, to a greater or lesser degree, influenced by their contact with the group. Scudder Mekeel, Lloyd Warner, Allison Davis, Joseph Lohman, and Edward Sapir may be mentioned in this connection.

Charlotte Babcock has helped to organize and has actively participated in a research team investigating the problems of acculturation of the Nisei group in Chicago. A different form of collaboration was demonstrated when Milton B. Singer applied a psychological thesis set forth by Piers to a critique of the anthropological literature on so-called "shame and guilt cultures."

A few papers concerned with literature and literary creation have been prepared by Alexander ("A Note on Falstaff"), Miller ("Balzac's *Père Goriot*"), and Grotjahn ("Ferdinand the Bull"). McLean has conducted seminars on the psychology of certain authors and their literary products. Harry Lee has given sustained attention to the psychological puzzle of artistic creation.

His main thesis, developed in a series of publications, asserts that (*a*) the old analytic concept of sublimation is very questionable and not apt to explain art and artistic production; (*b*) artistic creation is essentially a function of the ego and therefore "narcissistic"; (*c*) more specifically, it is a process of restoration of the maternal image which had been destroyed in a period of depression. Needless to say, this conclusion has been reached from analytic work with present-day artists.

Alexander has pointed out that the nature of esthetic appeal closely parallels the pleasure in jokes and wit as delineated by Freud. ("Unconscious Factors in Aesthetic Appeal," also Chapter 8 in *Fundamentals of Psychoanalysis*.) The content of literary and other art products (usually not greatly varied) reflects tabooed wishes of humanity which constitute the "basic themes" in world literature. The *form* of the product works with the effect of early primitive mentation (rhyme, rhythm, condensation, displacement, and so on). In the fusion of these unconscious pleasures of content and form, artistic appeal is generated.

Psychosomatic Research

THOMAS S. SZASZ, M.D.

CONTRIBUTIONS from the Institute to the field of psychosomatic medicine have constituted the major part of its research activities. Several of these studies have come to be regarded as basic contributions in the applications of psychoanalysis to problems of organic medicine. Because of the large number and variety of publications relating to this field, an integrated presentation of these contributions will not be attempted. Instead, in reviewing this phase of the Institute's work, we will follow a chronological order whenever possible.

The Institute's First Decade of Research

Gastrointestinal dysfunctions, asthma, and the sexual cycle in women were among the subjects studied during the first ten years. The first contribution, a study of *gastrointestinal disturbances* (peptic ulcer, constipation, and diarrhea), was published by Alexander, Bacon, Levy, Levine, and Wilson in 1934, and was among the very first in the field to attempt to relate psychodynamic factors not simply to a disease-picture, as a whole, but rather to specific physiological mechanisms responsible for its development. For example, in the case of peptic ulcer, emphasis was shifted from the lesion in the stomach or duodenum to the (temporally) more primary physiological dysfunction of gastric hypersecretion and hypermotility. The physiological dysfunction was then linked with the "psychological factor" of oral intaking, regressively intensified on account of failure to master some current situation (conflict). It was thus suggested that these three symptoms—ulcer, constipation, and diarrhea—may be viewed as specific manifestations of the orientation of the individual to the external world. Gastric hyperactivity and peptic ulcer were related to receptive or intaking wishes, constipation to a retentive orientation, and diarrhea to a tendency to eliminate.

Alexander's paper, "The Logic of Emotions and Its Dynamic Background" (1935), grew out of the study of gastrointestinal dysfunctions. In it, and on the basis of the functioning of the gastrointestinal tract, Alexander suggested that receiving, retaining, and eliminating also express three fundamental psychological tendencies on the part of the organism toward the outer world. He called the investigation of given phenomena in terms of the relative participation of these three tendencies "vector analysis." This theoretical model influenced a large number of later psychosomatic studies, both within and outside the Institute.

The second major collaboration research program was devoted to the problem of *bronchial asthma* (1941). This study, it should be noted, was influenced by a number of previous publications, and notably by an early work of Edoardo Weiss (1922). The conclusions of this investigation were summarized as follows: ". . . first that the asthmatic attack is a reaction to the danger of separation from the mother; second, that the attack is a sort of equivalent of an inhibited and repressed cry of anxiety or rage; third, that the sources of danger of losing the mother are due to some temptations to which the patient is exposed." This latter factor was also related to the high value which confession plays in the lives of these patients. The asthmatic individual makes extensive use of this device in an effort to protect himself from the danger of estrangement from the mother; if this attempt at verbal communication fails, an attack of asthma is likely to supervene.

Concerning the theoretical and methodological orientation of this work, we may note the emphasis on the concept of overly great attachment to the mother and the fear of losing her. In this study also the psychological factors were connected directly with a physiological function, with the expiratory phase of respiration, which is inhibited. The expiratory act is directly involved in both speaking (confession) and crying, which are inhibited in these patients by their specific conflict.

In addition to, and concurrent with the foregoing studies, there appeared a large number of psychoanalytic investigations of various specific syndromes. Van der Heide (1940) published a study of two cases of *peptic ulcer,* confirming Alexander's hypothesis of the pathogenesis of this syndrome. Wilson (1941) reported on a psychoanalytic study of seven cases of *hay fever* and proposed the assumption "that the psychological component of the hay fever symptom is a result of unsuccessful olfactory repression. Probably the first and most important factor in determining this unsatisfactory repression is that of unsatisfied, thwarted, and inhibited sexual curiosity." The problem of *essential hypertension* was studied by Alexander, Miller, and Saul (1939). At this time, Alexander stated that "we come to the conclusion that the early fluctuating phase of essential hypertension is the manifestation of a psychoneurotic condition based on excessive and inhibited hostile impulses. As such it is the reaction of the individual to the complexities of our present civilization." This concept was expanded recently (1950).

Saul (1941) reported his observations concerning the occurrence of attacks of *urticaria* in a female patient undergoing analysis. These attacks occurred when the patient's "longings for love . . . were especially stimulated and frustrated." The frustration stimulated weeping, and ". . . the urticaria appeared when weeping was repressed and often terminated when the patient wept." In a psychoanalytic study of *eczema and neurodermatitis,* Miller (1942) noted the autoerotic aspects of the skin lesions, and showed that the illness satisfies masochistic needs. Conflicts over exhibitionism and voyeurism were also prominent in these cases. The exhibitionism may find expression in the patient's exposing to others his diseased skin.

A significant methodological departure characterized another major research program carried out jointly by a psychoanalyst (Benedek) and an endocrinologist (Rubenstein). The results of their studies concerning the *sexual cycle of women* were published in 1939. This study differed from most other investigations of its time in that the authors were not aiming at the problem of "psychogenesis," but investigated rather the manner in which emotional and physiological phenomena are interrelated during the hormonal variations of the menstrual cycle. The main conclusions of the authors can be briefly summarized as follows: (1) It was found that different phases of the cycle were paralleled by different kinds of psychological material, as observed in the course of psychoanalytic treatment, and (2) it was possible on the basis of the psychoanalytic data to predict the nature of the predominant hormonal influence in the patient.

This study represents a revival of one of Ferenczi's early psychosomatic concepts—namely, his idea of "patho-neurosis"—which was here put on a more solid scientific foundation. But whereas Ferenczi's ideas related to neurotic formations resulting from, or superimposed upon, organic disease or trauma, Benedek and Rubenstein demonstrated that essentially similar interrelations between somatic processes and psychological trends may be found under "normal" conditions, that is, during various phases of the menstrual cycle. This investigation also demonstrated a method by which the activity of certain physiological processes could be ascertained from psychoanalytic material.

The salient features of this method are as follows: The psycho-analytic data, particularly the patient's free associations and dreams, are looked upon from a particular point of view, namely from the viewpoint of the nature of the instinctual tendencies mobilized at a particular time, and the precise pattern of their attempted integration and discharge. There are two main trends observable during the menstrual cycle; one is under the influence of an increasing estrogen production and is psychologically manifested by a turning of the libido toward objects, by a heterosexual interest, and by a tendency toward genital discharge of tension. The other trend is under the influence of progesterone and is paralleled by increasing narcissistic regression, interest in the self (and in pregnancy), and a tendency toward pregenital types of tension discharge.

The Second Decade

(1) *Theoretical Studies.* Contributions to the general theory of psychosomatic medicine, as well as to problems related to individual syndromes, continued to appear from various members of the staff throughout the second decade of our work. We will first present a brief review of some of the theoretical work published during this period, and will then summarize the work on specific syndromes.

It has been noted that the first psychosomatic study to come from the Institute—an investigation of gastrointestinal dysfunctions—delineated the concept of a vegetative neurosis. However, the exact differences between the mechanisms of vegetative neurosis and hysterical conversion were not clearly formulated until Alexander's publication, "Fundamental Concepts of Psychosomatic Research: Psychogenesis, Conversion, Specificity" (1943). The basic concept is continued in this notation:

It seems advisable to differentiate between hysterical conversion and vegetative neurosis. Their similarities are rather superficial: both conditions are psychogenic, that is to say, they are caused ultimately by a chronic repressed or at least unrelieved emotional tension. The mechanisms involved, however, are fundamentally different, both psychodynamically and physiologically. The hysterical conversion symptom is an attempt to relieve an emotional tension in a symbolic way; it is a symbolic expression of a definite emotional content. The mechanism is restricted to the voluntary neuromuscular or perceptive systems whose function it is to express and relieve emotions. A vegetative neurosis consists of a psychogenic dysfunction of a vegetative organ which is not under control of the voluntary neuromuscular system. A vegetative symptom is not a substitute expression of emotion, but its normal physiological concomitant.

This distinction between two fundamentally different types of symptom-formation has become generally accepted, although it is often stated in somewhat different terms.

The foregoing theoretical constructs led Alexander logically to a more general theory concerning the pathogenesis of several so-called psychosomatic diseases (for example, peptic ulcer, colitis, asthma, neurodermatitis, hyperthyroidism, hypertension). Alexander called this the "theory of specificity" and formulated it in detail in his recent book, *Psychosomatic Medicine* (1950). "According to this theory, physiological responses to emotional stimuli, both normal and morbid, vary according to the nature of the precipitating emotional state. Laughter is the response to merriment, weeping to sorrow; sighing expresses relief of despair, and blushing expresses embarrassment. The vegetative responses to different emotional stimuli vary according to the quality of the emotions. Every emotional state has its own physiological syndrome. Increased blood pressure and accelerated heart action are a constituent part of rage and fear. Increased stomach secretion may be a regressive response to an emergency. Attacks of asthma are correlated with an unconscious suppressed impulse to cry for mother's help. How specific the physiological responses to various emotional stimuli are is still an open question. The proposed theory differentiates principally between two attitudes: (1) preparation to deal with an anxiety-producing situation by meeting it actively, and (2) retreat from it to increased dependence like the small child who turns to the mother for help instead of trying to meet the emergency himself. In accord with Cannon's concepts, the first type of emotional attitude goes with increased sympathetic, the second with increased parasympathetic excitation. Within these two large categories specific responses to different emotions can be distinguished." The second (parasympathetic) group of responses serves no physiologically useful function. These responses do not prepare the organism to meet an external danger, but rather constitute a "retreat reaction." Accordingly, Alexander called this type of response the "vegetative retreat."

One may note that this theory postulates a rather direct connection between "psychodynamic constellations" and certain specific diseases. As in the case of other scientific theories, the question remains not so much whether the theory is "right" or "wrong," but rather to what extent is it useful in explaining observable phenomena. Accordingly, we may anticipate additions to, or changes in, these concepts, particularly with regard to the problem of the nature of the economic function of various organic diseases for the psychic apparatus or the total organism.

Several recent publications throw some light on this problem. Bettelheim and Sylvester (1949) observed the occurrence of various physical symptoms in emotionally disturbed children. These symptoms seemed to serve as significant tension-discharge mechanisms when normal emotional maturation was blocked by environmental (interpersonal) difficulties. When emotional growth could proceed, the physical symptom disappeared. Similarly, in a psychiatric study of patients with duodenal ulcer treated with vagotomy, Szasz (1949) noted the development of a number of new symptoms in a relatively large percentage of patients. These studies emphasize the psychic-economic significance of organic disease (including vegetative neurosis).

Among the methodological contributions, the paper by French and Shapiro (1949) on "The Use of Dream Analysis in Psychosomatic Research" is noteworthy. The ideas expressed here grew from two sources: (1) from research on rheumatoid arthritis, and (2) from French's long-term study of the integrative functions of the ego. This paper shows how the activity of a particular physiological system may be deduced from the manifest content of the patient's dream. In this respect, these ideas are also closely related to Benedek's work on the sexual cycle of women.

A recent theoretical contribution is a paper by Szasz (1952) on "Psychoanalysis and the Autonomic Nervous System." This study draws upon Ferenczi's approach in Thalassa, designated by him as *bioanalysis* (that is, the application of psychoanalytic concepts to biological phenomena). A theory is proposed according to which autonomic functions may be understood as either currently adaptive or regressive. Cannon's emergency responses, mediated by adrenergic impulses, fall into the first category. These responses are considered "normal" when acute, and may lead to dysfunction and organic disease when chronic. Certain persistent sympathetic (adrenergic) excitations of organs or organ-systems were thus termed "concomitant innervations." Clinical syndromes illustrative of this mechanism are thought to include hyperthyroidism, glaucoma, Raynaud's disease, and others. Many of the so-called vegetative neuroses, on the other hand, are viewed as localized parasympathetic (cholinergic) hyperfunctions (for example, peptic ulcer, ulcerative colitis, asthma, and the like). These reactions are interpreted as specific regressions in the functioning of the autonomic nervous system, and are accordingly designated as "regressive innervations." Many of these parasympathetic reactions are the same ones as were designated by Alexander "the vegetative retreat." But whereas Alexander's concept interprets sympathetic and parasympathetic responses as over-all reactions in the organism, the concept of "concomitant" and "regressive innervations" emphasizes the circumscribed (localized) nature of the dysfunction.

Szasz then approaches the economic function of physiological disturbances by introducing the idea of a "physiological integrative mechanism" analogous to the ego. This "mechanism" is further subdivided into three hierarchies, the cerebrospinal, autonomic, and hormonal. It is suggested that the functional capacity of each of these systems, at any particular time, plays a significant role in the pathogenesis of syndromes affecting the various hierarchies.

(2) *Studies on Individual Syndromes.* A number of contributions to specific syndromes have been published by the Institute during its second decade of work. Some of the research begun during this time is still wholly or partly unpublished (for example, ulcerative colitis, diabetes, rheumatoid arthritis).

A collaborative study on *rheumatoid arthritis* was started in 1945. Preliminary findings were published by Johnson, Shapiro, and Alexander in 1947. This report was based on observations in female cases only. The authors' conclusions were: "In these cases the general psychodynamic background is a chronic inhibited hostile aggressive state as a reaction to the earliest masochistic dependence on the mother that is carried over to the father and all human relationships, including sexual. The majority of these personalities learn to discharge hostility through masculine competition, physical activity, and serving, and also through domination of the family. When these methods of discharge are interrupted in specific ways, the persistent increased muscle tonus resulting from inhibited aggression and

the defense against it in some way precipitates the arthritis."
Further observations, including physiological (electromyographic) studies, stemming from this research were published
by Gottschalk, Serota, and Shapiro in 1950. A few male patients
with arthritis have been studied since then. In these cases there
were marked difficulties in attempting to conduct prolonged
psychoanalyses. Some of the patients were overtly psychotic. In
others, paranoid trends emerged as therapy progressed.

Similar problems have been encountered in the work with
patients with *ulcerative colitis*. This project was begun in 1947.
The medical supervision of most of the patients accepted for
treatment with ulcerative colitis was carried out by Walter L. Palmer of the University of Chicago Clinics. The results
of this research are as yet unpublished.

A large body of information has been accumulated in the research program on *diabetes mellitus* which has been in progress
since 1947. The psychoanalysis of a number of patients with this
disease is still continuing. Some methodological aspects of this
study were described by Benedek in 1948. Detailed findings will
be published in the near future.

A paper based on a study of *infertility in women* was recently
published by Benedek, Ham, Robbins, and Rubenstein (1952).
They discussed the functional significance of this symptom in
terms of its meaning in the total equilibrium of the psychic apparatus. Infertility was thus considered to be a "psychosomatic
defense" against serious conflicts (anxieties) associated with
childbearing and motherhood. In part, this work was based on
and grew out of an earlier study of the psychosexual functions
of women by Benedek and Rubenstein (1939, 1942).

The role of psychological factors in *hyperthyroidism* was investigated by Ham, Carmichael, and Alexander. They suggested
a psychodynamic constellation characteristic of patients with
this illness, consisting of severe, early insecurity and a conse-

quent need for premature mastery by effort (self-help). Thus an over-compensatory tendency to help others frequently develops. Clinically, the central role of deep-seated anxiety in the form of a fear of death is the most constant finding. It was postulated that the struggle for the mastery of this "biological fear" may cause chronic activation of thyroid functions and eventually lead to thyrotoxicosis.

Szasz (1949, 1950) published some psychoanalytic observations on *hypersalivation* and suggested that this physiologic dysfunction is probably a frequent occurrence in patients suffering from peptic ulcer (gastric hypersecretion). This dysfunction was interpreted as a specific physiological regression of the upper part of the digestive tract.

On the basis of a psychiatric study of peptic ulcer patients treated by vagotomy, Szasz (1951, 1952) proposed a new hypothesis of the "psychogenesis" of *constipation and diarrhea*. Utilizing psychoanalytic observations in a patient with bulemia and another with ulcerative colitis, these ideas were expanded to show how oral mechanisms (or, changes in the upper gastrointestinal tract) influence the function of the colon and rectum, and may thus lead to hypo- or hyperfunction of these structures. This theory is a departure from the interpretation of these symptoms in terms of retention or elimination. Instead it was postulated that activation, satisfaction, or inhibition of oral impulses can, through a chain of physiological events (the gastrocolic reflex), secondarily lead to activation or inhibition of lower intestinal function. It was emphasized that the final physiological symptom may not have any primary psychological "meaning."

Bacon (1953) recently reported some psychoanalytic observations on *cardiac* pain.* This study was based on material ob-

* Read at Annual Meeting of the American Psychoanalytic Association, Atlantic City, 1952.

tained during the analyses of eight men and four women "who had frequent or rare cardiac pain." A hypothesis is put forward according to which "cardiac pain can arise when in the patient's unconscious, receptive impulses combine with combative ones or with anxiety. It is well known that oral impulses cause vagal stimulation as in eating and digestion, or as in noxious stimulation of the gastro-intestinal tract. Vagal stimulation of the gastro-intestinal system reflexly slows the heart, redistributes the blood away from the skeletal musculature and into the splanchnic area for the purposes of digestion. It also probably constricts the coronary arteries and arterioles. If this anabolic type of circulation with vagal preponderance is suddenly disturbed by rage and/or fear, the increased sympathetic stimulation interferes with the vegetative balance. This can result in a functional disturbance of the heart which can lead to ischemia and cardiac pain."

A major collaborative research program on *cancer* was begun in 1949. The first phase of this investigation was a study of female patients with *cancer of the breast*. A preliminary report about this work was published by Bacon, Renneker, and Cutler in 1952. The major behavioral characteristics of the forty patients studied were: (1) a masochistic character structure; (2) inhibited sexuality; (3) inhibited motherhood; (4) inability to discharge or deal appropriately with anger, aggressiveness, or hostility, covered over by a facade of pleasantness; (5) an unresolved hostile conflict with the mother, handled through denial and unrealistic sacrifice; and (6) delay in securing treatment. It was also emphasized that, "It is not the range or purpose of this brief report to attempt any profound psychobiological hypothesis. If there is any validity to the suspicion which this paper raises, namely, that it is possible for emotional forces at times to provide the catalyst for the cancer reaction, then more general and detailed research on all cancers in both sexes must provide the confirmation and the explanation." In the course of this work, the group became interested in the role of emotional factors in *disease resistance*. The "longevity project" within the cancer study is designed to investigate this subject.

Several of the staff members together with collaborators from other institutions are engaged in very intensive work on the *problem of specificity*. This project is based on what has been described as Alexander's theory of specificity, according to which certain "psychosomatic disorders" are characterized by "specific psychodynamic constellations." Methodologically, this study aims at establishing whether or not, or to what extent, psychiatric data provide clues to the diagnosis of seven syndromes (peptic ulcer, colitis, asthma, neurodermatitis, hypertension, arthritis, and thyrotoxicosis). This investigation is now in its fourth year. The results are as yet unpublished.

Publications, 1932-1952

THIS LIST includes all the publications, individual and collective, of members of the Staff of the Chicago Institute for Psychoanalysis during the period of their association with the Institute.

JOINT PUBLICATIONS

Alexander, F., and French, T. M., et al. *Psychoanalytic Therapy;* •
Principles and Application. New York, Ronald Press Co., 1946.

Alexander, F., and French, T. M., et al. *Studies in Psychosomatic Medicine: An Approach to the Cause and Treatment of Vegetative Disturbances.* New York, Ronald Press Co., 1948.

French, T. M., and Alexander, F., et al. *Psychogenic Factors in Bronchial Asthma.* Washington, D.C., National Research Council, 1941. 2 vols.

The Proceedings of the Second Brief Psychotherapy Council, January 1944. Chicago, Institute for Psychoanalysis. (Published in three parts, separately titled: *Psychosomatic Medicine; War Psychiatry; Psychotherapy for Children, Group Psychotherapy*).

The Proceedings of the Third Psychotherapy Council, October 1946. Chicago, Institute for Psychoanalysis.

FRANZ ALEXANDER

The Accident Prone Individual. *Trans. National Safety Congress,* 1948, Vol. 32, pp. 9–12.

Addenda to "The Medical Value of Psychoanalysis." *Psychoanalyt. Quart.,* 5: 548–559, 1936.

Aggressiveness—Individual and Collective. (In *The March of Medicine;* the New York Academy of Medicine Lectures to the Laity, 1943. New York, Columbia University Press, 1943, pp. 83–99).

Analysis of the Therapeutic Factors in Psychoanalytic Treatment. *Psychoanalyt. Quart.,* 19: 482–500, 1950.

The Bomb and the Human Psyche. *United Nations World,* 3: no. 11, Nov. 1949.

The Brief Psychotherapy Council and Its Outlook. (In *The Proceedings of the Second Brief Psychotherapy Council,* January 1944. Chicago, Institute for Psychoanalysis. Section: *Psychosomatic Medicine.* pp. 1–4).

A Case of Peptic Ulcer and Personality Disorder. (In *The Proceedings of the Third Psychotherapy Council,* October 1946. Chicago, Institute for Psychoanalysis. pp. 18–40).
(Also in Alexander, F., and French, T. M., et al. *Studies in Psychosomatic Medicine.* 1948. pp. 173–191. See under Joint Publications; and also in *Psychosom. Med.,* 9: 320–330, 1947. Title slightly changed).

Clinical Versus Experimental Approach in Psychosomatics; comments on Dr. John Whitehorn's statement on recent trends in psychosomatic research. *Psychosom. Med.,* 3: 330–339, 1941.

Concerning the Genesis of the Castration Complex. *Psychoanalyt. Rev.,* 22: 49–52, 1935.

Contribution to Psychological Factors in Anti-Social Behavior. *The Family,* 13: 142–146, 1932.

Correlations Between Emotions and Carbohydrate Metabolism in Two Cases of Diabetes Mellitus. (with Albrecht Meyer and L. N. Bollmeier) *Psychosom. Med.,* 7: 335–341, 1945.
(Also in Alexander, F., and French, T. M., et al. *Studies in Psychosomatic Medicine.* 1948. pp. 384–397. See under Joint Publications).

The Criminal, the Judge, and the Public. (with H. Staub) New York, Macmillan Co., 1931.

Defeatism Concerning Democracy. *Am. J. Orthopsychiat.,* 11: 643–651, 1941.

Development of the Fundamental Concepts of Psychoanalysis. (In *Dynamic Psychiatry.* Edited by Franz Alexander and Helen Ross. Chicago, University of Chicago Press, 1952. pp. 3–34).

(Discussion) A Postgraduate Psychoanalytic Training Program: Its Evolution, Principles, and Operation at the New York Medical College, by A. Gralnick. *Am. J. Psychiat.,* 106: 844, 1950.

Discussion of Dr. Bassoe's Article, "Spain as the Cradle of Psychiatry." *Am. J. Psychiat.,* 102: 408–410, 1945.

The Don Quixote of America. *News-Letter of the American Associa-*

tion of Psychiatric Social Workers, 7: no. 1, Summer 1937, pp. 1–2.

Dynamic Aspects of the Personality Features and Reactions Characteristic of Patients with Graves' Disease. (with G. C. Ham and H. T. Carmichael) *A. Res. Nerv. & Ment. Dis. Proc.* (1949) 29: 451–457, 1950. (*Life Stress and Bodily Disease*).

Dynamic Psychiatry. (with H. Ross as co-editor) Chicago, University of Chicago Press, 1952.

The Dynamics of Personality Development. *Soc. Casewk.,* 32: 139–143, 1951. (Also in *Proceedings of the Midcentury White House Conference on Children and Youth.* Raleigh, N.C., Health Publications Institute, 1951. pp. 100–105).

Educative Influence of Personality Factors in the Environment. *Human Development Series* (University of Chicago) 1: 29–47, 1942.

Emotional Factors in Essential Hypertension. *Psychosom. Med.,* 1: 173–179, 1939. (Also in Alexander, F., and French, T. M., et al. *Studies in Psychosomatic Medicine.* 1948. pp. 289–297. See under Joint Publications).

Emotional Maturity. *Illinois Society for Mental Hygiene Mental Health Bulletin,* 26: no. 5, Nov.–Dec., 1948, pp. 1–4.

Essentials in Psychotherapy. *J. Michigan M. Soc.,* 49: 549–551, 567; 1950.

Evaluation of Statistical and Analytical Methods in Psychiatry and Psychology. *Am. J. Orthopsychiat.,* 4: 433–448, 1934.

The Evolution and Present Trends of Psychoanalysis. *Congrès International de Psychiatrie,* Paris, 1950. *Rapports,* 5: 1–28, 1950.

Family Problems and Psychological Disturbance. *International Congress on Mental Health,* London, 1948. *Proceedings of the International Conference on Mental Hygiene,* 4: 148–157.

Frontiers in Psychiatry. (In *Frontiers in Medicine; The March of Medicine,* 1950. New York, Columbia University Press, 1951. pp. 3–24).

Functional Disturbances of Psychogenic Nature. *J.A.M.A.,* 100: 469–473, 1933.

Fundamental Concepts of Psychosomatic Research; psychogenesis, conversion, specificity. *Psychosom. Med.,* 5: 205–210, 1943. (Correction: *Psychosom. Med.,* 5: 400, 1943).

(Also in Alexander, F., and French, T. M., et al. *Studies in Psychosomatic Medicine.* 1948. pp. 3–13. See under Joint Publications; and also in *The Yearbook of Psychoanalysis,* Vol. 1, 1945. New York, International Universities Press, 1945. pp. 257–266).

Fundamentals of Psychoanalysis. New York, W. W. Norton & Co., 1948.

Gastrointestinal Neuroses. (In *Diseases of the Digestive System.* Edited by S. A. Portis. Philadelphia, Lea & Febiger, 1941. pp. 206–226).

Hugo Staub, 1886–1942. *Psychoanalyt. Quart.,* 12: 100–105, 1943.

The Human Spirogram. (with L. J. Saul) *Am. J. Physiol.,* 119: 396–397, 1937.

The Indications for Psychoanalytic Therapy. *Bull. New York Acad. Med.,* 20: 320–332, 1944.

Individual Psychotherapy. *Psychosom. Med.,* 8: 110–115, 1946.

The Influence of Psychologic Factors upon Gastro-Intestinal Disturbances: A Symposium. I. General Principles, Objectives, and Preliminary Results. *Psychoanalyt. Quart.,* 3: 501–539, 1934.
(Also in Alexander, F., and French, T. M., et al. *Studies in Psychosomatic Medicine.* 1948. pp. 103–133. See under Joint Publications).

Inner and Outer Worlds. *Survey,* 71: 207–208, 1935.

Introduction to *The Spectacle of a Man,* by John Coignard. New York, Duell, Sloan and Pearce, 1941.

Introduction to *What Man Has Made of Man,* by Mortimer Adler. New York, Longmans, Green and Co., 1937.

A Jury Trial of Psychoanalysis. *J. Abnorm. & Social Psychol.,* 35: 305–323, 1940.

The Logic of Emotions and Its Dynamic Background. *Internat. J. Psycho-Analysis,* 16: 399–413, 1935.

The Medical Value of Psychoanalysis. Second Edition. New York, W. W. Norton & Co., 1936.

Meeting Emotional Depression. *Hygeia,* 11: 215–218, 276–277; 1933.

Mental Hygiene and Criminology. *First International Congress on Mental Hygiene. Proc.,* 1: 745–773, 1932.

Mental Hygiene in the Atomic Age. *Ment. Hyg.,* 30: 529–544, 1946.

Neuroses, Behavior Disorders, and Perversions. (with L. B. Shapiro) (In *Dynamic Psychiatry.* Edited by Franz Alexander and Helen Ross. Chicago, University of Chicago Press, 1952. pp. 117–139).

A Note on Falstaff. *Psychoanalyt. Quart.,* 2: 592–606, 1933.

On Human Motivations. *Mental Hygiene Review,* 1: 72–80, 1940.

Our Age of Unreason. Philadelphia, J. B. Lippincott Co., 1942.

Our Age of Unreason. Revised Edition. Philadelphia, J. B. Lippincott Co., 1951.

(Panel Discussion) Proceedings of the Meeting on Gastrointestinal Disorders of the American Society for Research in Psychosomatic Problems. Detroit, May 1943. *Psychosom. Med.,* 6: 74–76, 1944.

Preliminary Report on a Psychosomatic Study of Rheumatoid Arthritis. (with A. M. Johnson and L. B. Shapiro) *Psychosom. Med.,* 9: 295–300, 1947.

(Also in Alexander, F., and French, T. M., et al. *Studies in Psychosomatic Medicine.* 1948. pp. 489–498. See under Joint Publications).

Present Trends in Psychiatry and the Future Outlook. (In *Modern Attitudes in Psychiatry; The March of Medicine,* 1945. New York, Columbia University Press, 1946. pp. 61–89.

(Also in Alexander, F., and French, T. M., et al. *Studies in Psychosomatic Medicine.* 1948. pp. 14–33. See under Joint Publications).

The Price of Peace. *Child Study,* 25: 71–73, 1948.

The Problem of Psychoanalytic Technique. *Psychoanalyt. Quart.,* 4: 588–611, 1935.

Problems of a War Time Society. Psychological Forces, Destructive and Constructive. Peace Aims. *Am. J. Orthopsychiat.,* 13: 571–580, 1943.

The Psychiatric Approach to Community Welfare Problems. *Indiana Bulletin of Charities and Correction,* No. 217: 487–492, March 1935.

The Psychiatric Aspects of War and Peace. *Am. J. Sociol.,* 46: 504–520, 1941.

Psychiatric Contributions to Crime Prevention. *Federal Probation,* 4: no. 2, May 1940, pp. 10–16.

Psychoanalysis. (with G. J. Piers) (In *Progress in Neurology and Psychiatry.* Vol. I. Edited by E. A. Spiegel. New York, Grune & Stratton, 1946. pp. 681–694).

Psychoanalysis. (with G. J. Piers) (In *Progress in Neurology and Psychiatry.* Vol. II. Edited by E. A. Spiegel. New York, Grune & Stratton, 1947. pp. 500–517).

Psychoanalysis and Medicine. *Ment. Hyg.,* 16: 63–84, 1932.

Psychoanalysis and Social Disorganization. *Am. J. Sociol.,* 42: 781–813, 1937.

Psychoanalysis Comes of Age. *Psychoanalyt. Quart.,* 7: 299–306, 1938.

The Psychoanalysis of the Total Personality. (Second Printing). New York, Nervous and Mental Disease Publishing Co., 1935.

Psychoanalysis Revised. *Psychoanalyt. Quart.,* 9: 1–36, 1940.

Psychoanalytic Aspect of Mental Hygiene and the Environment. *Ment. Hyg.,* 21: 187–197, 1937.

Psychoanalytic Study of a Case of Essential Hypertension. *Psychosom. Med.,* 1: 139–152, 1939.

> (Also in Alexander, F., and French, T. M., et al. *Studies in Psychosomatic Medicine.* 1948. pp. 298–315. See under Joint Publications).

Psychoanalytic Training in the Past, the Present and the Future: a Historical Review. Chicago, Institute for Psychoanalysis, 1951, 8 p.

Psychological Aspects of Medicine. *Psychosom. Med.,* 1: 7–18, 1939.

Psychological Warfare. *Dis. Nerv. System,* 4: 223–224, 1943.

Psychology and the Interpretation of Historical Events. (In *The Cultural Approach to History.* Edited by Caroline F. Ware. New York, Columbia University Press, 1940. pp. 48–57).

The Psychology of Dreaming. (In *Elements of Psychoanalysis.* Edited by Hans Herma and Gertrud M. Kurth. Cleveland, World Publishing Co., 1950. pp. 58–75).

The Psychosomatic Approach in Medicine. (with T. S. Szasz) (In *Dynamic Psychiatry.* Edited by Franz Alexander and Helen Ross. Chicago, University of Chicago Press, 1952. pp. 369–400).

Psychosomatic Disturbances of the Gastrointestinal Tract. (In *Diseases of the Digestive System.* Second Edition. Edited by S. A. Portis. Philadelphia, Lea & Febiger, 1944. pp. 826–844).

Psychosomatic Medicine. New York, W. W. Norton & Co., 1950.

A Psychosomatic Study of Hypoglycaemic Fatigue. (with S. A. Portis) *Psychosom. Med.,* 6: 191–206, 1944.

> (Also in Alexander, F., and French, T. M., et al. *Studies in Psychosomatic Medicine.* 1948. pp. 359–383. See under Joint Publications).

A Psychosomatic Theory of Thyrotoxicosis. (with G. C. Ham and H. T. Carmichael) *Psychosom. Med.,* 13: 18–35, 1951.

Quantitative Dream Studies: A Methodological Attempt at a Quantitative Evaluation of Psychoanalytic Material. (with G. W. Wilson) *Psychoanalyt. Quart.,* 4: 371–407, 1935.

Recollections of Berggasse 19. *Psychoanalyt. Quart.*, 9: 195–204, 1940.

The Relation of Persecutory Delusions to the Functioning of the Gastro-Intestinal Tract. (with W. C. Menninger) *J. Nerv. & Ment. Dis.*, 84: 541–554, 1936.
(Also in Alexander, F., and French, T. M., et al. *Studies in Psychosomatic Medicine*. 1948. pp. 192–205. See under Joint Publications).

The Relation of Structural and Instinctual Conflicts. *Psychoanalyt. Quart.*, 2: 181–207, 1933.

Remarks About the Relation of Inferiority Feelings to Guilt Feelings. *Internat. J. Psycho-Analysis*, 19: 41–49, 1938.

Respiration and Personality—A Preliminary Report: Part I. Description of the Curves. (with L. J. Saul) *Psychosom. Med.*, 2: 110–118, 1940.

Review of Freud's "New Series of Introductory Lectures on Psychoanalysis." *Psychoanalyt. Rev.*, 21: 336–346, 1934.

The Role of the Scientist in Society: A Symposium. (In *Orthopsychiatry 1923–1948: Retrospect and Prospect*. Menasha, Wis., American Orthopsychiatric Association, 1948. pp. 342–358).

Roots of Crime. (with W. Healy) New York, Alfred A. Knopf, 1935.

Section Meeting on Culture and Personality (1938). (Round Table: Dr. Alexander presiding). *Am. J. Orthopsychiat.*, 8: 587–626, 1938.

Sigmund Freud: 1856–1939. *Arch. Neurol. & Psychiat.*, 43: 575–580, 1940.

Sigmund Freud: 1856–1939. *Psychosom. Med.*, 2: 68–73, 1940.

The Significance of Emotional Attitudes in the Psychoanalytic Situation. *Am. J. Orthopsychiat.*, 3: 35–43, 1933.

The Social Problem and the Individual. *Parent Education*, 3: no. 4, Feb. 1937, pp. 19–26.

The Sociological and Biological Orientation of Psychoanalysis. *Ment. Hyg.*, 20: 232–248, 1936.

(Symposium) Looking Ahead in the Fields of Orthopsychiatric Research. *Am. J. Orthopsychiat.*, 20: 73–78, 1950.

(Symposium) Research in Orthopsychiatry; the 1942 Symposium. *Am. J. Orthopsychiat.*, 13: 241–244, 1943.

(Symposium) "Unraveling Juvenile Delinquency"; a symposium of reviews. *J. Criminal Law and Criminology*, 41: 751–755, 1951.

Teaching Psychodynamics. *Am. J. Orthopsychiat.*, 17: 605–608, 1947.

A Tentative Analysis of the Variables in Personality Development. *Am. J. Orthopsychiat.*, 8: 587–591, 1938.

The Therapeutic Applications of Psychoanalysis. (To be published in *Mid-Century Psychiatry*. Springfield, Illinois, C. C. Thomas).

Three Criminal Types As Seen by the Psychoanalyst. (with L. J. Saul) *Psychoanalyt. Rev.*, 24: 113–130, 1937.

Three Fundamental Dynamic Principles of the Mental Apparatus and of the Behavior of Living Organisms. *Dialectica*, 5: 239–245, 1951.

Training Principles in Psychosomatic Medicine. *Am. J. Orthopsychiat.*, 16: 410–412, 1946.
(Also in Alexander, F., and French, T. M., et al. *Studies in Psychosomatic Medicine*. 1948. pp. 34–36. See under Joint Publications).

The Unconscious Motives of Men. *Frontiers of Democracy*, 6: 232–233, 1940.

Values and Science. *J. Soc. Issues*, 6: no. 4, 1950, pp. 28–32. (Contribution to "A Symposium of Commentaries" on: Values and Social Science, by George Geiger).

A Voice from the Past; some remarks on Dr. Bernard Sachs' protest against psychoanalysis. *Am. J. Psychiat.*, 13: 193–200, 1933.

"The Voice of the Intellect Is Soft . . ." *Psychoanalyt. Rev.*, 28: 12–29, 1941.

What is a Neurosis? *Digest Neurol. & Psychiat.*, 16: 225–233, 1948.

Wider Fields for Freud's Techniques. *New York Times Magazine*, May 15, 1949, pp. 15, 52–53.

A World Without Psychic Frustration. *Am. J. Sociol.*, 49: 465–469, 1944.

Zest and Carbohydrate Metabolism. (with W. S. McCulloch and H. B. Carlson) *A. Res. Nerv. & Ment. Dis. Proc.* (1949), 29: 406–411, 1950. (*Life Stress and Bodily Disease*).

CHARLOTTE G. BABCOCK

Emotional Needs of Nursing Students. *Am. J. Nursing*, 49: 166–169, 1949.

The Emotions and Food. *Food & Nutrition News*, 20: no. 1, Oct. 1948, pp. 1–2, 4.

Food and Its Emotional Significance. *J. Am. Dietet. A.*, 24: 390–393, 1948.

Problems in Sustaining the Nutritional Care of Patients. *J. Am. Dietet. A.*, 28: 222–227, 1952.

Psychologically Significant Factors in the Nutrition Interview. *J. Am. Dietet. A.*, 23: 8–12, 1947.

Report of a Study of Cases with Headache as the Presenting Symptom. *J. Am. M. Women's A.*, 2: 329–335, 1947.

The Social Worker in a World of Stress. *Social Service Review,* 25: 1–13, 1951.

Some Observations on Consultative Experience. *Social Service Review,* 23: 347–358, 1949.

CATHERINE L. BACON

The Influence of Psychologic Factors upon Gastro-Intestinal Disturbances: A Symposium. II. Typical Personality Trends and Conflicts in Cases of Gastric Disturbance. *Psychoanalyt. Quart.,* 3: 540–557, 1934.

(Also in Alexander, F., and French, T. M., et al. *Studies in Psychosomatic Medicine.* 1948. pp. 134–147. See under Joint Publications).

THERESE BENEDEK

Adaptation to Reality in Early Infancy. *Psychoanalyt. Quart.,* 7: 200–215, 1938.

An Approach to the Study of the Diabetic. *Psychosom. Med.,* 10: 284–287, 1948.

Climacterium: A Developmental Phase. *Psychoanalyt. Quart.,* 19: 1–27, 1950.

The Correlations Between Ovarian Activity and Psychodynamic Processes: I. The Ovulative Phase. (with B. B. Rubenstein) *Psychosom. Med.,* 1: 245–270, 1939.

The Correlations Between Ovarian Activity and Psychodynamic Processes: II. The Menstrual Phase. (with B. B. Rubenstein) *Psychosom. Med.,* 1: 461–485, 1939.

Defense Mechanisms and Structure of the Total Personality. *Psychoanalyt. Quart.,* 6: 96–118, 1937.

The Emotional Structure of the Family. (In *The Family: Its Function and Destiny.* Edited by Ruth Anshen. New York, Harper & Bros., 1949. pp. 202–225).

The Functions of the Sexual Apparatus and Their Disturbances. (In

Psychosomatic Medicine, by Franz Alexander. New York, W. W. Norton & Co., 1950. pp. 216–262).

Infertility as a Psychosomatic Defense. (To be published in *Fertility and Sterility*).

Insight and Personality Adjustment. New York, Ronald Press Co., 1946.

On the Organization of Psychic Energy: Instincts, Drives and Affects. (To be published in *Mid-Century Psychiatry*. Springfield, Illinois, C. C. Thomas).

Personality Development. (In *Dynamic Psychiatry*. Edited by Franz Alexander and Helen Ross. Chicago, University of Chicago Press, 1952. pp. 63–113).

The Physiological and Psychological Aspects of Normal Pregnancy and Childbirth (Their Significance in Illegitimate Pregnancy). (In *Proceedings Eleventh Institute of the Committee for the Study of Unmarried Parenthood of the Welfare Council of Metropolitan Chicago.* Chicago, April 11, 1951. pp. 2–7).

Psychosexual Function in Women. (In *Encyclopedia of Psychology.* Edited by P. L. Harriman. New York, Philosophical Library, 1946. pp. 667–678).

Psychosexual Functions in Women. New York, Ronald Press Co., 1952. (*Studies in Psychosomatic Medicine*).

The Psychosomatic Implications of the Primary Unit: Mother-Child. *Am. J. Orthopsychiat.,* 19: 642–654, 1949.

The Sexual Cycle and Personality. *J. Am. M. Women's A.,* 6: 335–340, 1951.

The Sexual Cycle in Women. (with B. B. Rubenstein) Washington, D.C., National Research Council, 1942.

Some Emotional Factors in Infertility. (with G. C. Ham, F. Robbins, and B. B. Rubenstein) (To be published in *Psychosom. Med.*)

EDWIN R. EISLER

Cultural Factors in Relation to the Emotional Problems of the Unmarried Mother. (In *Cultural Factors As They Relate to Unmarried Parenthood. Proceedings Tenth Institute of the Committee for the Study of Unmarried Parenthood of the Welfare Council of Metropolitan Chicago.* Chicago, March 29, 1950. pp. 14–21).

Mental Hygiene and Democracy. *Illinois Society for Mental Hygiene Mental Health Bulletin,* 24: no. 4, Sept.–Oct., 1946, pp. 4–5.

Regression in a Case of Multiple Phobia. *Psychoanalyt. Quart.*, 6: 86–95, 1937.

Technical Problems of Social Work in Relation to Clinical Psychoanalysis. *Am. J. Orthopsychiat.*, 12: 191–201, 1942.

THOMAS M. FRENCH

Akinesia After Ventriculography; a contribution to ego psychology and the problem of sleep. (with M. Grotjahn) *Psychoanalyt. Quart.*, 7: 319–328, 1938. (Also in Alexander, F., and French, T. M., et al. *Studies in Psychosomatic Medicine.* 1948. pp. 514–521. See under Joint Publications).

An Analysis of the Goal Concept Based Upon Study of Reactions to Frustration. *Psychoanalyt. Rev.*, 28: 61–71, 1941.

Brief Psychotherapy in Bronchial Asthma. (with A. M. Johnson) (In *The Proceedings of the Second Brief Psychotherapy Council*, January 1944. Chicago, Institute for Psychoanalysis. Section: *Psychosomatic Medicine.* pp. 14–21).

(Also in Alexander, F., and French, T. M., et al. *Studies in Psychosomatic Medicine.* 1948. pp. 249–258. See under Joint Publications).

Clinical Approach to the Dynamics of Behavior. (In *Personality and the Behavior Disorders.* Vol. I. Edited by J. McV. Hunt. New York, Ronald Press Co., 1944. pp. 255–268).

A Clinical Study of Learning in the Course of a Psychoanalytic Treatment. *Psychoanalyt. Quart.*, 5: 148–194, 1936.

Defense and Synthesis in the Function of the Ego; some observations stimulated by Anna Freud's "The Ego and the Mechanisms of Defense." *Psychoanalyt. Quart.*, 7: 537–553, 1938.

Dreams and Rational Behavior. (In *Dynamic Psychiatry.* Edited by Franz Alexander and Helen Ross. Chicago, University of Chicago Press, 1952. pp. 35–39).

Ego Analysis as a Guide to Therapy. *Psychoanalyt. Quart.*, 14: 336–349, 1945.

(Also in *The Yearbook of Psychoanalysis.* Vol. 2, 1946. New York, International Universities Press, 1946. pp. 49–61.

Emotional Conflicts and Allergy. *Internat. Arch. Allergy & Applied Immunol.*, 1: 28–40, 1949.

Emotional Reactions to External Events. *Hygeia*, 11: 221–222, 1933.

Goal, Mechanism and Integrative Field. *Psychosom. Med.*, 3: 226–252, 1941.

Insight and Distortion in Dreams. *Internat. J. Psycho-Analysis*, 20: 287–298, 1939.

The Integration of Behavior. Volume I. *Basic Postulates.* Chicago, University of Chicago Press, 1952.

The Integration of Social Behavior. *Psychoanalyt. Quart.*, 14: 149–168, 1945.

The Integrative Process. *Dialectica*, 5: 246–256, 1951.

Interrelations Between Psychoanalysis and the Experimental Work of Pavlov. *Am. J. Psychiat.*, 12: 1165–1203, 1933.

Physiology of Behavior and Choice of Neurosis. *Psychoanalyt. Quart.*, 10: 561–572, 1941.
(Also in Alexander, F., and French, T. M., et al. *Studies in Psychosomatic Medicine.* 1948. pp. 37–45 See under Joint Publications).

Psychoanalysis and Ethics. (with J. G. Miller and D. Riesman) *University of Chicago Round Table*, No. 638, June 18, 1950.

The Psychodynamic Problem of Democracy. (In *Civilian Morale.* Edited by Goodwin Watson. New York, Reynal & Hitchcock, 1942. pp. 19–29).

A Psychodynamic Study of the Recovery of Two Schizophrenic Cases. (with J. Kasanin) *Psychoanalyt. Quart.*, 10: 1–22, 1941.

Psychogenic Factors in Asthma. *Am. J. Psychiat.*, 96: 87–98, 1939.

Reality and the Unconscious. *Psychoanalyt. Quart.*, 6: 23–61, 1937.

Reality Testing in Dreams. *Psychoanalyt. Quart.*, 6: 62–77, 1937.

Research in Psychotherapy. *Am. J. Psychiat.*, 105: 229–230, 1948.

Social Conflict and Psychic Conflict. *Am. J. Sociol.*, 44: 922–931, 1939.

Some Psychoanalytic Applications of the Psychological Field Concept. *Psychoanalyt. Quart.*, 11: 17–32, 1942.

Some Psychodynamic Reflections upon the Life and Writings of Solon. (with B. Engle) *Psychoanalyt. Quart.*, 20: 253–274, 1951.

Study of the Integrative Process: Its Importance for Psychiatric Theory. (In *Feelings and Emotions;* the Mooseheart Symposium in Cooperation with the University of Chicago. Edited by M. L. Reymert. New York, McGraw-Hill Book Co., 1950. pp. 108–113).

The Use of Dream Analysis in Psychosomatic Research. (with L. B. Shapiro) *Psychosom. Med.*, 11: 110–112, 1949.

(Also in *The Yearbook of Psychoanalysis*. Vol. 6, 1950. New York, International Universities Press, 1951. pp. 123–128).

MARGARET W. GERARD

Bronchial Asthma in Children. *Nerv. Child,* 5: 327–331, 1946.
(Also in Alexander, F., and French, T. M., et al. *Studies in Psychosomatic Medicine.* 1948. pp. 243–248. See under Joint Publications).

Case for Discussion at the 1938 Symposium. *Am. J. Orthopsychiat.,* 8: 1–18, 1938.

Child Analysis as a Technique in the Investigation of Mental Mechanisms; illustrated by a study of enuresis. *Am. J. Psychiat.,* 94: 653–663, 1937.

Direct Treatment of the Child. (In *Orthopsychiatry 1923–1948: Retrospect and Prospect.* Menasha, Wis., American Orthopsychiatric Association, 1948. pp. 494–523).

Direct Treatment of the Pre-School Child. *Am. J. Orthopsychiat.,* 12: 50–55, 1942.

Emotional Disorders of Childhood. (In *Dynamic Psychiatry.* Edited by Franz Alexander and Helen Ross. Chicago, University of Chicago Press, 1952. pp. 165–210).

Enuresis. A Study in Etiology. *Am. J. Orthopsychiat.,* 9: 48–58, 1939.
(Also in Alexander, F., and French, T. M., et al. *Studies in Psychosomatic Medicine,* 1948. pp. 501–513. See under Joint Publications).

Orthopsychiatry and the Profession of Education. Physiological and Environmental Factors in the Learning Processes of the Preschool Child. *Am. J. Orthopsychiat.,* 13: 266–270, 1943.

Personality Development in Early Childhood. (In *Personality Development and Its Implications for Nursing and Nursing Education.* Proceedings of an Institute on Nursing Education. Springfield, Illinois, State Dept. of Public Health, 1949. pp. 17–37).

Problems of a War Time Society. The Modification of Pre-War Patterns. The Clinical Picture. *Am. J. Orthopsychiat.,* 13: 600–604, 1943.

The Psycho-Pathological Aspect in Child Guidance. (In *Handbook of Child Guidance.* Edited by Ernest Harms. New York, Child Care Publications, 1947. pp. 172–192).

The Psychogenic Tic in Ego Development. (In *The Psychoanalytic*

Study of the Child. Vol. II, 1946. New York, International Universities Press, 1947. pp. 133–162).

(Also in Alexander, F., and French, T. M., et al. *Studies in Psychosomatic Medicine.* 1948. pp. 455–488. See under Joint Publications).

Psychology of Pre-Adolescent Children in War Time. Psychological Effects of War on the Small Child and Mother. *Am. J. Orthopsychiat.*, 13: 493–496, 1943.

Trends in Orthopsychiatric Therapy. V. Treatment of the Young Child. *Am. J. Orthopsychiat.*, 18: 414–421, 1948.

ROY R. GRINKER

Cisterna Magna Lead for Electroencephalography. *Confinia Neurol.*, 3: 257–261, 1941.

A Comparison of Psychological "Repression" and Neurological "Inhibition." *J. Nerv. & Ment. Dis.*, 89: 765–781, 1939.

The Course of a Depression Treated by Psychotherapy and Metrazol. (with H. V. McLean) *Psychosom. Med.*, 2: 119–138, 1940.

Electroencephalographic Studies of Corticohypothalamic Relations in Schizophrenia. (with H. M. Serota) *Am. J. Psychiat.*, 98: 385–392, 1941.

Hypothalamic Functions in Psychosomatic Interrelations. *Psychosom. Med.*, 1: 19–47, 1939.

(Also in Alexander, F., and French, T. M., et al. *Studies in Psychosomatic Medicine.* 1948. pp. 46–84. See under Joint Publications).

The Interrelation of Neurology, Psychiatry and Psychoanalysis. *J.A.M.A.*, 116: 2236–2241, 1941.

The Nervous System. (In *Britannica Book of the Year*, 1941. p. 488).

Neurogenic Disturbances of the Gastrointestinal Tract. (In *Diseases of the Digestive System.* Edited by S. A. Portis. Philadelphia, Lea & Febiger, 1941. pp. 227–235).

Panel Discussion. Neurosurgical Treatment of Certain Abnormal Mental States. *J.A.M.A.*, 117: 517–527, 1941.

The Present Status of Electroencephalography in Clinical Diagnosis. (with H. M. Serota) *Dis. Nerv. System*, 2: 276–288, 1941.

Reminiscences of a Personal Contact with Freud. *Am. J. Orthopsychiat.*, 10: 850–854, 1940.

Studies on Corticohypothalamic Relations in the Cat and Man. (with H. M. Serota) *J. Neurophysiol.*, 1: 573–589, 1938.

MARTIN GROTJAHN

Akinesia After Ventriculography; a contribution to ego psychology and the problem of sleep. (with T. M. French) *Psychoanalyt. Quart.*, 7: 319–328, 1938.
(Also in Alexander, F., and French, T. M., et al. *Studies in Psychosomatic Medicine*. 1948. pp. 514–521. See under Joint Publications).

A Child Talks About Pictures; observations about the integration of fantasy into the process of thinking. *Psychoanalyt. Quart.*, 10: 385–394, 1941.

Dream Observations in a Two-Year-Four-Months-Old Baby. *Psychoanalyt. Quart.*, 7: 507–513, 1938.

Ferdinand the Bull. *Am. Imago*, 1: no. 3, 1940, pp. 33–41.

A Few Remarks About Brief Psychotherapy on Psychoanalytic Principles. *Illinois Psychiatric Journal*, 2: no. 1, March 1942, pp. 20–22.

The Process of Awakening; contribution to ego psychology and the problem of sleep and dream. *Psychoanalyt. Rev.*, 29: 1–19, 1942.

Psychiatric Observations in a Case of Involutional Melancholia Treated with Metrazol. *Bull. Menninger Clin.*, 3: 122–125, 1939.

Psychoanalysis and Brain Disease (Observations of Juvenile Paretic Patients). *Psychoanalyt. Rev.*, 25: 149–164, 1938.

Psychoanalytic Investigation of a Seventy-One-Year-Old Man with Senile Dementia. *Psychoanalyt. Quart.*, 9: 80–97, 1940.

Some Features Common to Psychotherapy of Psychotic Patients and Children. *Psychiatry*, 1: 317–322, 1938.

GEORGE C. HAM

Dynamic Aspects of the Personality Features and Reactions Characteristic of Patients with Graves' Disease. (with F. Alexander and H. T. Carmichael) *A. Res. Nerv. & Ment. Dis. Proc.* (1949) 29: 451–457, 1950. (*Life Stress and Bodily Disease*).

Hindsight and Foresight in Psychiatric Medicine. (To be published in *North Carolina M. J.*).

Psychiatric Investigation and Management of Gastrointestinal Diseases. (To be published in *New York J. Med.*).

A Psychosomatic Theory of Thyrotoxicosis. (with F. Alexander and H. T. Carmichael) *Psychosom. Med.*, 13: 18–35, 1951.

Some Psychodynamic Factors in Multiple Sclerosis. (with R. R. Grinker and F. P. Robbins) *A. Res. Nerv. & Ment. Dis. Proc.* (1948) 28: 456–460, 1950. (*Multiple Sclerosis and the Demyelinating Diseases*).

ADELAIDE M. JOHNSON

Analysis of a Disturbed Adolescent Girl and Collaborative Psychiatric Treatment of the Mother. (with D. Fishback) *Am. J. Orthopsychiat.*, 14: 195–203, 1944.

The Application of Psychoanalysis to the Team Work of Psychiatrist and Psychiatric Social Worker. (To be published in *Psychoanalysis and Social Work*. Edited by Marcel Heiman. New York, International Universities Press).

Brief Psychotherapy in Bronchial Asthma. (with T. M. French) (In *The Proceedings of the Second Brief Psychotherapy Council*, January 1944. Chicago, Institute for Psychoanalysis. Section: *Psychosomatic Medicine*. pp. 14–21).

(Also in Alexander, F., and French, T. M., et al. *Studies in Psychosomatic Medicine*. 1948. pp. 249–258. See under Joint Publications).

A Case of Migraine. (In *The Proceedings of the Third Psychotherapy Council*, October 1946. Chicago, Institute for Psychoanalysis. pp. 69–93).

(Also in Alexander, F., and French, T. M., et al. *Studies in Psychosomatic Medicine*. 1948. pp. 522–543. See under Joint Publications).

Collaborative Psychiatric Therapy of Parent-Child Problems. (with S. A. Szurek and E. I. Falstein) *Am. J. Orthopsychiat.*, 12: 511–516, 1942.

A Contribution to Treatment of Superego Defect. *Soc. Casewk.*, 31: 135–138, 1950.

The Genesis of Antisocial Acting Out in Children and Adults. (with S. A. Szurek) *Psychoanalyt. Quart.*, 21: 323–343, 1952.

The Growing Science of Casework. (with H. Ross) *J. Soc. Casewk.*, 27: 273–278, 1946.

Preliminary Report on a Psychosomatic Study of Rheumatoid Arthritis. (with L. B. Shapiro and F. Alexander) *Psychosom. Med.*, 9: 295–300, 1947.

(Also in Alexander, F., and French, T. M., et al. *Studies in Psychosomatic Medicine.* 1948. pp. 489–498. See under Joint Publications).

Psychiatric Interpretation of the Growth Process. Part I. The Earliest Years.—Part II. Latency and Adolescence. (with H. Ross) *J. Soc. Casewk.*, 30: 87–92, 148–154; 1949.

Sanctions for Superego Lacunae of Adolescents. (In *Searchlights on Delinquency.* New York, International Universities Press, 1949. pp. 225–245).

School Phobia. (with E. I. Falstein, S. A. Szurek, and M. Svendsen) *Am. J. Orthopsychiat.*, 11: 702–711, 1941.

Some Etiological Aspects of Repression, Guilt and Hostility. *Psychoanalyt. Quart.*, 20: 511–527, 1951.

IRENE M. JOSSELYN

The Adolescent and His World. New York, Family Service Association of America, 1952.

The Caseworker as Therapist. *J. Soc. Casewk.*, 29: 351–355, 1948.

Cultural and Emotional Factors in Their Relation to Unmarried Parents. New York, Episcopal Service for Youth, 1947.

Emotional Implications of Rheumatic Heart Disease in Children. *Am. J. Orthopsychiat.*, 19: 87–100, 1949.

Evaluating Motives of Foster Parents. *Child Welfare*, 31: no. 2, Feb. 1952, pp. 3–8.

Growing to Adulthood. (In *Our Children Today.* New York, Viking Press, 1952. pp. 175–186).

Marriage and Motherhood. (In *Patterns for Modern Living.* Chicago, Delphian Society, 1949. pp. 143–190).

Psychological Problems of the Adolescent. *Soc. Casewk.*, 32: 183–190, 250–254; 1951.

Psychosocial Development of Children. New York, Family Service Association of America, 1948.

Should Mothers Work? (with R. S. Goldman) *Social Service Review*, 23: 74–87, 1949.

Social Pressures in Adolescence. *Soc. Casewk.*, 33: 187–193, 1952.

Some Defenses Seen in the Unmarried Mother. (In *Proceedings*

Eleventh Institute of the Committee for the Study of Unmarried Parenthood of the Welfare Council of Metropolitan Chicago. Chicago, April 11, 1951. pp. 47–56).

Treatment of the Emotionally Immature Child in an Institution Framework. *Am. J. Orthopsychiat.*, 20: 397–409, 1950.

HARRY B. LEE

The Creative Imagination. *Psychoanalyt. Quart.*, 18: 351–360, 1949.

The Cultural Lag in Aesthetics. *J. Aesthetics and Art Criticism*, 6: 120–138, 1947.

The Influence of Psychologic Factors upon Gastro-Intestinal Disturbances: A Symposium. IV. Oral Trends and Oral Conflicts in a Case of Duodenal Ulcer. *Psychoanalyt. Quart.*, 3: 574–582, 1934. (Also in Alexander, F., and French, T. M., et al. *Studies in Psychosomatic Medicine.* 1948. pp. 161–167. See under Joint Publications).

On the Esthetic States of the Mind. *Psychiatry*, 10: 281–306, 1947.

Projective Features of Contemplative Artistic Experience. *Am. J. Orthopsychiat.*, 19: 101–111, 1949.

Spirituality and Beauty in Artistic Experience. *Psychoanalyt. Quart.*, 17: 507–523, 1948.

The Values of Order and Vitality in Art. (In *Psychoanalysis and the Social Sciences.* Vol. 2. New York, International Universities Press, 1950. pp. 231–274).

HELEN V. McLEAN

The Course of a Depression Treated by Psychotherapy and Metrazol. (with R. R. Grinker) *Psychosom. Med.*, 2: 119–138, 1940.

The Emotional Background of Marital Difficulties. *Am. Sociol. Rev.*, 6: 384–388, 1941.

The Emotional Health of Negroes. *J. Negro Education*, 18: 283–290, 1949.

A Few Comments on "Moses and Monotheism." *Psychoanalyt. Quart.*, 9: 207–213, 1940.

Group Tension. *J. Am. M. Women's A.*, 2: 479–484, 1947.

(Panel Discussion) New Problems and Methods for Research in Human Development, by Lawrence K. Frank. *Human Development Bulletin*, Fifth Issue, Spring 1952, pp. 50–52.

Psychodynamic Factors in Racial Relations. *Ann. Am. Acad. Pol. and Soc. Sci.*, 244: 159–166, 1946.

Racial Prejudice. *Am. J. Orthopsychiat.*, 14: 706–713, 1944.

The Status of the Emotions in Palpitation and Extrasystoles with a Note on 'Effort Syndrome.' (with M. L. Miller) *Psychoanalyt. Quart.*, 10: 545–560, 1941.

(Also in Alexander, F., and French, T. M., et al. *Studies in Psychosomatic Medicine.* 1948. pp. 333–344. See under Joint Publications).

(Symposium) Looking Ahead in the Fields of Orthopsychiatric Research. *Am. J. Orthopsychiat.*, 20: 78–85, 1950.

Treatment of the Neuroses. *Cincinnati J. Med.*, 29: 545–555, 1948.

Why Negroes Don't Commit Suicide. *Negro Digest*, 5: no. 4, Feb. 1947, pp. 4–6.

MILTON L. MILLER

Balzac's *Père Goriot*. *Psychoanalyt. Quart.*, 6: 78–85, 1937.

Blood Pressure Findings in Relation to Inhibited Aggressions in Psychotics. *Psychosom. Med.*, 1: 162–172, 1939.

(Also in Alexander, F., and French, T. M., et al. *Studies in Psychosomatic Medicine.* 1948. pp. 316–332. See under Joint Publications).

Facts About the Menopause. *Hygeia*, 18: 692–694, 740; 1940.

A Psychological Study of a Case of Eczema and a Case of Neurodermatitis. *Psychosom. Med.*, 4: 82–93, 1942.

(Also in Alexander, F., and French, T. M., et al. *Studies in Psychosomatic Medicine.* 1948. pp. 401–421. See under Joint Publications).

Some Emotional Problems of War-Time. *News-Letter of the American Association of Psychiatric Social Workers*, 12: no. 1, Summer 1942, pp. 20–27.

The Status of the Emotions in Palpitation and Extrasystoles with a Note on 'Effort Syndrome.' (with H. V. McLean) *Psychoanalyt. Quart.*, 10: 545–560, 1941.

(Also in Alexander, F., and French, T. M., et al. *Studies in Psychosomatic Medicine.* 1948. pp. 333–344. See under Joint Publications).

FRITZ MOELLENHOFF

The Price of Individuality; speculations about German national characteristics. *Am. Imago,* 4: no. 2, April 1947, pp. 33–60.

GEORGE J. MOHR

Dependent Mother or Dependent Child? *National Parent-Teacher,* 42: no. 7, March 1948, pp. 19–21.

Freud and Psychoanalysis. *Am. J. Orthopsychiat.,* 10: 858–860, 1940.

Influence of Mothers' Attitudes on Mental Health. *J. Pediat.,* 16: 641–646, 1940.

Mental Hygiene Aspects of Occupational Therapy. *Occup. Therapy.,* 18: 25–30, 1939.

Notes on the Trial of a Twelve Year Old Boy for Murder. (with I. C. Sherman) *Quart. J. Child Behavior,* 2: 1–31, 1950.

Orthopsychiatry—Fifteenth Year. *Am. J. Orthopsychiat.,* 8: 185–191, 1938.

Pediatrics and Child Psychiatry: A Symposium. Some Treatment Indications. *Am. J. Orthopsychiat.,* 11: 438–444, 1941.

Present Day Trends in Psychoanalysis. *Psychiatry,* 6: 281–284, 1943.

Psychiatric Problems of Adolescence. *J.A.M.A.,* 137: 1589–1592, 1948.

Psychiatric Services for Social Agencies. (In *Proceedings—Psychiatry in Hospitals and Agencies.* New York, Council of Jewish Federations and Welfare Funds, January 1948. pp. 46–50).

Psychoanalytical Theory of Personality. *Social Work Technique,* 4: 35–46, 1939.

Psychological Factors in Marital Maladjustments. (In *Successful Marriage.* Edited by Morris Fishbein and Ernest W. Burgess. Garden City, N.Y., Doubleday & Co., 1947. pp. 177–190).

Psychosomatic Problems in Childhood. *Child Development,* 19: 137–142, 1948.

Sexual Education of the Adolescent. *J. Pediat.,* 19: 387–391, 1941.

Therapy with Older Children As Seen by the Psychiatrist. (In *Proceedings of the National Conference of Social Work;* selected papers. Sixty-Seventh Annual Conference, Grand Rapids, Mich., 1940. New York, Columbia University Press, 1940. pp. 352–362).

The Threat of Divorce. *Child Study,* 25: 7–9, 1947.

GERHART J. PIERS

Psychoanalysis. (with F. Alexander) (In *Progress in Neurology and Psychiatry*. Vol. I. Edited by E. A. Spiegel. New York, Grune & Stratton, 1946. pp. 681–694).

Psychoanalysis. (with F. Alexander) (In *Progress in Neurology and Psychiatry*. Vol. II. Edited by E. A. Spiegel. New York, Grune & Stratton, 1947. pp. 500–517).

HELEN ROSS

Adolescents in American Culture. (with A. Davis, M. Gitelson, and W. Henry) *University of Chicago Round Table*, No. 576, April 3, 1949.

The Case Worker and the Adolescent. *The Family*, 22: 231–238, 1941.

Children in Wartime. *Junior League Magazine*, Oct. 1941.

Competition; a discussion of its psychological aspects. Published by the Leah Blumberg Memorial Fund, 1941.

Dynamic Psychiatry. (with F. Alexander as co-editor) Chicago, University of Chicago Press, 1952.

Emotional Needs of the Young Child. (In *Our Children Today*. New York, Viking Press, 1952. pp. 57–68).

Fears of Children. Chicago, Science Research Associates, 1951. 49 p.

Foreword to American Edition of: *Child Treatment and the Therapy of Play*, by Lydia Jackson and Kathleen M. Todd. New York, Ronald Press Co., 1950.

Freedom from Fear. *National Parent-Teacher*, 43: no. 4, December 1948, pp. 7–9.

Getting Along and Getting Ahead. *Child Study*, 27: 69–71, 1950.

Group Psychotherapy Related to Group Trauma. *Am. J. Orthopsychiat.*, 14: 609–615, 1944.

The Growing Science of Casework. (with A. M. Johnson) *J. Soc. Casewk.*, 27: 273–278, 1946.

Juvenile Delinquency Begins at Home. (with J. M. Braude and W. F. Byron) *Northwestern University Reviewing Stand*, 9: no. 17, November 2, 1947.

Learning to Live with People. *National Parent-Teacher*, 44: no. 3, November 1949, pp. 4–6.

Like Mother, Like Daughter? (In *Father of the Man*, by W. Allison

Davis and Robert J. Havighurst. Boston, Houghton Mifflin Co., 1947. pp. 148–168).

New Forces in Family Living: Emotional Values. *J. Soc. Casewk.*, 30: 55–58, 1949.

Problems of Adolescence. *Illinois Society for Mental Hygiene Mental Health Bulletin,* 1: no. 1, Jan.–Feb., 1948, pp. 1–4.

Psychiatric Interpretation of the Growth Process. Part I. The Earliest Years.—Part II. Latency and Adolescence. (with A. M. Johnson) *J. Soc. Casewk.*, 30: 87–92, 148–154; 1949.

Psychology of Pre-Adolescent Children in War Time. Emotional Forces in Children As Influenced by Current Events. *Am. J. Orthopsychiat.,* 13: 502–504, 1943.

Section on "Play Therapy" 1938 (as participant). *Am. J. Orthopsychiat.,* 8: 500–507, 1938.

Why Vacations? (with W. E. Parker and A. C. Van Dusen) *Northwestern University Reviewing Stand,* 12: no. 21, May 29, 1949.

LEON J. SAUL

Cerebral Action Potentials. (with R. W. Gerard and W. H. Marshall) *Proc. Soc. Exper. Biol. & Med.,* 30: 1123–1125, 1933.

A Clinical Note on a Mechanism of Psychogenic Back Pain. *Psychosom. Med.,* 3: 190–191, 1941.

(Also in Alexander, F., and French, T. M., et al. *Studies in Psychosomatic Medicine.* 1948. pp. 544–546. See under Joint Publications).

Electrical Activity of the Cat's Brain. (with R. W. Gerard and W. H. Marshall) *Arch. Neurol. & Psychiat.,* 36: 675–735, 1946.

The Emotional Settings of Some Attacks of Urticaria. (with C. Bernstein, Jr.) *Psychosom. Med.,* 3: 349–369, 1941.

(Also in Alexander, F., and French, T. M., et al. *Studies in Psychosomatic Medicine.* 1948. pp. 424–451. See under Joint Publications).

Hostility in Cases of Essential Hypertension. *Psychosom. Med.,* 1: 153–161, 1939.

(Also in Alexander, F., and French, T. M., et al. *Studies in Psychosomatic Medicine.* 1948. pp. 345–356. See under Joint Publications).

The Human Spirogram. (with F. Alexander) *Am. J. Physiol.,* 119: 396–397, 1937.

Incidental Observations on Pruritis Ani. *Psychoanalyt. Quart.*, 7: 336–337, 1938.

(Also in Alexander, F., and French, T. M., et al. *Studies in Psychosomatic Medicine*. 1948. pp. 422–423. See under Joint Publications).

A Note on the Psychogenesis of Organic Symptoms. *Psychoanalyt. Quart.*, 4: 476–483, 1935.

(Also in Alexander, F., and French, T. M., et al. *Studies in Psychosomatic Medicine*. 1948. pp. 85–90. See under Joint Publications).

Physiological Effects of Emotional Tension. (In *Personality and the Behavior Disorders*. Vol. I. Edited by J. McV. Hunt. New York, Ronald Press Co., 1944. pp. 269–305).

The Physiological Effects of Psychoanalytic Therapy. *A. Res. Nerv. & Ment. Dis. Proc.* (1938) 19: 305–317, 1939. (*The Inter-Relationship of Mind and Body*).

(Also in Alexander, F., and French, T. M., et al. *Studies in Psychosomatic Medicine*. 1948. pp. 91–100. See under Joint Publications).

Psychoanalytic Case Records. *Psychoanalyt. Quart.*, 8: 186–190, 1939.

Psychogenic Factors in the Etiology of the Common Cold and Related Symptoms. *Internat. J. Psycho-Analysis*, 19: 451–470, 1938.

Psychosomatic Knowledge in Case Work. *The Family*, 22: 219–227, 1941.

Respiration and Personality—A Preliminary Report: Part I. Description of the Curves. (with F. Alexander) *Psychosom. Med.*, 2: 110–118, 1940.

Section Meeting on Culture and Personality (1938) (as participant). *Am. J. Orthopsychiat.*, 8: 609–610, 1938.

Some Observations on the Relations of Emotions and Allergy. *Psychosom. Med.* 3: 66–71, 1941.

(Also in Alexander, F., and French, T. M., et al. *Studies in Psychosomatic Medicine*. 1948. pp. 547–554. See under Joint Publications).

Telepathic Sensitiveness as a Neurotic Symptom. *Psychoanalyt. Quart.*, 7: 329–335, 1938.

Three Criminal Types As Seen by the Psychoanalyst. (with F. Alexander) *Psychoanalyt. Rev.*, 24: 113–130, 1937.

Utilization of Early Current Dreams in Formulating Psychoanalytic Cases. *Psychoanalyt. Quart.*, 9: 453–469, 1940.

LOUIS B. SHAPIRO

Aseptic Lymphocytic Meningitis in the Case of Infantile Cerebral Palsy, Adult Form. *J. Nerv. & Ment. Dis.*, 97: 166–169, 1943.

A Case of Associated Facial and Intracranial Hemangioma. *Illinois M. J.*, 83: 272–274, 1943.

Neuroses, Behavior Disorders, and Perversions. (with F. Alexander) (In *Dynamic Psychiatry*. Edited by Franz Alexander and Helen Ross. Chicago, University of Chicago Press, 1952. pp. 117–139).

Preliminary Report on a Psychosomatic Study of Rheumatoid Arthritis. (with A. M. Johnson and F. Alexander) *Psychosom. Med.*, 9: 295–300, 1947.

> (Also in Alexander, F., and French, T. M., et al. *Studies in Psychosomatic Medicine*. 1948. pp. 489–498. See under Joint Publications).

Psychologic Conflict and Neuromuscular Tension. I. Preliminary Report on a Method As Applied to Rheumatoid Arthritis. (with L. A. Gottschalk and H. M. Serota) *Psychosom. Med.*, 12: 315–319, 1950.

> Also in *A. Res. Nerv. & Ment. Dis. Proc.* (1949). 29: 735–743, 1950. (*Life Stress and Bodily Disease*).

The Use of Dream Analysis in Psychosomatic Research. (with T. M. French) *Psychosom. Med.*, 11: 110–112, 1949.

> (Also in *The Yearbook of Psychoanalysis*. Vol. 6, 1950. New York, International Universities Press, 1951. pp. 123–128).

EMMY SYLVESTER

Delinquency and Morality. (with B. Bettelheim) (In *Psychoanalytic Study of the Child*. Vol. V. New York, International Universities Press, 1950. pp. 329–342).

Emotional Aspects of Learning. *Quart. J. Child Behavior*, 1: 133–139, 1949.

Milieu Therapy: Indications and Illustrations. (with B. Bettelheim) *Psychoanalyt. Rev.*, 36: 54–68, 1949.

Notes on the Impact of Parental Occupations: Some Cultural Determinants of Symptom Choice in Emotionally Disturbed Children. (with B. Bettelheim) *Am. J. Orthopsychiat.*, 20: 785–795, 1950.

Pathogenic Influences of Maternal Attitudes in the Neonatal Period. *Trans. Conference on Problems of Early Infancy*, 1: 67–70, 1947.

Physical Symptoms in Emotionally Disturbed Children. (with B. Bettelheim) (In *The Psychoanalytic Study of the Child*. Vol. III/IV. New York, International Universities Press, 1949. pp. 353–368).

The Preparatory Phase in Child Analysis. (To be published in *The Psychoanalytic Study of the Child*).

Therapeutic Influence of the Group on the Individual. (with B. Bettelheim) *Am. J. Orthopsychiat.*, 17: 684–692, 1947.

A Therapeutic Milieu. (with B. Bettelheim) *Am. J. Orthopsychiat.*, 18: 191–206, 1948.

THOMAS S. SZASZ

Factors in the Pathogenesis of Peptic Ulcer; some critical comments on a recent article by George F. Mahl. *Psychosom. Med.*, 11: 300–304, 1949.

On the Psychoanalytic Theory of Instincts. *Psychoanalyt. Quart.*, 21: 25–48, 1952.

Oral Mechanisms in Constipation and Diarrhoea. *Internat. J. Psycho-Analysis*, 32: 196–203, 1951.

Physiologic and Psychodynamic Mechanisms in Constipation and Diarrhea. *Psychosom. Med.*, 13: 112–116, 1951.

Psychiatric Aspects of Vagotomy: A Preliminary Report. *Ann. Int. Med.*, 28: 279–288, 1948.

Psychiatric Aspects of Vagotomy. II. A Psychiatric Study of Vagotomized Ulcer Patients with Comments on Prognosis. *Psychosom. Med.*, 11: 187–199, 1949.

Psychiatric Aspects of Vagotomy. III. The Problem of Diarrhea after Vagotomy. *J. Nerv. & Ment. Dis.*, 115: 394–405, 1952.

Psychiatric Aspects of Vagotomy. IV. Phantom Ulcer Pain. *Arch. Neurol. & Psychiat.*, 62: 728–733, 1949.

Psychoanalysis and the Autonomic Nervous System; a bioanalytic approach to the problem of the psychogenesis of somatic change. *Psychoanalyt. Rev.*, 39: 115–151, 1952.

The Psychosomatic Approach in Medicine. (with F. Alexander) (In *Dynamic Psychiatry*. Edited by Franz Alexander and Helen Ross. Chicago, University of Chicago Press, 1952. pp. 369–400).

Psychosomatic Aspects of Salivary Activity. I. Hypersalivation in Patients with Peptic Ulcer. *A. Res. Nerv. & Ment. Dis. Proc.* (1949). 29: 647–655, 1950. (*Life Stress and Bodily Disease.*)

Psychosomatic Aspects of Salivary Activity. II. Psychoanalytic Observations Concerning Hypersalivation. *Psychosom. Med.,* 12: 320–331, 1950.

The Role of Hostility in the Pathogenesis of Peptic Ulcer: Theoretical Considerations with the Report of a Case. (with E. Levin, J. B. Kirsner, and W. L. Palmer) *Psychosom. Med.,* 9: 331–336, 1947.

The "Schemm Regime" in the Treatment of Extreme Congestive Heart Failure: A Case Report. (with S. Elgart) *Ohio State M. J.,* 43: 926–928, 1947.

A Theory of the Pathogenesis of Ordinary Human Baldness. (with A. M. Robertson) *Arch. Dermat. & Syph.,* 61: 34–48, 1950.

CAREL VAN DER HEIDE

A Case of Pollakiuria Nervosa. *Psychoanalyt. Quart.,* 10: 267–283, 1941.

Psychosomatic Medicine. *News-Letter of the American Association of Psychiatric Social Workers,* 13: no. 1, Summer 1943, pp. 13–20.

A Study of Mechanisms in Two Cases of Peptic Ulcer. *Psychosom. Med.,* 2: 398–410, 1940.

(Also in Alexander, F., and French, T. M., et al. *Studies in Psychosomatic Medicine.* 1948. pp. 206–223. See under Joint Publications).

EDOARDO WEISS

Clinical Aspects of Depression. *Psychoanalyt. Quart.,* 13: 445–461, 1944.

History of Metapsychological Concepts. (In *Dynamic Psychiatry.* Edited by Franz Alexander and Helen Ross. Chicago, University of Chicago Press, 1952. pp. 40–62).

Paul Federn (Obituary). *Internat. J. Psycho-Analysis,* 32: 242–246, 1951.

Paul Federn's Scientific Contributions: In Commemoration. *Internat. J. Psycho-Analysis,* 32: 283–290, 1951.

Principles of Psychodynamics. New York, Grune & Stratton, 1950.

Projection, Extrajection and Objectivation. *Psychoanalyt. Quart.,* 16: 357–377, 1947.

Sense of Reality and Reality Testing. *Samiksa,* 4: 171–180, 1950.

Some Dynamic Aspects of Dreams. *Samiksa*, 2: 209–226, 1948.
(Also in *The Yearbook of Psychoanalysis*. Vol. 5, 1949. New York, International Universities Press, 1950. pp. 128–145).

GEORGE W. WILSON

The Analysis of a Transitory Conversion Symptom Simulating Pertussis. *Internat. J. Psycho-Analysis*, 16: 474–480, 1935.

The Influence of Psychologic Factors upon Gastro-Intestinal Disturbances: A Symposium. III. Typical Personality Trends and Conflicts in Cases of Spastic Colitis. *Psychoanalyt. Quart.*, 3: 558–573, 1934.
(Also in Alexander, F., and French, T. M., et al. *Studies in Psychosomatic Medicine*. 1948. pp. 148–160. See under Joint Publications).

John Wilkes Booth: Father Murderer. *Am. Imago*, 1: no. 3, 1940, pp. 49–60.

A Prophetic Dream Reported by Abraham Lincoln. *Am. Imago*, 1: no. 3, 1940, pp. 42–48.

Quantitative Dream Studies: A Methodological Attempt at a Quantitative Evaluation of Psychoanalytic Material. (with F. Alexander) *Psychoanalyt. Quart.*, 4: 371–407, 1935.

The Red-Headed Man. *Psychoanalyt. Rev.*, 25: 165–169, 1938.

Report of a Case of Acute Laryngitis Occurring as a Conversion Symptom During Analysis. *Psychoanalyt. Rev.*, 21: 408–414, 1934.
(Also in Alexander, F., and French, T. M., et al. *Studies in Psychosomatic Medicine*. 1948. pp. 259–265. See under Joint Publications).

Some Facts and Fallacies Regarding Psychoanalysis. *Illinois M. J.*, 73: 248–254, 1938.

A Study of Structural and Instinctual Conflicts in Cases of Hay Fever. *Psychosom. Med.*, 3: 51–65, 1941.
(Also in Alexander, F., and French, T. M., et al. *Studies in Psychosomatic Medicine*. 1948. pp. 266–286. See under Joint Publications).

The Transition from Organ Neurosis to Conversion Hysteria. *Internat. J. Psycho-Analysis*, 19: 23–40, 1938.
(Also in Alexander, F., and French, T. M., et al. *Studies in Psychosomatic Medicine*. 1948. pp. 224–239. See under Joint Publications).

REPORTS AND BROCHURES

Review for the Year 1932–1933.
Review for the Year 1933–1934.
Review for the Year 1934–1935.
Five-Year Report 1932–1937.
Supplement to the Five-Year Report 1932–1937.
Ten-Year Report 1932–1942.
Report of the Five Year Period 1942–1947.
The Discovery of the Self. 1940.
Exploration of the Mind. 1940.
Psychotherapy for the People. 1940.
Living Together, by Edwin R. Embree. 1941.
Psychoanalysis in Medicine, by Alfred E. Cohn. 1941.
Proceedings of the Brief Psychotherapy Council. October, 1942.
Growing Up in a World at War. 1942.
Women in Wartime. 1943.

Faculty, 1952

Franz Alexander, M.D.
Charlotte Babcock, M.D.
Catherine L. Bacon, M.D.
Therese Benedek, M.D.
Hugh T. Carmichael, M.D.
Edwin R. Eisler, M.D.
Joan Fleming, M.D.
Thomas M. French, M.D.
Margaret W. Gerard, M.D.
Roy R. Grinker, M.D.
Adelaide M. Johnson, M.D.
Irene M. Josselyn, M.D.
Bernard A. Kamm, M.D.
Harry B. Lee, M.D.
Maurice Levine, M.D.
Helen V. McLean, M.D.
Albrecht Meyer, M.D.
Fritz Moellenhoff, M.D.
George J. Mohr, M.D.
Gerhart Piers, M.D.
Richard Renneker, M.D.
Louis B. Shapiro, M.D.
Thomas S. Szasz, M.D.
Lucia E. Tower, M.D.
Adrian H. Vander Veer, M.D.
Edoardo Weiss, M.D.
George W. Wilson, M.D.